RUTHLESS MARKETING

BY T.J. ROHLEDER

11 PROVEN SECRETS TO GAIN AN ALMOST UNFAIR ADVANTAGE OVER YOUR COMPETITORS.

Also by T.J. Rohleder:

The Black Book of Marketing Secrets (Series)
The Ultimate Wealth-Maker
How to Get Super Rich in Opportunity Market
Four Magical Secrets to Building a Fabulous Fortune
The Ruthless Marketing Attack
$60,000.00 in 90 Days
How to Start Your Own Million Dollar Business
Fast Track to Riches
Five Secrets That Will Triple Your Profits
25 Direct Mail Success Secrets That Can Make You Rich
24 Simple and Easy Ways to Get Rich Quick
How to Create a Hot Selling Internet Product in One Day
Secrets of the Blue Jeans Millionaire
Shortcut Secrets to Creating High-Profit Products

FIRST EDITION

ISBN 1-933356-31-6

TABLE OF CONTENTS

INTRODUCTION

by T.J. Rohleder

"Little hinges swing big doors."

Congratulations on your decision to read this book. After all, most businesspeople and entrepreneurs 'claim' they want to make more money, but how many are willing to pick up and study a book that can help them do it? I'm ashamed to say that the answer is very few.

Yes, most people want all of the benefits <u>without</u> paying the price to get them. Earl Nightingale called this *"the strangest secret"* and recorded one of the first audio programs over 50 years ago to describe this phenomenon... Unfortunately, this is even a bigger problem today than it was when Earl recorded his classic program. Nowadays it seems as if almost everyone is looking for a free ride or something for nothing. Very few people are willing to pay the price to get what they want. *This is bad news for them...*

But it's great news for YOU!

Why? That's simple. You see, the people who are unwilling to do whatever it takes to build their business includes <u>most</u> of your competitors. Because of this, you can dramatically gain an almost unfair advantage over all of these individuals and companies. This book shows you how. You can use the Secrets inside the eleven chapters of this book to...

Become a dominant competitor in your market and start getting all of the money that could and should be yours.

The eleven secrets in this book really are *'secrets'* because most of your competitors don't know about them. As you'll see, each of these secrets is easy to understand and simple to use. There's nothing complicated about any of this. But don't let this simplicity fool you. Even though these secrets are simple to understand and easy to use, each one really does have the awesome power to make you huge sums of money. And together...

All eleven of these secrets will create a synergistic force that lets you GAIN AN UNFAIR ADVANTAGE over all of your competitors!

So don't let the size of this small book fool you. You see, *"Little hinges really do swing big doors."* The eleven marketing secrets in this book truly can triple your profits in no time flat! Using all eleven of these secrets will help you quickly attract and retain more customers within your market area. That's what marketing is all about, by the way.

The word *marketing* is thrown around a lot these days and used rather loosely... **But my definition is so simple a grade school kid can understand it.** Here it is:

> "Marketing is made up of all the things you do to attract and sell to the right people who are perfectly suited for whatever you offer — and then all the things you do to re-sell as much as you can to these people (and perhaps their closest contacts) for as many years as possible."

This clear definition tells you *exactly* what you must do:

A: Attract the right prospective buyers to your business.

B: Then re-sell to them (and perhaps their closest associates) for as many months and years as possible.

Forget the complicated theories. Good marketing is simply **attracting and retaining the right kind of customers — who will do the largest amount of repeat business with you** over the longest period of time. (Why more college business schools don't teach this will always be a mystery to me.)

So that's our definition of marketing. Simple. Clear. Direct. There's no confusion here. In fact, there's nothing complicated about any of this. You see, building a business is actually a very simple process... There are only three ways to do it:

#1: You can increase the number of new customers who are attracted to your business.

#2: You can increase the frequency of repeat business these people do with you (in other words, you can do things to get them to re-buy more often).

#3: You can increase the average profit of each repeat transaction you do with your ever-growing base of customers.

THE ELEVEN MARKETING SECRETS in this book can be applied to all three of these business-building areas. Do this and you will see dramatic improvements right away... Then within 90 days or so — your take-home profits can be double or triple what they are now!

Still sound unbelievable? If so, that's okay. But please study this book carefully and prove to yourself that this is true. Just spend some time thinking about all of the ways that you can use these eleven key secrets. Spend some time doing this every day and let these very simple, but powerful secrets help you triple your profits in no time flat.

And to reward you for reading this book, I have...

A great FREE business-building gift for you!

Yes, I have a gift waiting for you that can help you make huge sums of extra money! Here's what it's all about: Throughout this small book are some additional marketing secrets that came from

---

a special eBook I have just written, called; *"265 of the Greatest Marketing Secrets You Can Use to Dominate Your Market."* This Electronic Book is on the Internet and ready for you to download right now! It normally sells for $27.95 — and is worth every penny. But for a limited time it can be yours — absolutely FREE — by simply going to my Web-Site and giving me your contact information.

Why am I giving you this $27.95 eBook for free? That's simple. You see, I have other products and services that were developed to help you make the maximum amount of money that I would love to tell you about. So I'm more than happy to give you this brand new Electronic Book that gives you 265 of my greatest marketing secrets if you'll give me your contact information (which I will not give out to anyone). IT'S EASY TO RECEIVE THIS FREE GIFT: just go to **www.RuthlessMarketing.com/freegift** and immediately download this very special Electronic Marketing book. And don't worry, although I <u>will</u> add your name to my mailing list and send you additional information, there is NEVER any cost or obligation for you to purchase anything else from me, now or in the future. This FREE gift will be my way of thanking you for taking the time to read and study this book.

So with all this said, let's begin…

SECRET ONE:

Establishing Your USP

In this chapter, we're going to talk about building a Unique Selling Position — what's also known in the industry as a Unique Selling Proposition or, more succinctly, a **USP.** If you have no idea what a USP is, then what you learn in this chapter alone will be worth every penny you paid for this book. Even if you already know all about USPs, by the time we're done here you'll have learned a lot you didn't know already, and you'll have supercharged your understanding of this valuable marketing strategy.

Ask yourself this one question as you read this chapter: why do your clients buy from you instead of your competitors? If you can't answer that question, it means one of two things: either you're offering your clients a unique set of advantages that you've never bothered to identify, or you offer *no* unique advantages; so you're lucky to have any business in the first place. If that's the case, there's no compelling reason for your customers to keep doing business with you. Therefore, **anytime your competitors offer your customers a unique advantage, they can steal those customers away.**

You can't let that happen! In this chapter, I'm going to show you how to build your own Unique Selling Position: a USP that completely separates you from all of the other competitors in your market, and makes people want to keep doing business with you over and over again. So, please: read carefully, and take plenty of notes.

What a USP Is, and Why It's Important

Ask a dozen marketing experts what a USP is, and you'll get a

Direct-marketing is a personal medium.

- Write and speak to only one person.

- The art is to make the person you are communicating with seem special.

- The more you can make them feel you are only speaking to them — the better.

dozen answers — but they'll have a lot in common. At its most basic, **a USP is a clear statement of the unique benefits your customers get from doing business with you. It's something that sets you apart from your competition.** No matter what field you're in, all your competitors are usually saying the same thing. A USP is something — a benefit, an idea, a concept — that helps you say something your competitors don't, so that when people look at your business, it stands out against the rest of the field and looks unique to their eyes.

The most unique USP possible would be to have a product that everybody wants and nobody else has. The only problem there is that 99.99% of businesses *don't* have that. They've got plenty of competition. It doesn't matter if you're a chiropractor, a dentist, an attorney, a plumber, or an air conditioner repairman: whatever you're doing, chances are you've got competition up the kazoo. A USP is important because it defines you and your company, and gives potential customers a very compelling reason — or even several reasons — why they should favor you over all those competitors.

You can **look at a USP as simply what you do better or differently than everybody else. In most cases, you should be able to get your USP down to a few words.** Here are three great examples I picked up from a website. Burger King says, "Have it your way!" Enterprise Car

Rental says, "We'll pick you up." Bounty Paper Towels call themselves "The Quicker Picker-Upper." The best USP is a condensed catchphrase that tells your customers why they should do business with you instead of your competition. **Your answer has to telegraph a very clear and direct benefit to your prospect or customer, in a concise, distinct, fulfilling way.**

For example, if you were to say, "Melts in your mouth, not in your hands!" everyone would know you were talking about M & M's. That's a classic USP, and it's sold millions of dollars worth of candy over the years. A good USP like that one stays with a person, etched into both their subconscious and their conscious mind, so when they walk away and later think about buying a product in that particular category, they'll think of you first. Here are a few more great examples: take Avis Rent-A-Car. They couldn't be #1 in their market — that was Hertz — so they came up with this USP: "We're #2. We try harder!" And here's Federal Express: "When it absolutely, positively has to be get there overnight." And then there's the old USP for Domino's Pizza, which is my favorite, though the government actually court-ordered them to stop using it because of a lawsuit. It was so brilliant: "Fresh hot pizza in 30 minutes or less!" What could be clearer than that?

The USP, then, is whatever you can offer that your best prospects or customers want the most that nobody else has — and it's up to you to discover or create that. I'm going to show you how in this chapter. But just as important, I'm going to show you exactly what a USP is *not*. If you flip through the Yellow Pages or a newspaper advertising section, you'll see plenty of examples of what a USP is not: and that's just your name, your address, your telephone number, how many years you've been in business, the fact that you're "family-owned," and so on. That's what you see in most advertising — but that's not a USP. It doesn't telegraph any benefit. You need to give people not what they *need*, but what they *want*. And **what people want is to solve their problems or to fulfill their desires, as quickly, easily, and painlessly as possible.**

Taming the Wild USP

Now we'll get into the meat-and-potatoes of what a USP really is, and how to find the one that's right for you. This isn't an easy process for the inexperienced marketer. First of all, how do you get started? That's usually a little daunting, because you may not be sure exactly what a USP is, although you should have some general idea by now. **The first question you should always ask yourself is, "What needs are going unfulfilled in my industry, or in this segment of my target market? What problems need to be fixed?" The second question is, "What great value, service, or benefit will people receive from my business that will justify them doing business with me?"**

So... is a USP a slogan? It is indeed, in its most basic sense, but even then you have to gather together all your raw material before you try to put it into a statement. An easy way to do that is to compile a Claims Matrix. A Claims Matrix is a chart, a visual representation of what's out there, who's saying what, and what's available. Frankly, very few companies are in a position so unique that they don't have direct competition. Even if you have a unique service that everybody needs and no one else provides... well, you're a very rare bird, and you won't be in that position for very long. If you're trying something new, it's either going to succeed because of its uniqueness, or you're going to discover that the product is unique because there was no demand for it in the first place. Even if you do succeed, you'll have imitators very quickly. Imitation may be the sincerest form of flattery, but it can hurt you severely if it steals away dollars that should be yours.

Here's how you create a Claims Matrix to get all the raw data to work from. You can do it on paper, on a computer spreadsheet, or even in your head if you can handle all the data that way. Down one side of the chart, list all the benefits and features you can think of that pertain to your product or service. Include all the features and benefits your competition is claiming. That might be that they have 24 stores and locations, free delivery, same-day service, or whatever. You should include as many as you can think of.

Then, across the top of the chart, write the names of all your competitors. Once you've done that, go down the chart and put a checkmark next to each feature or claim that's being made by each competitor. So, if it's fast delivery and there are three competitors who make that claim, you put the checkmark in the spaces for those three businesses. Go right on down the line, and spend a little while doing this. You'd better come back after a day or so, because more features and benefits will dawn on you. When you complete this simple task, you'll have a visual representation of what other people are doing, and you'll very likely see big, open spaces where no competitor is making a claim. These open spaces offer a whole list of ideas you can claim: they're the raw data you can work from to create your own USPs. And don't be scared to have more than one, especially if you have different divisions within your company.

Here's one of the prime lessons you should take away from this chapter: *even if you're not unique, you can be unique in saying what no one else is saying.* Once you've put together a nice list of benefits and features, you can translate any of those features into additional benefits.

As you go down that list, you'll read a feature and ask yourself, "So what?" For instance, here's a typical claim: "We have the most locations." So what? "Well, that means you're never more than ten minutes away from one of our stores." So what? "That means you're only 20 minutes from having food at home that's still hot and fresh." Aha! There's your *real* benefit.

Keep going down the list. Suppose someone claims, "We have the largest inventory." So what? He has the biggest selection; what does that mean? "That means you can always find the hard-to-find items that the other stores don't carry." *Now* you have a clue.

Once you complete your Claims Matrix, you have the raw

The right marriage between message to market — the closer marriage — the more money Formula

a. Right message/offer

b. To right market

c. Through the right media

data to begin crafting your USP. Your list can be very long in the beginning, but then you can start editing it down until you end up with a single statement that says everything you want to say. It tells the customer, "Here's why you should do business with me; this is a unique benefit you'll get." You're claiming something in the marketplace that none of your competition is claiming. That will help you get started. This is an ongoing process, and it may take you a few days just to get some preliminary ideas about what you want to do. But that's okay; this is something you need to hammer out right now before you even open your doors. Figure out what your point of difference is going to be. What are you going to offer to your customers and prospects that's different from everybody else? You've got to answer this question, and it has to be something that will compel them to do business with you rather than your competitors. That said, keep in mind that a USP isn't necessarily set in stone. It evolves; you're constantly asking yourself these questions, so your USP is a process rather than a static thing that just pops into your head full-grown and never changes. **Your best ideas will come from the time you put into process.**

Here's one of the things that makes this process so useful: if you talk to most businesspeople about developing a Claims Matrix and adding up all the benefits and features, they'll look at you like you're speaking a foreign language. That's because hardly anybody puts in the effort to do this, or even knows they should. This is your real advantage here. It's your edge in the marketplace: the fact that most people won't take the time to do this.

The best evidence of that is most businesses are saying the same thing — they're "me too" businesses. Drive through any town, and you'll see hundreds of little businesses. Not that there's anything wrong with that, but these little businesses are all the same: little gift shops, hole-in-the-wall restaurants, antique stores, and the like. It's obvious that so many people have poured their hearts, lives, and all their assets into opening a business, without ever wondering how that business is going to succeed. They do no market research; they have no idea why people would do business with them, as opposed to all the other shops that are offering the same thing. They just open their doors and say, "I offer that, too."

You've also got to take care to avoid marketing pitfalls in creating your USP. Let's say you decide to carve out a niche in the printer cartridge industry. It's a very competitive market, so you might decide to build your USP around your price. Here's where you have to be careful, because the prices are more or less the same throughout the industry for specific printer cartridges. Quality? That's about the same, too. Delivery? Yep, that's about the same. So how do you differentiate yourself? How do you create a USP that gives you that competitive advantage? One individual did this: he sent out an email reminder when it was about time to replace a cartridge one of his customers had purchased.

There's always something there that research will uncover if you do it correctly, especially if you do your matrix chart first. Often, business owners and marketers talk about the benefits to the buyer, but we fail to appreciate that the important part is taking that feature and showing the customer how buying a product conveys the benefit to them. That's what your USP does. It takes the person from asking, "Should I or shouldn't I buy this product?" to a point where they say, "I can't live without this product, because it benefits me *this* way."

You May Think That's a USP, But It's Not

Wanna know a secret? Here it is: ***You only have to be a little better than everybody else in order to get all the business you can handle.*** One reason is that most businesses out there don't have a clue what a USP is, let alone *have* one. I'd say at least 98% of businesses out there, in any field, have no real understanding of the concept of the USP. They're not telegraphing any benefits to their prospects or customers. They hang a sign in the window that says "OPEN," and feel that's a compelling enough reason to get people stampeding through the doors. It just doesn't happen.

In order to understand what truly comprises a USP, you need to understand what a USP isn't. When I look at the ads in the newspaper, the Yellow Pages, and other venues — even the mail — I see advertisers talking about quality and service. Here's a common refrain: "We offer exceptional quality and service!" Well, holy-moly, that's going to make me run down and buy everything you have! Yeah, right. Frankly, **in most cases "quality" and "service" are empty words. They're repeated over and over by so many businesses that they've become meaningless to the consumer.** It's too often the case that the businesses using these empty words just aren't delivering on their promises. And here's the kicker: often the employees of those businesses have no idea what the company's USP is, so they don't even realize they aren't delivering on their promises. They're totally clueless — totally disconnected from the USP.

That's not to say that simple things like quality, price, and service can't make good USPs; they can, but you have to use them very, very carefully. **Because they're so simple, they're often weak, and present hazards that can kill a young business.** Here's a great USP, *if* you can back it up: your price is the lowest. It's a dangerous USP, too, because if your price is the lowest, your profit margin is small, and that may hurt you. You can only make it with this USP if you have a product that you really can cut the price on, so you can cut down the competition along with your price. This works like magic if it's still profitable. McDonald's does it with burgers, and Wal-Mart does it with discount consumer goods. Most of us can't make a dangerous USP like this work, and I'll tell you why later on.

High quality is also good USP material, but you have to explain, exactly, everything that people want to know about the quality. You can't just use those empty words I mentioned before. Greater choice can be a USP, but only if you really do have a tremendous selection. **Exceptional service is always a good USP, as long as you define your service and make it known exactly what it is you're offering.** In other words, if you offer help after the sale, you tell your customers, "Here's what we'll do for you after the sale, and how we'll be there to help you if anything comes up." **A superior guarantee can be a powerful USP,** but it should be a long guarantee, without a lot of escape clauses, that people can readily see is advantageous to them.

Danger, Will Robinson!

Quality, price, and service: these are all USPs that are viable, but they're weak. That is, they can work under certain circumstances, but you really, really have to know what you're doing to use them well. **In my opinion, lowest price is absolutely the worst of all the workable USPs you can try.** I'm speaking from experience here, because 20 years ago, when I started my first business, that was my USP: I was a cheap date. I was the lowest-priced provider in my market — and I'm telling you, it's horrible.

First of all, any idiot can offer the lowest price. It takes no imagination whatsoever; it takes no creativity. It's dumb for a lot of reasons, but part of the reason it's dumb is that with all of the unforeseen costs in business, you need to charge premium rates just so you can afford to develop the kind of infrastructure that's needed to support the levels of service that keep your customers

MARKETING SECRET #3

Overview of a successful marketing campaign...

a. Take the best sales points and "schemes" that have worked before...

b. Find new ways to hook them together... new themes, new angles

c. Then smooth it out... So it sounds new and different.

coming back. In my case, I was the lowest-priced carpet cleaner in my market. I couldn't afford to upgrade my equipment. My level of service was poor, because I was always running from one job to the next, and my whole business model required me to spend as little time at each job as possible. So everything suffered.

Here's another reason that offering the absolute rock-bottom lowest price is a bad idea, short and to the point: **it can backfire on you.** Some people will choose a product or service on price, and that's always the way they're going to shop — period. But **if they're willing to buy on price, they'll leave you on price, too.** Others shop on price because they don't know any better. The first question they ask when they call a new company is what the price is, because they don't know any other question to ask. Most businesses can't give them a better question to ask, because they don't operate with a USP.

I can't emphasize enough how important a USP is to your business. While it's true that most people shop according to price at least occasionally, they're often willing to choose goods and services based on benefits. If you can provide a USP that gives your prospect a reason to do business with you instead of the low-priced guy, they're going to choose you. **With a strong USP, you can easily justify higher prices and get them, because you're not competing on price: you've got other**

FREE GIFT! Go to www.RuthlessMarketing.com/freegift

things to offer. The cream is going to rise to the top: you're going to get better customers who are easier to deal with, who have money and are willing to spend it, if you offer things that appeal to those customers.

Build It, and They Will Come

In this section, I'm going to tell you how to built a powerful USP that will attract customers for years to come. I'll start with three secrets that will practically force your customers to do business with you instead of your competition. These are conceptual items that, if you'll keep them in mind as you develop your USP, will help you fashion one that does the job in a potent and consistent manner.

Number One: The More Unique You Are, The Better

There's a reason it's called a *Unique Selling Position*. At its root, **a USP is really just what separates you from your competition,** whether that's one thing or several; it's what makes a person choose to do business with you rather than the guy down the street. That means you have to think about what makes you different from the next guy selling the same thing.

Let's say you sell a certain type of widget, and there are hundreds of people in your market selling that widget. There are still ways you can set yourself apart from your competitors. This could be anything from a catchy name or slogan, to how fast you ship your product. Maybe everyone else takes four to five days to ship the widget — but you do it in 24 hours. These are just a few off-the-cuff examples: there are all kinds of things you can come up with if you put a little skull-sweat into it. **Your USP can even be so unique that it's controversial. That makes it newsworthy. That, in turn, leads to free publicity.** If you have the right USP in place, it's going to give you a competitive advantage, because you're the company the media is focusing on — and as a result, you're the business that your target market is going to focus on.

Here's a related point. **As much as you want to attract the right people to your business, it's equally as important to repel the *wrong* people.** What that means is, you've got to have enough courage to not worry about ticking off the wrong people. You're looking for just one type of person; that's all you care about, and that's who your message is aimed at. The more controversial it is, assuming that you don't repel the kind of people that you're looking for, the better. Many businesses, I think, are preoccupied with trying to be lukewarm. They're trying to attract everybody, and their messages have no real power to their potential customers whatsoever. It's like jumping up and down in the ocean instead of in a puddle.

Number Two: Know Your Competitors Better Than They Know Themselves

You can't assume that just because you sell the same widget as your competitors, you understand how those competitors operate. Take Sam Walton, the founder of Wal-Mart; he knew better. When he was starting out, he spent more time in K-Mart than most K-Mart managers! He knew that the best way to make Wal-Mart successful was to know the competition extremely well — to know it inside and out. He spent months learning how they did business, what their prices were, and the products they sold — and in the process, he got kicked out of several K-Marts. Obviously, that didn't stop him.

If you have a physical storefront, you need to visit other stores selling the same types of products to the same types of customers, or at least stores selling related products. **You need to spend time in the store of anyone you consider a direct competitor.** Talk to their employees; if you can do it and they don't know who you are, that's great. But if they're smart and they're running their business right, they know who you are — so you might have to send someone else in to do some covert operations for you. If you're an Internet business and don't have a physical storefront, you can do this online as well; it may even be easier, because to a large extent,

---

FREE GIFT! Go to www.RuthlessMarketing.com/freegift

it's anonymous. Spend plenty of time looking at other websites that sell the same kinds of products to the same types of customers. Spend some time on Google or Yahoo doing research. Search for the kinds of products you think your customers will be searching for when they find your website. If you're using Pay Per Click advertising on the search engine, spend lots of time searching the same phrases that you're advertising, in order to see what other people who are running the same keywords are advertising.

Knowing your competition, however you do it, is the best market research you'll ever do, and probably the least expensive, so it gives you the best return on your investment. Look at their literature, look at their processes, know what they're doing so you can do it better and faster and easier for the consumer. That's inexpensive education that can give you an unfair advantage over the competition. Shopping with them can also help you — so go ahead, order one of their products. How fast do you get it? What's in the package when you get it? What are they offering as an upsell or a back-end? How do they handle customer service complaints? How do they handle returns? You can get a wealth of information about your competition simply by ordering one of their products, or making a phone call inquiring about it.

Number Three: Be Specific About the Benefits You Offer

Generally speaking, being general is generally not a good way, in general, to come up with a USP. Did you get that? Obviously, I threw "general" in there several times to make the point that your USP can't be generic. *It's got to be specific*. **The reason a good USP works is because it makes your customer choose to do business with you over your competitors.** It makes people want to seek you out. A broad USP can't do this: it doesn't provide enough punch to get your customer to do business with you.

Look at Domino's Pizza, which had the best USP ever until the law made them change it: "Fresh, Hot Pizza Delivered In 30

- It's fresh. (A lot of pizza isn't; it's anything but fresh.)

- It's hot.

- It's delivered within 30 minutes.

- That's guaranteed, or it's free.

It doesn't say the pizza tastes good, by the way. I think that's important. However, this simple statement is very clear, very compelling, and leaves nothing to the imagination. It delivered a specific benefit that used to separate Domino's from all the other pizza joints.

Be forewarned, however, that with specificity comes a built-in problem. **Your USP can come back to haunt you if you aren't careful when you construct it, to make certain that you're able to deliver on your promises.** If you advertise the "fastest delivery in town" and your delivery is slow, that works against you. People who never paid attention to the speed of your delivery before will notice it now, and then they won't trust you. If you make a promise, make certain it's a promise your business can support; otherwise, you're better not to mention it at all. Too many companies, in presenting their USP, will add features that sound good but that they're not capable of delivering. That doesn't advance your business at all; in fact, it's just the reverse. It's suicide.

MARKETING SECRET #4

The E-Factors that influence every sale:

- Pride — Desire to be better than others…

- POWER

- Love

- Fear

- Greed

- Guilt

That's it!

These are the 5 reasons people buy anything and everything! Every reason to buy can be linked back to these 5 powerful emotional factors.

Let's look at Domino's again. If they hadn't been able to deliver pizza in 30 minutes, you would have been unhappy. But if you'd called a regular pizza delivery shop and it took 45 minutes or an hour to get there, you would have been perfectly satisfied, because that was normal service. Once you make a promise and it raises that expectation, failure to deliver puts you in an unfavorable light. So you have to make certain that your USP is understood clearly in its statement, that you can deliver on that USP, and more importantly, that everyone working for you knows that it's a statement you're making publicly, and that they're expected to comply with it. That's your responsibility as a business owner. If you're writing the ads, running the business, and responsible for the cash flow, you've got to make sure that your employees are in tune with your marketing message.

Refine Your USP

Here's something I want to reiterate. Your USP, whatever you come up with, isn't set in stone. **The right USP might not even come immediately; and even if it does, it may take some tinkering to get it just right.** Here's an interesting story that makes that point, one that my good friend Don Bice heard from the original Advertising Manager for Federal Express. Their classic tagline, "When it absolutely, positively has to get there overnight," took them a while to come up with — but it's made them tons of money. Here's what happened: they'd been having meeting after meeting, trying to work out a good USP, and the early efforts weren't working at all. It seems their Shipping Manager happened to be dropping some things off at one meeting, so they turned to him and said, "We're struggling with how to position our service and sell it to people." He said, "Oh, that's easy! You use us when it absolutely, positively has to get there overnight." And they said, "That's it!"

You never know where that inspiration will come from. Sometimes it comes right from your customers. **One of the secrets to developing great USPs is to hone in on the problems your**

customers are having, and some of the challenges they face on a daily basis. All this is work; there's no question about it. It really does take a lot of time and effort, and it's probably not going to come overnight. But once you find that competitive advantage, you can build your entire marketing effort around it.

C'mon, Everybody Does It

An easy way to come up with your own USP is to look closely at your own company. It's funny, **but you can actually create a USP not by doing something differently than all your competitors, but by advertising things that *everybody* does in the marketplace but that your customers don't know about.** For example, let's say you do something behind the scenes that your customers never know about, and let's say everyone else in the same marketplace does the exact same thing. You can stand up and say, "Look, this is how we do it. This is the care that we take. This is how we process orders. This is how we handle *your* order." Just by bringing that to the forefront, all of a sudden you've got a USP. Any of your competitors can say, "We do that too!" But if they do, all of a sudden they become the "me too" person, following *you*.

Here's an excellent story of how this works. In 1919, Claude Hopkins, a famous copywriter and marketing expert, was hired by Schlitz Beer. At the time, Schlitz was in something like tenth or fifteenth place in beer sales. They were desperate to boost their sales, so they hired Hopkins. He went in and asked all sorts of questions about what they did in their business, so they walked him through the factory and showed him the brewing process. He was shown how they washed the beer bottles repeatedly, how carefully they chose the yeast, and all the copper kettles and other equipment they used. He was absolutely fascinated by the entire process, so he went to the people at Schlitz and said, "Look, why aren't you telling people about this? This is absolutely amazing! People would love this!" The Schlitz people replied, "But everybody else does the exact same thing." And Claude Hopkins pointed out, "Yes, but nobody *knows* that. If you use your marketing to tell everyone how you brew your beer, it'll put you above and beyond everybody else. You'll be the first in this category, even though your competitors do these things too."

The Schlitz people did what Hopkins told them. They told people how beer was made, and in six months' time Schlitz was the best-selling beer in America. Did they have to change anything they did? No; **all they did was tell their customers about something they were already doing for them. They made the product interesting. It's a common product in a very competitive market, but they got around that by telling people what most brewers would assume everybody already knew. They brought it to the forefront, and that became their USP.** You see, sometimes you've got to educate your customers. You have to teach them what makes you special; don't just take it for granted. Then dramatize those facts to make them appealing to people so that it really *does* interest them, and they'll appreciate that.

That's why when you're doing your research, you should think about whatever it is you're already doing just like everybody else, but that maybe nobody knows about. If you tell your customers about it, it sounds like inside information, or a revelation, or something new and different, maybe even a breakthrough — *even if everybody else in your field is doing it.*

You're Selling What Now?

Here's something that many people never even consider when developing their USP. Obviously you're selling a product or a service, and you know what that is. But here's how it fits into crafting a USP. **You have to ask yourself, "What am I really selling?"**

A perfect example is a company I know of that markets an office prospecting system. This is a management and organization service that shows you how to prospect for new clients, how to handle the clients once they're in your system, and how to get all the employees on the same page as to how this all works. That was how they marketed the product at first, plain and simple. Then at some point they asked themselves, "What are we *really* selling?"

Here's the USP they developed. The headline for their ad was, "It puts your office on autopilot so you can spend the afternoon playing golf." Why would they do such a thing? Because they took time to back away and take a good look at their market. They asked themselves, "Who's most likely to give us money for what we're offering?" They discovered that many of the people who use this kind of system are golfers, who are looking for any excuse to get out of the office, hold all their messages, and get out on the golf course. When they realized this, they crafted their USP to target those people, and they recreated their product. In other words, they're no longer selling this unique system with all the software that does this and that and has all these wonderful features. They're selling golf time. Their whole selling point is that it frees you up and puts everything on autopilot so you can go play golf. It's a great example of how you should deconstruct what your service or product is and ask yourself, what are you *really* selling?

A Few Other Options to Consider

I think making things risk-free can be a great USP. For example, a company called Investment Rarities in Minnesota offers a two-year, money-back guarantee when you buy gold bouillon or gold coins from them — which is ideal if the market takes a downturn. Seaside Buick in San Diego offers another great example. When you buy a car from most dealers, you lose thousands of the dollars the instant you drive it off the lot — but what Seaside Buick does is offer a five-day money-back guarantee. For most products and services, five days doesn't count for much; but when you're buying a new car, it counts big-time! You take the car, you drive it anywhere you want for five days, and if you didn't like something about it, you can bring it back and get your money back in full.

My company, M.O.R.E., Inc., produces information products. In our marketplace, which is loaded with skepticism, one of the USPs we used for years was a lifetime money-back guarantee, until our lawyer made us change it — he told us it wasn't legal. For years, that was the deal our company offered: if you weren't happy with the product anytime within your lifetime or ours, you could get your money back — no questions asked. It blew the customers away, because they were used to dealing with lots of hassles with other companies whenever they tried to get their money back, even after ten or twenty days, let alone years after they made the purchase!

Offering special incentives is another great way to refine your USP. Give people something extra. This works especially well if your competitors are selling the exact same products as you. Another good USP is to zero in on the needs of your market. If you're a sporting goods store, tell your customers that you have all the products they need for fishing, hunting, golf, or archery, or that you specialize in serving people with special health needs.

Here's another thing to keep in mind: **try to get your USP in everything that describes what you do.** For example, you can

---

clearly telegraph a benefit, or at least what it is that you're selling, through the name on your business cards. When somebody asks you what do you do, describe what you do. Turn *that* into a USP. Don't just say, "I provide financial services," if that's what it might be. **Figure out what you're really selling, find the benefits that you can telegraph to that customer or prospect, and use that to describe what you do.** You don't need to use catchy, cute, clever phrases in your USP or business name — everybody else does that.

Instead of playing around with words, **create a name for your business that telegraphs the major benefit of what you're offering,** so people don't have to scratch their heads and wonder. Make it so that when they see you listed in the Yellow Pages, they can determine, just from the title of your business, exactly what it is that you're offering. If you're creating products, make sure that the product name telegraphs your USP and makes that benefit clear. Promotions work the same way. If you want to name the promotion, try to integrate your USP into the name of that promotion so people don't have to figure it out on their own. I'm not trying to say that your customers are stupid, but they'll appreciate it if you make life a little bit easier for them.

It's easy to get caught up in being the business owner and to forget what it's like to be the customer. What you need to do is take off the business-owner hat for just a moment, put on a consumer's hat, and pretend you've got a problem your customer wants solved. Write down the things people might be looking for. What's their exact problem? What's the exact end result they want? What do they have going on in their minds when they're looking for the product or service you're providing? In doing that, you're going to achieve some insight you didn't have before.

If you're so close to the business that you can't do this yourself, it wouldn't hurt to talk to some of your consumers; or you might be able to talk to some friends who've used your product and services. **You have to get into that customer's mindset;** don't keep working from your own mindset, saying to yourself, "Well, they *should* want this," and, "They *should* want that," and, "They *should* be interested in this." What they *should* want doesn't matter. It's what they *do* want that actually matters. Once you find out what they *do* want, you can build your USP around that.

Cop a Realistic Attitude About Your USP

Remember this painful fact: not everyone is as enamored with your business as you are. You may love your company and your products, but you also have to realize that we live in a busy culture that's saturated with marketing. People are busy; they've got their heads full of all kinds of different things, and the bottom line is this: most people just don't give a damn about your business. That's the one thing a lot of businesspeople never stop to consider, and sure, it's understandable. Our companies are our livelihoods; they're extensions of ourselves. We love what we do, and so naturally we suffer from the delusion of thinking that other people give a damn — but they really don't. I hate to break it to you, but sometimes even our own families and friends don't really give a damn about our businesses.

Many entrepreneurs make the mistake of thinking that people care about their product or service, or that all they have to do is put an ad in the Yellow Pages and say that they're in business at a certain location, and the people will come. But remember, this is exactly what a good USP isn't. Most people won't spare something like this a second glance. It's not necessarily that they're lazy and apathetic; in most cases, they're just plain busy. On top of that, they're so bombarded with marketing that they usually don't have the time to think about or care about what they're hearing. If anything, they feel like they're overwhelmed with advertising messages.

If you can realize that most people not only don't give a damn about your advertising, your company, and what you're

---

trying to sell them, but on the contrary, actually hate it — then you're of the proper mindset. Once you realize how fed up with advertising people are, you can start adjusting your message so it really does do all the great things I'm talking about here. Whatever it is you're selling, you have to get people to stop and pay attention — and that's what a USP is all about. If you can't get them to pay attention to you, they've got plenty of other things to do to keep themselves occupied.

Avoid Change for Change's Sake

If a USP just isn't working for you, don't hesitate to change it — but beware of changing a successful USP just because you've grown bored with it. This happens far more often than it should: marketing people get tired of the same old advertising, even though it works. **Somebody goes through a tremendous amount of time, money, and effort to develop a USP, to put together some great marketing campaigns, business just grows by leaps and bounds, and then they get bored and start changing everything.**

A good example is the Schlitz story I mentioned earlier. Several years after Hopkin's innovative idea, some not-so-bright marketer said, "You know, we need a catchphrase for our Schlitz Beer," and they changed the whole marketing strategy to this: "Schlitz, the beer that made Milwaukee famous." And now Schlitz Beer is nowhere in the Top 10, or even Top 20, of all beer sold in America. In fact, the company barely exists as such these days. This shows you how you can have the right USP, and how you can go back and change it and get the wrong one.

In advertising they have a saying: "By the time the client gets bored with the message and wants to change, it's probably making its first impression on the public." Here's a word to the wise: **get a good thing going and keep it going. A great way to think of your marketing is to picture it as a parade.** Your business is on a parade float, and at the beginning you're all excited about being on the float and you see the flowers, and the papier-mâché, and you're waving at the people and having a good time. Then, after about 30 minutes you're getting hot, and you realize that the papier-mâché is flaking off, and you're sweating and you hate it, and you want to jump off that float and get onto another. What you don't realize is that the people the parade is passing by are seeing you for the first time. They're excited. They're waving. Down the way a bit, there are even more people who've never seen you before, and they're excited to see you. Further on down, there are even more people happy to see you!

The long and the short of it is, most companies just get bored, because they see the same marketing every day. They want to jump off that float, even though it's still effective. "Oh, that slogan is so old. These sales letters are bad. Our USP is worn out; we've had it now for six months." So what? Some companies keep the same USP for years and years. Why would they do that? Because it continues to work. Don't change your USP just because you're bored. If it's working, if it's making money — stick to it.

In business, we tend to monkey with things more than we should, when if we'd let the customers continue to tell us what they want by studying their buying patterns, we'd be a lot better off. If the USP stops working because sales are low, then by all means change it; find a new USP, adjust it, tweak it, do whatever you need to. But to change your USP just because you're tired of it or bored with it is a bad idea. If the customers still like it and your sales are good, keep riding that baby as long as you can!

Summing It Up

As I wind down this chapter, I want to give you a quick recap of the things I've talked about here. **In a way, these concepts are entirely unfair to your competitors — because if you use them to create your USP, they'll separate you from every other competitor in your marketplace and let you dominate that marketplace.** But hey — there's a reason this is called the Ruthless Marketing System, right? You've got to be ruthless if you want to stay alive in our increasingly competitive marketplace.

Identify the Enemy

Take a look at the people who sell the exact same goods and services in your marketplace. **Who are your top five competitors, and why?** You've got to figure out what they're doing right, what they're doing wrong. What do they do to attract and retain the best customers and clients? You've got to spy on them, study them, become a customer. You've got to know them better than they know themselves. You've got to know their strengths and weaknesses and try to focus in on those, because nobody makes money by accident. If they're doing well consistently, they're doing something right.

Identify the Biggest Problems and Unfulfilled Needs in Your Market

What are the three biggest problems your prospects and customers face on a daily basis? **What do your best prospects and customers want and need that they're not getting anywhere else?** Answer these questions right, and you'll have a great USP. Build your Claims Matrix, so you can find where the gaps are. Where are the unfulfilled promises? Where are the biggest dissatisfactions? Work to create the great solutions to the biggest problems. To do this, you've got to brainstorm, brainstorm, and brainstorm!

Make Your Benefits Clear To Your Customers

Every USP requires a clear statement of benefits. Don't assume that your customers know what they'll get when they deal with you instead of "Joe Blow" down the street. **Tell them exactly what you can do for them, and why they should come to you instead.** If you've got the best-quality muffins in town, flaunt it. If your service is unique, take advantage of that. People need to know how you're going to make their lives better.

Just Get Your USP Out There

I can't overstate the importance of formulating your USP and getting it out there where your clients can see it. It's too easy to get caught in the paralysis of analysis. You say to yourself, "It has to be perfect! I've got to get it just right!" Well, no, it doesn't. As I've made clear, you can refine your USP after you've launched it, as long as you don't overdo it. Don't think your USP has to be perfect right out of the box. As the owner of a small business, you have the ability to be flexible. **If you can come up with a great USP right now, and if down the road there's an ever better one and an even better advantage to your business, then you can change it.** Take a little bit of time and effort, get your USP out there and, believe me, even if it's not the best of the best of the best, you're going to be head and shoulders above the rest of your competitors.

Refine That USP

This one goes hand-in-glove with the previous point. Once your USP's out there, you can refine it as needed. Here are some good guidelines to follow: **keep it short and clear. Keep it benefit-oriented. Make your claims believable.** Make them measurable, if possible, as in time or quantity. Avoid defining your USP on price

---

alone; someone can always beat you on that. Make your claim unique, and use your proposition everywhere you can.

That's a good place to end this chapter. I hope you understand a little better the fact that putting together a decent USP and making money with it really does take an intimate understanding of your best customers, their likes and dislikes, the challenges they face, the problems that keep them up at night, and the frustrations with which they live. The more you know about all of that, plus the more aware you are of those few competitors who are out there kicking butt in the marketplace, the better. Watch them closely. **Good companies are few and far between; that makes them easy to spot, if you know what to look for.** Keep a close eye on them, and you'll find the right type of messages, through experimentation, because your customers will respond. They'll respond with their checkbooks, their credit cards, and their cash.

SECRET TWO:

Direct-Response Marketing

In this chapter, I'll introduce you to Direct-Response Marketing, and show you how you can use this powerful tool to dramatically increase your profits. The tips, tricks, and strategies I'll reveal to you here can make you huge sums of money, but you're going to have to read this chapter several times to really understand it. **Direct-Response Marketing is a complicated subject that deserves in-depth study.**

At its most basic, **Direct-Response Marketing is whatever you do to get your customers to respond to you directly.** It's not the kind of brand awareness you see when Pepsi or AT&T run a commercial on TV. That's not really asking you to do anything; it's just them getting their name out there. Direct-Response Marketing, on the other hand, is meant to get people to respond to you directly: to pick up the phone and call you, or to fill out an order form and fax it or mail it to you. **It's anything you do in business to get people to order from you, or to request more information, or to take a specific action.**

In some ways, I consider Direct-Response Marketing an art form. It's the process of identifying the audience most likely to purchase your product or service, and then approaching them directly at the right time to solicit their business, using a direct-to-consumer advertising medium. This can be postcards or other mailings, sales calls, special emails, handing out discount cards — **any form of advertising that directly targets potential and existing customers,** rather than something just thrown out there in hopes that someone will remember you when it comes time to fix the muffler or buy roses for Mother's Day. I call it an art form because it takes a while to understand and perfect the strategies you *must* use to truly match the right people with the right message at the right time.

But Direct-Response Marketing is also very much a science. It's an organized, multi-step system for selling, which starts off by targeting and contacting the people who might be interested in what you're selling, in such a way that you get them to respond and make their interest clear. Then the system kicks in, working to elicit their response again and get them more involved in what it is you're offering. This works whether you do it through direct-mail, on the Internet, in seminars, or even one-on-one. **The science is also in the mechanics that make it all work: the ability to put together a database, to build a list, and to market to various elements of that list.** Regardless of the advertising media or strategies you choose, you have to immerse yourself in the science if you want to even get close to achieving art.

You have to employ the mechanics of Direct-Response Marketing in a way that makes sense to **the people with whom you want to build relationships.** You have to get their attention, you have to grab their interest, you have to create desire, and then you have to get them to take action. If you do that right, eventually you'll be able to create your masterpiece — the kind of life you want to live, lubricated by copious amounts of money.

The Name of the Game

Your goal with Direct-Response Marketing is to get an immediate action from your prospect, whether it's a visit to your business, a call, an order, a purchase, a request for more information, or a promise. To accomplish any of these things, you need to create **salesmanship in print**. Not only does your Direct-Response Marketing strategy need to evoke an immediate action, but it also has to do everything a real salesman would do, in terms of generating that response. **Just like a living, breathing**

salesman, here's what that a good Direct-Response Marketing campaign does:

- It tells the prospect about the benefits of the product;
- It overcomes objection;
- It answers questions;
- It provides a guarantee; and
- It makes promises.

A good Direct-Response Marketing campaign does all these things and more; it has to, in order to succeed. I think the biggest benefit of Direct-Response Marketing over face-to-face salesmanship or even tele-marketing is that you have the power to let Yellow Page ads, sales letters, classified ads, or display ads in the newspaper, magazines or on the Internet generate the response you want. Direct-Response Marketing allows you to multiply your effort, to reach a lot more people, and generate a lot more responses without wasting your time — and that makes it a very powerful strategy indeed.

In order to work effectively, **Direct-Response Marketing has to be a very targeted form of marketing.** Think of a rifle, versus a shotgun. With Direct-Response Marketing, you don't just blast out a message to everyone at random: **your message is delivered in the clearest and most compelling way possible, to the specific people who are most likely to buy and then continue to buy from you.** Those people could be highly qualified prospects that you've identify through various methods, or they can be established customers, people with whom you already have an ongoing relationship.

Marketers use lots of metaphors to describe Direct-Response Marketing. In addition to being a combination of art and science, to many of us it's also a combination of sport and war. This is a fun way of making money. You can be very strategic using this marketing method, just as a couple of generals would be when planning how to stage an attack on their enemy. Because make no mistake: no matter how much you'd like to believe otherwise, **your direct competitors are your enemies**. They're out there trying to get the same dollars you're trying to get, and you can't let that happen.

Laying a Firm Foundation

Direct-Marketing is a system for selling, and if **you don't have a system for selling, then you're at the mercy of your customer's system for buying — and they don't have one.** What most businesses do — sadly for them, but fortunately for you — is the direct opposite of Direct-Response Marketing. They set up shop, put up some signs, and maybe run the occasional radio ad or newspaper spot, but they do it in such a way that it's mildly effective at best. They're not using Direct-Response Marketing to get people into their selling system.

Now, in order to do Direct-Response Marketing right, you need to start with a firm foundation. One excellent way to do this is to achieve an intimate understanding of what I call the *Three Keys to Effective Direct-Response Marketing*. These keys will help you preform Direct-Response Marketing right; I've seen a lot of people make a lot of mistakes that could easily have been avoided if they'd just done the simple things I'm going to tell you to do here. The Three Keys are relatively straightforward, and they strip Direct-Response Marketing down to its basic elements. Without further ado, here's what's required for effective Direct-Response Marketing:

- The right message
- The right audience
- The right time

Or to put it all together into one sentence, you've got to **carry the right message to the right audience at the right time.** I consider this the Golden Rule of Direct-Response Marketing.

Many marketers boil this concept down to what they call the KISS Principle, where KISS stands for "Keep It Simple, Stupid." I think that's a little offensive, so I'll use my own term, thank you. Now, if you don't get the right message to the right audience at the right time, you're going to hear "no" a lot more than you'll hear "yes." **Instead of using a shotgun, pull up that high-powered rifle**, identify exactly who the prospect is who's most likely to buy your product, and go directly to that consumer using a direct-to-consumer advertising medium. In the following sections, I'm going to discuss all these things in greater detail, and in the order I think is most important.

Key One: The Audience

If you don't play to the right audience, you're never going to have a very good response to anything you do. You've failed right from the beginning: game over, time to go home. Identifying the right people is the most important key to successful Direct-Response Marketing, and I suggest you use three methods to accomplish this.

First is what I call "customer hijacking" — or **letting your competition do your work for you.** This is simply where you go out and rent a list of your competition's customers and then try to make them your own. It's not possible for every industry, but it's the number one tactic I suggest *if* it's possible. So if you're Sears, and J. C. Penney is selling appliances, you try to get a list of those people to whom they've recently sold appliances. Then you can send them a Direct-Mail piece that gives them the option of buying their next appliance from you.

Second is demographic profiling: analyzing your target audience and **coming up with the profile of your ultimate customer or target audience.** In using demographics like age, gender, income level, and location, you're basically looking for anything that helps you identify who's most likely to buy your products and services. Once you've figured that out, you can go out and acquire a list of clients who meet those criteria. You're going to use list brokers for both customer hijacking and demographic profiling.

Third is customer corralling. This is where you capture information on your past or current customers, and add them to a list so you can continue to solicit business. Keep in mind that **the easiest sale you're ever going to make is to a customer to whom you've already sold.** A good example of this is Harrah Casinos' Loyalty Programs. You go in there to gamble one time, they get you on a little card, and pretty soon you're getting more mail than you've ever known — and you're going back to Harrah's a lot more often.

Key Two: Your Message

Now, let's talk about the right message. You need to **study your products or services from your customer's perspective.** Remember, it's all about them; you have to keep in mind their view, which can be summarized as WIIFM — *What's In It For Me?* That's what your prospects want to know. So build your message around the strongest benefits to your customer, and keep in mind that there are only five real reasons people buy anything: greed, guilt, fear, pride, or love. We marketers call this the *psychographic* of your audience, as opposed to the demographic; and **the two most important of those psychographic motives are greed and fear.** That's why you see so many commercials that play on people's greed, or that make them afraid that they're doing something wrong: raising their children wrong, not brushing their teeth enough, or not wearing the right deodorant.

You need to **understand the emotional reasons that people buy products and services. Make sure you build your benefits toward one or more of those reasons.** Identify your customer's strongest motives to buy, and you're going to do very well identifying the right message.

Key Three: the Right Time

Once you've identified the right audience and the right message, **you need to identify the time your prospects are most likely to purchase your product or service.** For example, if you run a mortgage company, aim your message at people who are selling their houses. If a person's selling a house, they'll most likely need to buy a new house shortly thereafter — so if you hit them with a mortgage opportunity right then and there, there's a good chance they'll take it. If you wait three weeks or a month after your prospect puts his property on the market, chances are that he's already found another mortgage if he was planning to buy another piece of property. Therefore, you need to respond within a few days, no more. If you plan this properly and do it correctly, the time *will* be right.

Effective Direct-Response Marketing is all about the right audience, the right message, and the right timing. And while I've discussed Direct-Response Marketing as an art form, don't worry about going out there and trying to paint the *Mona Lisa* right off the bat. **It's kind of like playing chess. You might start out a bit slow, but you're going to get better at it the more you do it.** Like chess, Direct-Response Marketing takes a day to learn and a lifetime to master; but use these guidelines, and you'll have a solid

---

foundation on which to build your business.

What Kind of Bait's on Your Hook?

One thing you should be aware of from the get-go is that **Direct-Response Marketing isn't cheap.** If you use it right you can make millions, but as the old saying goes, it takes money to make money. Continuing with the mortgage example, here's an interesting way that some people have attracted new customers. They combine the right message with the right audience at the right time, they send their message by Federal Express — already an expensive proposition — and then they sweeten the proposition by throwing a $100 bill in that Federal Express package. That's right — a $100 bill. You see, they know it's a numbers game, but it's also a game of finding the right people to deliver your message to, and knowing that **you can spend a lot more money to reach that right person** (assuming that other things — your price points and your profit margins — are high).

So these marketers are throwing a $100 bill in a Federal Express envelope, and then sending a personalized letter along with it. There's none of that "Dear Friend" crap — that's counterproductive. Instead, they're saying, "Dear John: Why have I sent you a $100 bill by Federal Express? Two reasons: **1)** Your time is very valuable, so I'm paying you well to spend a good, solid hour looking over everything in this package; and **2)** I believe you're the type of person I'm looking for, and I'm willing to back up my beliefs with a solid investment." That's an excellent example of getting the right message to the right prospect at the right time, and not being afraid to spend a lot of money in the process.

So many people fail with Direct-Response Marketing, and they don't have to. This is a $300 billion a year industry; so why doesn't it work for them? When you dig a little deeper, it turns out that **they didn't have their hearts in it**. They sent out some postcards, they didn't get the results they expected, and they gave up. They thought they were doing Direct-Response Marketing — but they're really weren't. *You have to spend money with Direct-Response Marketing to make money.* It could be worth it to send out $100 bills once you know what your customers are worth. You want to get their attention, and their time is valuable, and paying them for it is a great way to grab them by the throat and make them give you a fair hearing.

P. T. Barnum, who is one of my heroes — a great, great marketer — once said, "Don't try to catch a whale by using a minnow as bait. **"If there's one general mistake I see a lot, one that people who are brand new to Direct-Response Marketing are making over and over, it's that they want huge results from the very beginning**. They're expecting enormous things from this form of marketing, which it can and does deliver to the people who understand how to use it. But they're starting out trying to capture a whale by using a minnow as bait, and in doing so they're being *far* too conservative. **As long as you've found the right customer and the right message, and the rest of your mechanics are in place, you can afford to spend a ton of money to reach that person."**

If I said this approach always works, I'd be lying. You don't know for sure what's going to happen. Even if it's the right thing to do, you're going to reach a certain percentage of people who can't follow through because other things are going on in their lives. Maybe, for example, they've just broken their leg, or they're getting a divorce, or they've lost their job. So you won't catch every prospect, but remember: you won't catch any if you use the wrong bait. Don't be afraid to gamble a little, because if you're trying to catch a whale by using a minnow as bait, you'll never have any real success.

Knowing What You're Doing

Here's another thing I'd like to add about the person who says, "Well, I sent out a postcard one time and I didn't get any responses." When I hear that, I say, "Let me see your sales material." Usually, I find that they've done a terrible job of getting their message across. Sometimes people believe they're great writers, and they're not; or they're not focusing on right kind of communication. They may write copy that sounds really good and has a lot of big words in it, and what those big words do to a lot of people is turn them off. Many of their readers might not understand them, and **a confused mind says "no" automatically.** Also, if a prospect doesn't understand a word, they may subconsciously feel like they're stupid. They shut off at that point.

There are all kinds of factors that go into Direct-Response Marketing that a novice isn't even aware of. They may have written a postcard, and had their buddy with an English degree edit it so it's grammatically correct and looks nice, but it just doesn't elicit the response they wanted — because they didn't really know what they wanted it to do, or they didn't know how to compel people to say "yes." **In order to solicit business, you need to get into those psychographic factors I mentioned before (fear, greed, guilt, love, and pride), as well as the nuts-and-bolts science of what makes people say yes.**

If you don't know how to do this, don't try to wing it: either hire people who do, or go find people who've done it and emulate them. Don't steal from them, but model your copy after what they've done. **Do the things you know have already been**

---

successful for others, then fine-tune those strategies so they can work for you. There are a lot of strategies floating around out there, and lots of little ways to tweak your performance. Even the colors of your postcards can make a difference in response. As a Direct-Response Marketer, you're going to have to do a lot of things you've never done before. Think of all these things as broadening your education.

You'll want to continue to market to your prospects in a systemized manner, using follow-up campaign sequences — one following the other. This will cost you some money, but it's justified. Once you implement the three keys I talked about earlier — getting the right message to the right people at the right time — you're not done. That's really where you start. Do those things right, and you're going to grab a nice percentage of your target audience; they'll go through your selling process, and you'll make some money. But you need to continue to market to them! Once you've gotten the responses from a mailing, do a second mailing, and then another. **The great thing about Direct-Response Marketing is that you know the results very quickly** — with direct-mail, for example, it may take a couple of weeks, at most. Online it's even faster.

Once again, remember this: your offer does need to be tweaked and made more efficient, but it doesn't have to be a masterpiece from the word go; it just has to be good enough. Once you've got everything together and you've followed all the steps, go for it. Send it out, and learn from what happens. You don't have to flood the market right away, either — you can test and improve on your message quickly if you **start out slowly**. Start mailing, testing, sending out little bits and pieces, and see what happens.

AIDA Ain't Just an Opera

Here's an interesting acronym that some of my fellow marketers find useful: AIDA. It stands for:

- **A**ttention
- **I**nterest
- **D**esire
- **A**ction

MARKETING SECRET #10

The Slack Adjuster — Develop and promote at least one super high-profit item that helps build your overall net profits.

- This is crucial. You must develop this super high-profit margin to make up for all of the high expenses that eat into your bottom line margins.

AIDA dovetails nicely with the three keys we've already discussed here. But these four elements have more to do with the overall process once you've already targeted your prospects and figured out what you want to say, and you know you have the timing down.

Once you've done all these things, look at the actual Direct-Marketing media available: the piece, the letter, the ad, the email message, or whatever it is. **First of all, you need to grab your prospect's Attention**, and typically you're going to do that with your headline. That's what it'll be in print or on a website; if it's an email, it's your subject. If you're addressing people in a conference, it's the first thing you say. If it's a postcard, it's in bold print. The headline has to grab their attention and make them want to read further. That's its only purpose — to grab their attention, and get them interested in continuing to read.

One of the greatest headlines ever was Dale Carnegie's "How To Win Friends and Influence People." "How to" headlines are not only often the easiest to come up with — because you already have the first two words down — but quite often they're also the most effective. What should that "how to" promise? **It needs to be benefit-laden**. I've mentioned "What's In It For Me?" already. WIIFM is the essence of writing your headline.

Once you get their attention, **you need to grab their Interest. Quite often, this is done with a sub-headline that states your Unique Selling Proposition.** As I made clear in the last chapter, a USP is what sets you apart from everyone else. It answers the question in the prospect's mind: "Why should I deal with this person or company, or buy this service, or get involved in this, or even accept this free report over all the others out there?"

Your next goal is to stimulate a Desire as they get into your offer. Most people think in words, but they take those words and put them into pictures. A picture is a stronger, more effective way of thinking. Most people, being visual, require the painting of these word pictures in their minds, and that's what you want to do as you tell your story. You want them to be in this story; they're the star of the show you're creating here. **That's how you really create desire in people: by the way you place them in the copy, and the way you overcome their initial apprehension.** Testimonials from people who have benefited from what you offer can work wonders here.

Now we come to the second "A," which is Action. You have to **make sure that it's easy and convenient for prospects to become customers.** This is where you ask for their response, whether it's an order, or for them to call an 800 number, or to send an email — whatever it is you want them to do. This is where you make it convenient for them to respond. Give your prospects several ways to get in touch with you. You don't want to give them too many choices, ever, on anything, but you want to give them basic choices. This is where understanding your customer is really important. Some people may have misgivings about certain ways of responding to you, so you want to give them options that are comfortable for them. Maybe the psychodemographics of your customer base makes them more likely to pick up the phone and call a number; or maybe they'd prefer to FAX their order in. You should also give them the option to mail their order in, even if you're strictly doing an online transaction. That's a big mistake I often see online: not even offering that option. The way a lot of websites work — you put your credit card in or you don't buy, and that's a mistake. Some people just don't feel safe putting their credit card number out there in cyberspace.

Calls to Action

Let's go back to something I touched on earlier: the way that **many businesses try Direct-Response Marketing, then dump it quickly because it doesn't work for them.** That's because they're not using it right. I've discussed using the right bait, and this next point plays into that concept: you have to give your customers a great offer. Some businesses try Val-Pak, where you get all these little full-color inserts about various businesses; you've probably gotten these packets yourself. But that's not Direct-Response Marketing. That's just coupon marketing. Most of the coupons are horrible because they're either designed by the advertiser, who doesn't know how to market properly, or they're designed by a person who wants to get the work done and move on to the next customer. Yes, you're sending that coupon out to a list of human beings, but it's not targeted, and the ads are uninspired. If you look at them, basically what they're saying is, "Hey, we're your plumber! We've been in business for 80 years. We're the best in the business!" That's not Direct-Response Marketing, because that doesn't evoke an action. Someone who gets that will say, "Wow, they've been in business 80 years. I'd go crazy if I had to do plumbing for 80 years! Poor suckers!" And then they throw it away.

You have to give people an offer that will evoke an action. Maybe you've done some image advertising, where you just try to get your name out in front of people, say through postcards or in the Yellow Pages, and hope that somebody will contact you because your ad just happened to appear when they had a plumbing problem, or they needed an attorney, or whatever your business is

---

— but that's not going to happen very often. You absolutely have to target your market, you have to get the right message to them, and you have to use the right timing. **You need to capture their attention by making them an offer that will actually get them to take an action — whether that's calling your business, coming by, or purchasing something from you.**

One great example is a gentleman by the name of Bob Stupak, the founder of the Stratosphere Casino in Las Vegas. As you know, most Las Vegas casinos do image advertising. They don't say, "Come on in, we've got this special deal for you," and things like that; instead, they've got these beautiful billboards and beautiful ads, and they show the fountains out in front and the people gambling and having fun inside. That's supposed to be enough to evoke an action in you, to have you come to their casino. Well, Bob Stupak was a great marketer as well as a great gambler. **When he started out, the Stratosphere was a tiny casino, and he needed to pull people in, so he created an offer: for $198 you got a three-day, two-night stay at his casino. You paid this in advance, before you ever showed up, and you had an entire year to use it.** He ran his ads in *Parade* magazine and did Direct-Mail and got his ads out everywhere. It wasn't an image ad; it was an actual *offer*. For $198 you got a three-day, two-night stay at the casino, but you also got two tickets to their headliner show, several meal coupons, as much as $500 in slot tokens, and $200 in casino chips.

People bought into Stupak's offer like crazy. He was selling literally tens of thousands of these packages, and that's how **he built the Stratosphere into a multi-billion dollar business.** It was a hot offer, and he continued to make it better and throw in more bonuses over time. Here's the kicker: plenty of people bought the offer, but only a relatively small percentage ever actually showed up at his casino. So all those people who didn't show up, didn't take up space in the room, didn't come to get their chips — they'd still paid all that money, and he got to pocket that.

Now you're thinking, "Okay, that's a casino. How am I going

Prepare for the worst
possible outcomes,
— Set up your
company so you can
still make money
with terrible
numbers.

- Set your margins
  high

- Keep your costs
  low

- Factor in low
  response rates...

- Plan for poor
  results. How?
  Figure out a way
  to make each
  promotion work
  — even if the
  numbers are bad.

to make a hot offer like that to my customers?" **Use your imagination. There are people in every business niche — plumbers, attorneys, restaurateurs — who are making hot offers people can't turn down.** There aren't very many of them, but they're out there. Here's another example: there's a certain restaurateur who realized early on that the lifetime value of each of his customers was very high. He knew that if he could get people into his restaurant to sit down and eat a meal, they'd come back not one or two times, but five times, 20 times, 100 times. They'd be coming back for many years, which made the lifetime value of the typical customer literally thousands of dollars.

So, what was his offer? He mailed out sales letters to people in his area, and offered them a free meal. That's right. I'm not talking about a "buy one, get one free" deal, or a child's meal free if you bought an adult meal. There were no strings attached: he offered an actual free meal. You got the entrée, you got an appetizer, you got your drink. Every single thing was free! In his sales letter, he told the truth about why he wanted you to come in and enjoy this free meal: it was because he knew you would come back again and again, since the food was so great. **His business practically exploded, because people thought that was an incredible deal.** They'd come in, enjoy the meal, and then come back again and again.

This takes us back to the concept of how much money you're willing to spend to get people into your business. A lot of business people are scared to go too far out on a limb; they don't want to spend too much of their limited advertising budget. Maybe a few cents for postage on a postcard is all they think they can afford. **But if you're delivering the services people want, and you're giving great value, and you have customers with a very high lifetime value, you can afford to make great offers in order to get prospects in the door.** You can go negative on that initial offer and still make money.

Your offer doesn't even have to be a price deal. Let's say you're stuck on your price: maybe you can't give your customers the lowest price out there, or maybe you don't even want to try. Instead, give more for what you're selling. For example, let's say you're a dentist. You can offer a lot more things than just a regular cleaning. You might say, "Come in, and we're going to give you a regular cleaning and a personalized toothbrush. Then we're going to have a customer appreciation party, and every six months you can get a free ticket for yourself and your family. We've got free drinks and free food." You can throw anything in there! **There's all sorts of crazy stuff you can do to create a great offer that catches prospects and brings them in.** If you make good on your promises, you're going to keep them.

So get over your fear of trying something wild to draw your customers in. The response can be phenomenal. Make a tremendous offer; do things that shock people; do things that would scare most business owners to death. Now, you don't have to be a fool about it. **One of the greatest things about Direct-Response Marketing is that you can test all kinds of wild and crazy and outrageous ideas to a small group of customers, so you're not really risking a lot of money if it doesn't work.** You can make sure you take what we call a stratified sample of your list and market to that — assuming you've built up a list.

You can stratify or segment your list by the products and

services your customers buy, or by the dollar amount they spend, or by the last time they did business with you. The reason you do this is because, first of all, you can tell everything about a person from their actions. When somebody's buying a certain type of product or service from you, that speaks volumes. Or, if you have a few customers who are spending ten times more money than the rest of your customers, those people are showing, by the money they spend, a certain level of seriousness that the rest of your customers aren't showing. **You've got to be able to segment those smaller groups of better customers or to segment for other reasons so that you can speak directly to those groups of people in a different way than you speak to the rest of your customer list.**

So don't drop a Direct-Mail campaign to your entire customer list with some crazy new idea that you're not sure is going to work. You want to see how a stratified sample is going to respond before you stretch your neck out too far. **Take little pockets of customers from your customer base and use them to test your wild and crazy stuff**, so you don't end up with a fiasco where everybody wants what you're offering, and you can't supply it to them all.

This brings up another point. When you're building your offer, you can also add a line like this one: **"While supplies last."** This will invoke urgency in your prospects, because now they know they'll need to hurry to get all the extra things you're throwing into your offer. In addition, this covers your bases in case you get an overzealous response. Your prospects won't mind being part of a small, select group, because when you market to a stratified sample, you're actually treating those customers special. Go ahead and tell them what you're doing; they'll appreciate being treated special. And to you, they *should* be special, because by marketing to them first, you're lowering your overall risk.

Common Sense — It's So Uncommon

It's easy to wonder why more people don't try test-marketing offers the way I've outlined above. I think one of the big reasons they don't do it is that they don't know *how* to do it. **Most people learn marketing by looking at other marketers in their field**. So if their major competitor is running a half-page Yellow Pages ad, they think they'd better do that — instead of thinking, "Okay, maybe this isn't the right way to do it." Well, sometimes in marketing **you have to go against the flow, and do something that makes you stand head and shoulders above the crowd**. Then, once you know that, you have to get past the fear. If you own a restaurant, you may be thinking: "Good Lord, I can't even imagine giving away a free meal. I've got staff, I've got food costs, and I've got overhead. I can't even imagine making that type of a deal." You've got to break through that fear barrier.

So once you've got your offer, **test it to a small portion of your list, and see what happens.** You don't have to mail it out to 20,000 people in your area; you can mail it out to a couple of hundred people and see what the response is. If it does well, roll it out to more people. **If it doesn't do well, try something else.** It's important to at least make that offer. Because if you don't, you're going to continue to market like everybody else and continue to get the same type of response as everybody else — and in most cases, that's a pretty poor response.

If you don't already have a list, you need to build one. A lot of businesses are of the opinion that they don't need one: "I don't have a list. People come in, they buy, they leave." But not creating a list that they can use for Direct-Response Marketing is where a lot of people stumble. **There's gold in your customer list, because you're able to go back to those people, make more offers, and get them back into your business — as opposed to always going out and trying to bring brand new people in, hoping that the people who did business with you one time will remember you the second time.** If you're hoping, instead of actually mailing to a list that you've created, you're not going to be making as much money as if you were smart enough to get some simple database software, ask people for their names and contact information, and actually mail to the resulting list.

You must put as much of your time, attention, energy, passion, and skills into the specific areas that bring your business the largest profits. FOCUS! Identify these areas and put everything into these activities.

- Focus only on these activities — and let other people do most of the other stuff.

Most merchants aren't even gathering up their customers' names to begin with — and frankly, that's just ridiculous. **If you ask most business owners how much money they spend on communicating and building relationships with their existing customers, most would say, "Huh?" They may spend money to** *attract* **new customers, and they think that's what advertising and marketing is. Real marketing, however, is customer relationship marketing** — and that's now an accepted way of running a business, thanks to a lot of us Direct-Response Marketers who've proven that it's successful to build and maintain those relationships. It makes sense, but so many businesses out there just don't grasp it, and they don't spend a dime to develop and maintain relationships with their customers.

Then again, **you could just do like just about everyone else, and sit around and wait for customers to come to you.** Let me share with you a story I heard from my good friend Russ von Hoelscher. He knows a guy who has a print shop in a little strip mall, and the guy's always whining and complaining about how bad business is. Russ likes the guy, but he gets sick and tired of hearing him moan. So one day Russ said, "Look, John, there's got to be 400 businesses within a five-mile radius of here. Since you've got those printing presses, why don't you just print up some sales material and I'll help you, and we can target all those businesses, and you can get them to start coming to you." And here's what the guy said to Russ: "People want printing, they can come to me." That was his whole attitude! It's ignorant, it's horrible, and it's unbelievable. Apparently, **it's easier to whine and cry and complain about how bad things are than to do a thing to change it.** Unfortunately, that mindset is more common that you might think.

It's Two, Two, *Two* Mints in One!

In the introduction to this chapter, I pointed out that Direct-Response Marketing is often considered both an art and as science, and I want to focus on that perception in this section. I want to clarify the fact that there's absolutely no way to achieve art, or even get close to it, without understanding the science involved in Direct-Response Marketing — and it's immense. So how are you going to master such a big topic, with all the variables it includes? You can start by breaking it down: learn the technology that's used to reach your market, for starters. If you're using a specific medium, you've got to understand how the process works, how to get the best rates, and what resources you have at your disposal to let you best use this medium, whether it's TV, radio, the Internet, or print. **Knowing the technology used to reach your market is one key to your success, and it's all part of the science.**

Another part is database management. Building or finding a list of highly qualified prospects is key. **Knowing and tracking your market is also crucial.** You need to know what they've purchased in the past and why they bought what they bought, because this will help you to sell them in the future.

Something I've mentioned several **times is understanding the psychological aspects of marketing — the emotional factors that prompt people to buy or to act.** Those are, again, pride, love, fear, greed, and guilt. **Practice weaving those psychological factors into your copy, into your message, into your headlines, and into your sub-headlines, because that will ultimately produce the actions you're wanting.** Now, you just can't say to

---

yourself, "Okay, I'm going to really concentrate on pride," and whip out something that sucks in the customers. **It takes practice. It takes time to understand your style, and how you're going to invoke these factors in your audience.**

Another important factor here is communication: learning to use plain, direct, and simple words and ideas, because a confused mind says "no." If you're writing something and you think, "Man, that's really clever, the way I did that," then you might be overthinking things. There's no need to be cute with this type of writing. You want to grab them by the heart or grab them by the gonads or grab them by the mind, and the best way to do that is to do it with plain, direct speech.

Here's another big factor: **testing.** Yes, I'm repeating this too, because I want to make you see how important it is. **You don't want to commit tons of money to something you're not even the least bit sure is going to work.** Our example is the guy who tried a bunch of postcards and failed; we've talked a lot about him. He went out there, spent a lot of money on getting them printed up and on the postage to send them out — and it flopped dead. Well, that money is just gone, because he didn't test his postcard before he sent it out. He wasted his advertising dollars.

As I mentioned at the start of this section, **there's no way to achieve art without understanding the science.** It's like when you first learned to ride a bike and you had training wheels, and it was fun. You learned that you pedaled and it made you go, and you learned how the brakes worked. But then you took those training wheels off, and pretty soon you were building ramps so you could jump your bike and do crazy stunts. The same thing goes with immersing yourself in the science of Direct-Response Marketing. You learn how it works, you learn the ins and outs and how to do it cost-effectively, and next thing you know you're jumping from ramp to ramp and you're building success on success. The art simply won't come unless you understand the science. **The science allows you to know your audience, know where to find them,**

know what to say, and know how to say it.

You may never get to where Direct-Response Marketing is an art form for you, but that's a goal you can set for yourself — and maybe, someday, you'll end up painting the ceiling of the Sistine Chapel. You're always striving for that masterpiece. I've already told you that **marketing is something that takes a day to learn and a lifetime to master.** The real art comes only after a lot of work. It's no accident that the best freelance Direct-Response Marketers are charging thousands of dollars for every piece they write, plus a nice chunk of the residual royalty income from the gross sales. These people have one thing in common: they've been doing it for a couple decades. There are some exceptions, but they're rare. The people in this world who are the best at this form of marketing, who really know how to do this, have been doing it for a long time.

Good Enough for Government Work

You're not going to create a perfect Direct-Response Marketing campaign from the start, but that shouldn't discourage you from trying. Remember, good enough is good enough, especially when you're starting out. You don't necessarily have to become an expert marketer before you take the plunge. The truth is, **some of the best marketing I've ever seen wasn't written by professionals — it was written by sincere business people who really love what they're doing, who really want to connect with the prospect, and who don't know all the fancy tricks and marketing secrets that somebody who's been in the business 20 years might know.** What they do have is *heart*. They have an understanding of a few of the basic principles, an understanding that you have to make an offer and you have to go to the right market with the right message at the right time. Knowing that, they're able to go out with a message that really hits home and drives business in.

Most people are convinced that advertising is best done by

Write down your best ideas when they are new — and when you are first getting started and very excited!

- These ideas are HOT! And you'll need them later on when you are cold!!!

- Ideas are like slippery fish! Hard to hold on to! So you must capture them!

The best ideas come to you in the heat of the moment!

experts. The advertising agencies of the world want to convince you that all this is so damn complicated that you've got to be educated to do all this stuff. One of the definitions of Direct-Response Marketing I mentioned at the beginning of this chapter is that Direct-Response Marketing is salesmanship in print. I promise you, **the best salespeople aren't the ones who went to college and got a degree (with some very notable exceptions, of course). The best salespeople are the ones out there in the trenches, face-to-face, belly-to-belly, eyeball-to-eyeball with their best customers.** They've got relationships with those people. They know what those people want. They know how to give them what they want. They're out there serving them like crazy. Oftentimes the best Direct-Response Marketing doesn't look pretty; some of it really looks like crap! But it does a powerful job of getting the right message to the right customer at the right time. **It's just salesmanship: one person wanting to do business with another person.** Those are the people you want to emulate — the ones who are getting the job done, actually seeing results and generating a profit.

You're going to get better over time. Even better, once you've got it down, it's a skill you'll have forever. You're not relying on another company to create turnkey materials for you, take your money, and disappear. **You're able to create and make offers whenever you want, and that's a real power — a power to generate cash**

whenever you need it. In that way, Direct-Response Marketing is the power to create money on demand. It's the opposite of just sitting around waiting for customers to come to you, which is what most people do. Good marketers are proactive: they're out there attracting people. They're not pushing; they're *pulling* people in with their messages. You can become one of those effective marketers. Once again, you don't really have to be perfect at it when you start out — it's actually quite a forgiving business. **You can make a ton of mistakes and still make a ton of money.**

Don't Overthink It

As human beings, we tend to overcomplicate things — and here's a good example. When NASA decided to send astronauts into space, on the first mission they discovered that the common ballpoint pen wouldn't work in zero gravity. So they spent millions of dollars developing a pen that would write in outer space. Now they've got one that writes underwater, upside-down, in temperatures over 100 degrees, on ice-capped mountains — in just about any condition that anyone could possibly imagine. But the Russians did something else that was pretty elegant: they used pencils instead.

There's a tendency, when you're coming up with all these ideas and strategies, to get a little overwhelmed. But **there's no need to make your marketing more complicated than it has to be. Don't try to do everything at once. You can learn one strategy and implement that strategy, then learn something else.** Look at what other people do, then tweak and fine-tune your strategy at the level you're currently at. You don't have to do everything with every promotion. There are so many different, elegant, and simple ways to make money in Direct-Response Marketing.

Why Don't More People Do Direct-Response Marketing?

Most business owners don't do more Direct-Response

Marketing because they don't understand it, and they don't realize it's one of the most cost-effective ways of advertising. They've been duped into thinking that other types of ads work better. Radio and television is what a lot of local businesses specifically focus their dollars on, at least in the very beginning — because it's a new business, the medium is glamorous, and they need new customers. Those media are actually training those advertisers to buy in that manner, and so advertisers often don't have the time to even consider Direct-Response Marketing.

And, of course, **there's hardly anybody showing up at their door to sell them good Direct-Response Marketing.** You've got the Yellow Pages guy, who keeps bugging you to get a bigger ad. You've got the advertising specialty people, who want you to print up everything with your name on it. The newspapers and some radio and TV stations — those guys bug the hell out of you. But you don't have anybody coming along saying, "Look, I specialize in good Direct-Response Marketing that's relationship-building and long-term, using strategies that will let you quadruple your profits — or, in some cases, make more than ten of your competitors combined." There's nobody out there who's doing that as a profession.

A Dearth of Decent Offers

Here's one reason a lot of people don't do Direct-Response Marketing: they don't know how to define and create decent offers. They're simply buying the advertising they can afford, when they can afford it. Most advertisers think that Direct-Response Marketing has to be very expensive. Sure, you've got to cut through all the radio, TV, newspaper, and magazines ads, and all the crap your prospects are getting in their mail and on the Internet. Does that mean it has to cost a lot of money? No. You can give something away that has a large perceived value, but may not cost that much. It depends on exactly what your prospect wants.

Sadly, many advertisers don't even know what a decent offer

---

is. I'll give you a good definition: **an offer is a reason to buy. It can be anything: a low price, unusual products, a special sale, special bonuses and extras — all the things you're offering to the customer in exchange for the money you want them to give to you.** Too much of the advertising out there doesn't have any real offer attached. People are spending their good, hard-earned dollars running this advertising — and they're not really trying to *sell* anything. They're not giving their prospects a clear and compelling reason to come do business with them right now.

In creating an offer, you should ask yourself what the prospect wants. If you're a restaurant owner, what do they want when they come into your restaurant? Let's say, for example, that you want to make a special offer for Valentine's Day, and normally you'd do "two-for-one," or you'd offer a free dessert, or something like that. Those aren't really eye-popping offers. Instead, think deeply about what your customers *really* want on Valentine's Day. They want the whole romantic feel, right? So how about this: you offer a "Valentine's Day Lovers Package." If they come in as a couple, the female of the party is going to get a bunch of roses, and there's going to be free champagne and there's going to be chocolate-dipped strawberries. There's going to be a person going around playing romantic music on the violin. By creating that type of special offer, you're going to set yourself apart from all the other restaurants out there who want that Valentine's Day business. And as I mentioned before, make it a limited offer. Say something like, "There's a limited number of spaces so you'd better act fast, because these Valentine's Day packages will go quickly."

Here's a good idea about which my colleague Randy Charach told me. He was going to the same hairstylist quite often, and one day he noticed that she had a little sign hidden behind her box of scissors and some business cards that said, "Please refer me." She asked him, "You're the marketing expert. How can I get more business?" He said, "It's really simple. You can make yourself as busy as you want by doing what I'm going to tell you right now. I hope you do this, because I know it will work. Give out a card to

A business is very similar to a living organism...

- The marketplace is its life and livelihood.

- It feeds off its market.

- It changes, grows, and adapts to the changes in its environment.

- Many outside forces can kill it. Some slowly. Some quickly.

- Keeping it alive for a long time can be a delicate thing.

every one of your customers that gives a free haircut, on the first visit, to anybody they give that card to. All you're doing is giving a free haircut once to one person."

Now, that's going to attract a lot of people to come for a free haircut. She does a good job, her price is reasonable, she's nice to talk to, and there's no reason for them not to come back. The only reason they may not even take her up this offer is that they're afraid to leave whomever they currently go to. That isn't the case with most people.

See? You don't have to spend much money to get good results from Direct-Response Marketing. If you can spend money, that's fine — maybe it's more profitable for you to do that. **You can afford to sell something for $50 that cost you $70, if you know the lifetime value of your customer is $1,000.** You've just got to do the numbers. Direct-Marketing is psychology and math, that's all it is: figuring out what the people want and then calculating the metric. Most advertisers don't bother, just as they don't bother to build a decent customer list.

Summing It Up

There's a lot of money out there that's just lying on the table — and it's waiting for you to pick it up. This chapter shows you the tip of the iceberg regarding what Direct-Response Marketing can do for you.

So let this be something that whets your appetite, and gets you hungry for more. By all means, go on to the next chapter, but be sure you come back to this chapter and read it again. **Do everything possible to learn everything you can about Direct-Response Marketing, because it's something that can increase your profits dramatically and give you an unfair advantage in your marketplace.**

MARKETING SECRET #15

Almost all profits come from the back-end...

- Spend more time, money, and effort — doing more business with your existing customers.

- 80% marketing to existing customers

- 20% to get new customers.

Front-End and Back-End Marketing Systems

In this chapter, I'm going to discuss front-end and back-end marketing systems, and why it's imperative that you develop your own. These systems are extremely important to any business, and if you'll practice the things I'm going to teach you here, you'll benefit dramatically.

Put simply, **front-end and back-end systems are the methods you use to attract customers, and then to sell to them again later.** I look at front-end sales as low-cost hand-raisers that you use as an introduction to new prospects, so they can express an interest in what you have to sell. But every front-end system is created and offered with the intention of making a back-end sale of a much higher-priced item. Your front-end breaks the ice; it's the secret to breaking through your inability to sell high-ticket items to people who don't know you. It lets you make that initial introduction, and identify those who are interested in what you've got to offer.

You should **look at your sales system as a funnel.** You're trying to bring in a large number of would-be buyers and get them into that huge opening at the top. You use a low-cost (or even a *no*-cost) offer to do this, but only to get them acquainted with you and what you have to offer. **The back-end is where you really make your money.** Once you've broken the ice, most of your would-be customers will fall by the wayside; and that's okay, because you're looking for the wheat, not the chaff. You simply have to take in a huge amount of people to get that small percentage of customers who will buy in the back-end, and then continue to buy from you in the future.

What it all boils down to is this: the front-end sale — **that first sale at the top of the funnel — is meant to get a prospect on your buyers list.** That's all it's for; it's not about profit, although it's nice if you can make a little. This is where a lot of people make their biggest mistake: they think that the front-end sale is the thing they're going for. Perish the thought! That's just to get the prospect to the point of being a customer, and to get their name on your house list. The back-end is the next sale and the next, and that's where you make your money.

That said, your front-end and back-end systems are actually interlocking components of a complex whole — the overarching Ruthless Marketing System that forms the basis of this book. Once again: **with the front-end system you're bringing people into your marketing funnel. On the back-end, you're nurturing the relationship with those people, and helping those people who give you more and more money.** It's a lot like running an automobile. The front-end is the key that starts the engine; it's small, and doesn't cost much by itself. The back-end system is the fuel that drives the vehicle. It costs a little more, but it's what really drives your business.

In the largest perspective, all this is just marketing — part of the package of things you use to attract and re-attract the best customers. **An effective marketing system is one that does it all for you automatically: the front-end automatically attracts the right people, and a back-end system automatically re-sells them.** I see the front-end/back-end interaction as something like the plate-spinning people you used to see on the Ed Sullivan Show, and that you can still see in some carnivals and circuses. They start spinning those plates, and eventually they get 14 or 15 plates spinning simultaneously. Once they're spinning, all the performer has to do is casually walk back and flip the first one, and then the second, and the third, and so forth. They can keep 15 plates spinning with a minimum of effort — but it does take effort, or they all come crashing down. That's how it can be for your marketing, too. **You can put systems in place that attract and then re-attract all the best customers, with a minimum of effort on your part.** Think of it as a kind of self-perpetuating money machine.

In its simplest manifestation, **your front-end is your lead generation system.** It's the process of taking all the prospects out there and determining which of them you can convert to actual clients. **The back-end becomes the continual marketing to those clients already on your customer list.** The marketing is different for those two aspects of business, since the marketing you'll use to get people to try your service is going to be different from the marketing you'll use to keep selling to the same customers repeatedly. Ultimately, front-end and back-end marketing systems are the best way to build business and create cash on demand.

Gaming the System

Like so many of the components of the Ruthless Marketing System, **front-end/back-end marketing is a systemized way to make on-going, automatic sales.** You should always develop your products and services with this approach in mind, because it's so valuable and proven. My good friend, Alan R. Bechtold, is in the process of developing a new marketing course, for example, and that's exactly how he's going about it. His new course is based on a series of recorded tele-seminars and a live workshop that he recently conducted. He led a whole group of people through this process in real time, and they each paid a princely sum to be a part of the group; but it goes without saying that it was all recorded, so it could be turned into a course for later use.

First, he recorded five preliminary calls. These calls served two purposes. The first was that they helped those people who paid for the original coaching, and kept them happy until the project officially got started. Second, Alan knew, in the back of his mind, that he was creating a front-end product that he could sell for $17 or $27 — maybe more, maybe less, based on the test marketing —

to find prospects who most want to buy the complete course, which he'll sell for a lot more. Now, Alan knows that he'd have very little luck going out to strangers on the street and trying to sell them a course for $997 or $1,499. **But if he sells them the $27 introductory course and follows up with the right pieces, and maybe even a few phone calls, then the sale is very easy** — because he's giving them a chance to get started very inexpensively. Those first five calls and the tons of information on that one CD-ROM make up almost one-third of the course.

Here's a similar example: Video Professor. They have all these information products that teach you how to use your computer, and what do they do? They offer you the basics on a free disk; all you pay is $6.95 for postage and handling. It's a fantastic method that's used everywhere in the business. Similarly, almost every infomercial you see is a front-end offer of one type or another. **Start paying close attention to those offers.** Call up some of them, and express your interest in buying. Listen to what they have on the back-end, because every offer you see for a low-cost product is a front-end offer, a set-up for the higher-priced back-end offer from which the marketer derives his profit.

The idea is to **introduce yourself to the prospect by over-delivering on a low-cost hand-raiser that's worth many times more than what the prospect paid.** At the risk of sounding sexist, **it's a bit like courting a woman.** You may get her attention initially, but you're not going to propose on the first date. Of course, by nurturing that relationship and getting her interested, at some point you can pop the question and expect a reasonable chance of making your "sale." That's what Alan is doing by leading with his $27 offer, and then introducing the bigger course later. His customers are going to be amazed and excited about paying him $1,000 when they think, *Imagine what I can get for $1,000 if I got all this for just $27!* And here's a point to keep in mind: when making a front-end offer of this sort, be sure to charge something to **qualify the prospects.** Otherwise you'll get a lot of people who aren't serious, and some who are will avoid your offer, because they'll think you can't be serious if you're giving it away for free.

Here's something that a lot of people overlook; I've already mentioned it here, but it's worth re-emphasizing. **You have to understand that a front-end sale is simply a customer's entry point onto your house list; it's the subsequent sales that are the source of your real profit.** I can't tell you how many items I've purchased through the mail, over the Internet, or whatever — and never heard from that vendor again. Obviously, they had no idea what they were doing; they were going for that first sale, and that was it. They got my money, they sent me the product, and it was over; they were on to the next sale. They're spending more money chasing new prospects to get that one front-end sale. It's like the two guys with the potato cart, where at the end of the day they lose money, and they figure, "Well, tomorrow we'll just have to sell more potatoes." But you can get by on fewer new potato sales, as you'll just implement a back-end system so you can rake in the profits by selling to previous satisfied customers. Do that, and you're going to have a huge, unfair advantage over 80-90% of the advertisers out there.

Catching a Clue

It's a sad fact of life that most businesses — especially

mom-and-pop operations — have no front-end offer to get people in the door. Their philosophy seems to be, "OK, I'm located at 608 Main Street here and I have a sign in the window that says OPEN FOR BUSINESS. That should be enough." Well, that's the wrong approach. You need a front-end offer to get people into your store — or if you're a service provider, a reason to get them to call your business. It should be something that costs you very little, but has a high perceived value. Don't make the mistake of either having no front-end, or of having a shoddy front-end that nobody wants. On the other hand, it shouldn't cost you too much to sell it at a big discount or give it away for free.

If you're a business owner, you have to keep asking yourself, over and over again, **"What's next?"** I think you should even put it on your wall in 200-point type, where you can look at it all the time: "What's next?" When you've got somebody who's interested and passionate about whatever it is you're selling — whether it's knitting supplies or Army boots — those people are insatiable. They'll keep buying and rebuying. It's up to you, though: **the responsibility is on your shoulders to keep dreaming up new things to sell them.**

Most business owners are either out there chasing the next sale, and wearing themselves out in the process, or they're not doing anything. **Remember Russ von Hoelscher's story from Chapter 2,** about the printer who worked in the strip center close to his office? He was always complaining about how there was never enough business. Russ finally told him, "Look, you've got to get some people in — there are hundreds of businesses within a mile of here. Paper them with flyers, go after the business, and be aggressive." But the printer said something amazingly stupid: "Look, pal. I'm open for business. I've got a printing press. If they want printing, they can come to me."

Now, he's on the backside of a strip mall, and he's unwilling to make that effort to sell his product. That's an absolute recipe for disaster, and it's hard to feel sorry for him! But **he verbalized the**

way that most people think, as rotten as that attitude is. That kind of attitude will only work if you've got a printing press back there and you intend to *print* the money you need to survive. Or, hey, you could print your own "GOING OUT OF BUSINESS" sign. Why not?

In my experience, the people who have that attitude are, for the most part, the people who've opened a business because that's what they've always dreamed of doing. They're already going into it with an attitude that they're the king on the throne, ruling over their new kingdom — their business — and the great unwashed masses are just going to come through the door and be thankful that they've thrown the "OPEN" sign in the window. Sorry, that's not the way it works. It's true that there are some people who do that and actually make a profit, but that only works under certain circumstances; if you have a dynamite location and you give good service, you might be able to survive, a least temporarily. But even if you do, you're losing so much more. If you're not serving the customers properly, you're leaving room for someone to come and take them all away.

If, on the other hand, you'll do the things I'm talking about here, **you won't just survive — you'll thrive.** It's easy: offer a great, cheap offer to get them to come in the first time, let them get comfortable with you and understand a little about your business, then hit them with your back-end offer. Try handing out samples, if your business is amenable to that kind of thing. If you've got a hairdressing salon, offer a $5 perm. Once they're in, make sure you over-deliver, and they're going to be back.

Servicing the Client

Even if you have a great front-end offer on which you over-deliver, **you can't count on every customer to come back on his own.** A good front-end system is useless unless you couple it with an effective back-end system, so you can take advantage of that goodwill and sense of reciprocity you've generated with your front-

Your marketing Mantra: What are the 3 BIGGEST THINGS your customers want — and how can you give it to them?

a. Find the answer to that question

b. Tweak it — work with it — refine it — polish it

c. Then shout it as loudly as you can!!!

Let the people in your market hear it in the clearest and most compelling way!

end offer. What comes next is a regular, systematic communication that goes out to those customers and gives them a specific reason to keep coming back and buying from you. **Even the people who know how valuable a customer list is are losing a whole lot of money that should be theirs, simply because they're not aggressively re-inviting their customers to come back and buy from them on a regular basis.**

You see, your customers are (silently) begging to be acknowledged. They want to be nurtured; they want to be responded to. If you take that first order and do nothing with it, then you're doing a great disservice to the customer. So the obligation you have as a marketer is to massage the egos of your customers, and help them give you more reasons to serve them. **So many times we worry about making that first sale, when in reality what's important is our ability to help our customers improve their lives, fulfill their desires, and solve their problems.** We do that by continually offering them new products, related products, and related services. They may not even know what direction to go in after they've bought that initial product; so if you just pitch them something at that point, they'll probably come back and buy from you again. So what if it costs you a cent for a postcard and a few cents for postage? That's just a dollar or so per customer per year, and those who respond will spend at least a hundred times that on repeat business with you. What business owner wouldn't exchange a dollar for a hundred dollars every day, and as many times during that day as they possibly could?

Now, this goes right back to what I said earlier about what you, as a marketer, should always be asking yourself: "What's next?" The customer is *already* asking that question, even before you ask it yourself. Sometimes they're asking it even as they purchase that first product. In other words, **they're looking for reasons to do more business with you,** and you've got to be able to answer that question instantly.

An Offer They Can't Refuse

The combination of aggressive front-end and back-end marketing works well with just about any advertising medium, from the Internet and direct-mail to infomercials. Just combine this method with the other techniques in this book, especially Direct-Response Marketing, and you've got yourself a well-oiled moneymaking machine.

In order for this strategy to work most effectively, however, **you've got to start out with an excellent, high-value offer that your prospect will think they'd have to be a fool to refuse.** A lot of us in the business accomplish this by offering a free report or even a free book as a lead generator. If you want to charge a dollar or two for the book, go ahead; most people appreciate things for which they have to pay. But in the case of a report, which is really a glorified sales letter, just give it away free. That'll bring a whole bunch of people into your funnel (you remember the funnel, don't you?).

Let's say I'm selling a book distributorship; I'd offer them the distributorship for several hundreds of dollars on the back-end. But like most people who market information products, I use a 1-2-3 approach with most items. That is, **1)** to get the people into the funnel, **2)** to make a medium-sized sale on the back-end, and then — the third spoke on the wheel is the most important — **3)** offer them an even bigger package: maybe reprint or resell rights for a bunch of tapes and books, at a price that could be $1,000 or more.

My friend Russ von Hoelscher has owned a number of retail bookstores. An effective offer he once used was to have people sign up for a $250 free book-shopping spree every month. All three of the stores he operated at the time used the promotion in their ads, and that enticed people in. There was no obligation, and no purchase necessary. They just signed a card and dropped it into a big bowl. But Russ found that with book customers, even browsers — well, they couldn't just come in and drop the card. They'd start looking at the books, and Russ would often get a sale. Another thing he did, when faced with heavy competition from some of the huge conglomerate bookstores, was to give away, at cost, his top ten bestsellers. It was an effective strategy; he never made much profit with them anyhow. **But by giving a discount of 40% off — literally giving them away at cost — people would come in to get the hot books, but then they'd go deeper in the store**. They'd look at some of the other books and audio programs, and often they'd leave not just with a couple of bestsellers, but two or three other items that made Russ a nice profit.

That brings to mind an especially effective front-end/back-end offer that a lot of different businesses can and do use: a low-cost yearly membership that includes a free report or a free product. You see this kind of thing at Barnes & Noble and at large record stores all the time, but it could be used with just about any business. You start out with a good front-end that leads to bigger and bigger back-end purchases, plus customer loyalty. When people are members of something, they feel better about themselves and what they're buying. Remember, **people want to feel important.** It's almost like they're running around with these invisible signs flashing, "MAKE ME FEEL IMPORTANT, PLEASE!"

We all want to feel special. **When you make your customers members of something, or give them some association they can join, the real purpose is to develop them as customers and to**

sell them more stuff. If they're a part of some membership, it makes them feel like they have that inside angle or that inside scoop on everyone else. And to a certain extent, they should. You should segment your client list so that your "Gold" or "Platinum" customers get an especially nice deal — for example, a sharp discount, or maybe you open the store only for them on particular days. That can really get some excitement going.

Now, maybe at its root the whole membership thing is phony, since you're more interested in them spending their money than in developing a club — but the more real you make it, the better. Then you're able to educate the customers. If you're selling knitting supplies or beads or books, you can have all kinds of workshops and seminars and bring in book authors to speak. **You can do all kinds of things to get people more addicted to whatever it is that you're selling.**

If you don't have a club for them to join, then have people come in and sign up for a drawing to win a grand prize, the way Russ did. Of course, only one person will win that; but by the end of the promotion, you'll have captured the names of everybody who participated. Remarkably, everyone can be a second-place winner, and get a discount on whatever you're selling! Just send them a little letter that says, "Unfortunately, you're not a first-place winner, but…" and then play up the fact that they *did* win second place. Little do they know that everybody else did too — but that's not important. **Coming in second makes them feel important; it makes them feel appreciated; and again, it gives them a reason to come back in.**

Here's another thing that a contest does, as it relates to the front-end. **The only people who sign up for any kind of contest are those who are already interested in whatever the prize is that you're giving away.** In my first business, I tried everything to get customers. You name it, I tried it — as long as it didn't cost very much; after all, I was on a limited budget. I used to knock on doors till my knuckles bled. The one method that worked best for

The best selling messages and offers grow and develop as you work on them.

- You must take the leap of faith — and develop it gradually as you go.

- Whatever you focus on expands! So keep focusing on improving each offer.

- More often than not, your best ideas will come as the deadline approaches!

me was a giveaway. This was when I had a carpet cleaning business, by the way — several years before I got into mail order and information products. I had a contest that ran continually, to give away three rooms of carpet cleaning, absolutely free. I put these little boxes up in different places around town, and I'd go collect my leads every day. I'd call them up and I'd give them the bad news, which was that they didn't get the three free rooms worth of cleaning. The *good* news was that they'd won the consolation prize, which was conditional. I'd do some free work for them if they would take a minimum amount of other work. Then, once I got in their house, I'd try to run the bill up as high as I could. I was closing between 30% and 50% of all of the people who were signing up for the contest, and the reason **I was closing those people is because they were pre-qualified to begin with.** Only a fool would enter a contest to get three rooms of free carpet cleaning, if they weren't interested in getting that done.

You can always make your consolation prize a lead generation tool, where they get so much off the goods and services you're selling. If you're working with a women's clothing store, like my friend Kris Solie-Johnson, you can run a contest where the winner gets a free outfit, while all the second-place prizewinners get 20% off all their purchases. But you can sweeten the pot a little, too; so why not offer 25%-30 off their purchases if the second-place prizewinner brings in a friend who hasn't been to the store before? **Set it up that way, and you'll have customers bringing in customers who are like them,** people you *know* will like what you have to offer — because why would you bring one of your girlfriends to a store if you knew she'd hate the clothes? This can work not only to bring in more customers, but to get everybody back into the store a second time.

You Can't Have a Front Without a Back

Here's something I wish I'd known when I got started: make sure, **once you've got that front-end attractor in place, that you've got something with which to back it up.** Once that system's in place to attract new customers, you've got to have your "What's next?" ready to offer to that new customer as the back-end sale. Let me say this again: you need to have that decided and worked out before you even think about making that first offer to the customer, or your front-end can backfire on you!

The last thing you want to do is to get all excited and worked up about your front-end and then go scrambling to find a back-end to offer your customers. Oh, you can certainly do it that way, but it's a pain. Instead of scrambling when you get that first order, instead of running around trying to figure out what you're going to do, you need to have that already mapped out in your marketing model. You want to put that offer in the fulfillment package for the front-end product. In other words, **whatever it is you're using for your front-end sale** — whether it's a book or a report or free yarn — **when they open that package up, there needs to be that back-end offer staring them right in the face.** Because, remember, people are going to be asking themselves right away, "What's next?" And you want to be there with the answer.

That's one of the reasons that **I love information products: because you can always use a piece of that information product as your front-end, and you know already what your back-end is.** But if yours is a physical product, consider the possibility of planning your front-end offer from the back-end offer. You need your goal — *What am I going to do?* — on the front-end to get them in. What will raise that hand? Now, the worst thing you can do is let that hand-raiser get cold. They're eager to buy *now*. They've just met you, and they're excited about you. They're more excited about you when you deliver that front-end product than they will be for the rest of your relationship, probably. Why on Earth would you wait and let them cool off for three weeks while you think of what else you're going to offer them? You want another offer to go in there — preferably with the front-end package, but if nothing else, immediately following.

Here's another tip: **never have a front-end offer that isn't related to the back-end.** I don't just think that's important, I think it's *essential*. Your front-end offer must dovetail with your back-end approach; otherwise, the person raising their hand isn't necessarily interested in what you're going to sell on the back-end. In fact, in many cases, your back-end can be the same product as your front-end; for example vitamins or supplements. The front-end sale is the product, and **the back-end sale is more of the same.** Sometimes you can get the back-end sale at the same time you make the front-end sale, but that's a whole other strategy.

Think it all through so that **your front-end gives them a small sampling of what they're going to get, so they get to like it.** Be like the Chick-Fil-A or Mrs. Fields cookie people; they're out there passing out free samples. The people who take those samples say, "Thank you" and walk about 20 steps, and all of a sudden they turn around and come back and buy a dozen cookies.

What the Heck *is* a System, Anyway?

Now, *there's* a question that's been begging to be asked: what is a system? By definition, it's a group of interacting or interrelated parts that make up a whole. When you're developing a front- or back-end system, at first glance the whole thing may seem overwhelming; it may seem too complex for you. **The best thing** to do is to look at this system as a set of pieces that all fit together to create, first, that front-end system, and then the associated back-end system.

Your front-end system is designed to promote new products, or generate leads, or sell an order to a first-time customer. But within that front-end system, you may have a series of mini-systems that compose the system itself. Maybe you've got a mini-system that generates leads for your business; then you might have a system in place that you use to create a new offer or new products for customers. Then, of course, you may as well have a system that sells the prospect. Maybe it's your Direct-Mail System, where you regularly and systematically contact those leads on a week-to-week or month-to-month or semi-annual basis. (I'll discuss this possibility in more detail in a later chapter.)

The back-end, of course, is the system where the real money really is. It's designed to ethically extract money from the pockets of clients and customers and prospects, and put that money into your bank account — into your own pocket. (Notice, again, that it's important you do this ethically — if not because you want a clear conscience, then at least because you don't want your misdeeds to jump up and bite you on the rear someday.) You might have a mini-system within your back-end system that progressively and aggressively follows up with your clients every 15 or 30 days. If you do that systematically, you're going to see your sales and your profits grow substantially.

The secret is to bridge the gap between that front-end system and the associated back-end system. The front-end system lets you leverage off your knowledge of your industry, your experience, your background, what you do best; **the back-end system lets you leverage off what you know about your clients.** It's important that you have a system in place that lets the clients tell you what they want. As the old saying goes, "The only votes that count are the ones that are paid for," and your customers vote by paying for products that you offer on the front-end. You know that on the back-

MARKETING SECRET #19

Emergency money-making generator...

- When times get hard

- When business gets slow

- When you need cash-flow to feed the monster...

All you do is:

a. Go to your best customers...

b. Make them an irresistible offer!

c. Have a special sale that will blow them away!

They'll stand in line with money in hand!

end, you're going to offer them more and more products related to that first purchase.

Most business people are too focused on the front-end, though, to ever make any money on the back-end. They get so excited about making that first sale that it's just like almost being on a narcotics high. But what happens when the sale is over? They've got to immediately go get another high by making another sale. In doing that, they're just leaving money on the table. If they would just work the back-end properly, they could create five or ten times more income and business for their company. You see, **your largest marketing expense is always new-customer acquisition. The easiest business is selling to people who already trust you, who've already bought from you.** Knowing that, you want to create products on the back-end that appeal to those people.

A good example of a back-end system is what happens at Amazon.com. If you go there and buy a book, that's the front-end. But when you go through the process of purchasing that book, you're going to see a page that says, "People who bought this book also bought..." Well, that's a back-end offer. Or you may go to a concert, and spend $70 for a ticket. When you get there, they're going to try to sell you a T-shirt, a cap, a CD, or something else. That's the back end. You may end up spending $150 or even more, all told.

The question is, how do you develop a good back-end system? First if all, take a good look at your business. What do you sell to your customers? In what are they interested? Can you upsell them — that is, can you get them to buy something bigger and better? Can you cross-sell to them — can you get them to buy something that's related to that product that you sold them on the front-end? **The ideas you come up with will help you create a back-end system for your business.**

I look at as being it like riding a bike up a tall hill. That's the vision I have of getting new customers. Man, it's difficult! I'm riding that bike up on a hot summer day, and I'm pedaling and I'm breathing hard, and I can't even ride all the way. I actually have to get off and walk the bike up the rest of the way. But then, when it comes to reselling those customers again and again, it's like coasting that bike right down the same hill. I've got my arms up like I'm on a roller coaster ride, and I'm not even putting in any effort: I'm zipping right on down the hill. **The fun part of the business is *not* getting the first sale.** The fun part of the business is developing relationships with customers who love you and trust you, who let you get inside their heads and inside their hearts. You get to know them better than they know themselves; and then, whatever you want to sell them, **you create the money at will.**

You've got to realize in business that you're going to spend a certain amount of money to acquire any customer; I discussed this fact in some detail in Chapter 2. All your customers come with a price, whether it's what you spend in ads, or what you spend in time and energy to attract them. **But it's worth it if you can figure out the average lifetime revenue of every new customer you acquire.** You can literally lose money in the short-term while attracting your customers, if you determine that their value, down the road, is many times more than what you're spending now.

Let me reiterate: *you can afford to lose money on your front-end sale.* You can sell something at less than your cost, if you must. A good 90% of your competition won't do this, because they won't do anything that affects their bottom line. But if you lose a few bucks on the front-end to entice people to come to you, and *then* have great, related items on which you can make a huge profit — then so what if you lose money on the front-end? There's tons of money to be had on the back-end. The most important part of this is knowing what the lifetime value of the average customer is. If you know that, you can go negative on the front-end, because you know that you're going to recover any losses.

Some people call these kinds of offers "loss-leaders." I prefer to think of them as investments towards future profits. If you do everything possible to know your best customers intimately, and make them the kinds of repeat offers to which you know they'll be attracted, you'll make money hand over fist.

But Why Doesn't Everyone Use This Method?

Some people are just too softhearted for their own good to make a system like this work. This all sounds somewhat ruthless — because you're trying to extract every last dollar of disposable income from your customers. But if you're providing products and services that represent true value to your marketplace, then there's nothing ruthless about it. It's more *aggressive* than anything. **I wish more business people would realize the tremendous amount of money they're losing by failing to vigorously resell to their customers.** As a business owner, you should always try to do more business with people who've already shown a certain level of trust in you.

Then again, many business people feel that the high point in their business is getting that first customer. They've never developed the art and science of attracting customers, and they never will. But if you know your system and your customers well enough that you can lose money on the front-end — if you know the lifetime value of your customers, and really nurture relationships with them and help them become not just customers but an integral part of your own life — then there's value there for everyone. The problem with most marketers today is that they only see the quick money, the upfront money, the easy money. They want the get-rich-quick money — when in reality, getting rich is in the *back-end*. It's in the long-term. And hey, let's be honest about it: **a lot of marketers are just flat-out lazy.** They don't want to go through all the necessary steps, and they don't want to take the initiative to do those things that need to be done to make it a business instead of just a hobby.

Another part of the problem may simply be that things have changed in the business world in the last few decades, and people haven't gotten used to thinking about, much less using, this new way of doing business. Twenty years ago, if you were the only grocery store on the corner, people went there. Think of it as the Field of Dreams business model: "If you build it, they will come." **But there are so many choices today that we've gotten a bit jaded and cynical about the different marketing messages we see. So the smaller business owner, especially the home-based business, needs to stand out from everybody else out there.** The Field of Dreams business model is mostly dead in America. You have to compete vigorously, and provide additional services that the Big Box companies aren't going to provide.

The key is establishing reciprocal relationships with your customers so your business can survive in the long-term. Let's say you're a novice knitter, and you don't know how to cast off the needles. You're not going to go to Wal-Mart and have someone show you how to do that — because, frankly, they're not going to. You have to go to a smaller neighborhood store that's going to have some of the personal service that the Big Boxes lack, a place that's willing to build a relationship with you. But if they don't pitch to you and don't market to you, you may not know what to ask them. Whereas, if a little knitting store regularly sends you a postcard to tell you they have beginner classes or new types of yarns, **they're educating you,** and you'll probably spend more money with them. Therefore you'll enjoy your hobby more, and they'll get more sales — it's win-win all around.

Hubba Hubba!

Sometimes **it's the worst things in life that provide the best examples,** if only so we can draw parallels to the good things. **So I'm going to discuss pornography** for a while. I realize it's a controversial subject, and I'm going to keep this PG-rated all the way. But there's this story I heard a long time ago; I've never forgotten it, and I think it illustrates something very important when it comes to understanding the power of front-end and back-end marketing. It's the story of Hugh Hefner.

As most people know, Hugh Hefner was the man who started *Playboy* magazine in the early 1950's. At that time, it was a revolutionary idea — though maybe "revolutionary" is the wrong word, because some people are so anti-porn that they may think it was a *terrible* idea. But in any case, it was new; let's just put it that way. Hefner was the first to go this route, and he was very insecure about the fate of his little publication — which, by the way, is rather innocent by today's standards. My wife gets the Victoria's Secrets catalog in the mail, and it's a lot racier... not that I ever look at it or anything!

Anyhow, the first *Playboy* was very innocent compared to today, but at that time it was new and unprecedented. Hefner was so unsure about it that he didn't even print a date on his first publication, since he figured it might just sit on the newsstands for a year or two before it sold out. He printed 5,000 copies, hoping that he wasn't going to lose all his money. But all 5,000 copies sold out in just a few days, and the rest is history.

Some people saw his success and started saying, "Hey, here's a guy who's found a new market!" One of the very first magazines to take him on was *Penthouse*. The story I heard was that when *Penthouse* went into business to compete against *Playboy*, all the experts in the publishing world said, "Look, there's no way this marketplace is big enough for two of these magazines. There's just absolutely no way!" And they did everything possible to advise the people behind *Penthouse* not to do it. "Don't spend your money! The marketplace just isn't big enough for two!" Now, of course, we can see what a ridiculous statement *that* was. Nowadays there isn't just *Playboy* and *Penthouse*; there are about a hundred other publications out there, and some are really quite pornographic.

Here's my point. It has nothing, really, to do with pornography, except as a means of illustration. The point is that **people are insatiable. They can't get enough!** The person who collects one gun is going to have a dozen before long. If there was just one fishing book on the market, that would be ridiculous, because readers would have an insatiable appetite for more — and so there's hundreds of them. The same's true for poker books, and hunting, and stamp collecting. **We're a nation of people who get involved with something and want more, more, more.**

Certain products and services lend themselves more to this emotional intensity than others. Look at casinos. When the government made it so that any Indian tribe in the country could start a casino, everybody said, "Well, there's the end of Vegas. There's the end of Atlantic City." When VCRs first came out in the 1980s, all kinds of people were saying, "There goes the movie industry." When it became possible to download free music on the Internet, all the experts said, "There goes the whole music industry right there. People can get it for free." Well, as you know, none of that has happened. **The marketplace is absolutely, positively** *insatiable*, and the people buying this stuff from you right now will buy from you again and again, *if* you make them the right offers and make it easy for them.

The problem is that **you have to be creative enough to come up with all kinds of different products and services that somehow relate to what you're selling** — and it really does take some creativity. You can do exactly what Hugh Hefner and all those other guys have done, only you don't have to do it with something like pornography. You can build an empire! You can resell, and you can copy someone who's doing something right. This is especially useful for the small business owner. Find out what your competitor is doing. If he's making a lot of money doing something, you want to do the same thing — only try to do it better than he does. **Don't steal from them, but borrow their best principles.** Even what some people would consider old, crowded markets can be revitalized if you work them right.

The bottom line is that the market is absolutely insatiable. If you grow a garden, next year you'll want to know how to grow a better garden. If you raise a rabbit, you'll like to know how to breed rabbits and sell them to other people. In other words, you — the customer — want to know more. One key to success is *not* looking for the place where there's no competition, but focusing on the place **where there *is* competition that's making money in spite of the fact that they don't understand front-end/back-end marketing** — places where they aren't even using those techniques but are still raking in the cash. Now you can step in and dominate that category and they'll be left in the dust, shaking their heads, going, "Wow! What happened here?"

So if you're looking to start a new business, **look for the places where there are plenty of competitors, because that shows just how rabid the market is.** You want to find a market that's not only hungry, but spending money too. Look for people already making money in spite of the fact that they don't know what you know. Let's go back to the pornography example for a minute. My wife once asked me, "What's wrong with men? Don't they realize that when you've seen one picture of a naked woman, you've seen it all?" And she's right — what else is there to see? But this illustrates the fact that people buy for emotional reasons. If everybody thought logically, then you'd see a picture of a naked person and you'd say, "Oh, well, that's interesting," and that would be it. But people can never get enough. While there are certain markets that are more prone to this insatiability, everybody buys for emotional, not logical, reasons. **It's up to you as the business owner to determine what those emotional reasons are, so you can use that as your ammunition and go out and try to get every disposable dollar you can from your customer base.**

There are a few businesses that, at first glance, you might think are *not* emotional — and I've run one. That would be carpet cleaning. But believe it or not, carpet cleaning can be a very emotional thing, because most of my customers were women. Generally, men couldn't care less about whether or not their carpets are dirty; my female customers, on the other hand, were all extremely emotionally attached to their homes. Their homes were important to them, and the more involved they were with social life, the more deeply they cared about what all their friends, family, and neighbors thought. Anybody walking through their home was judging them by the appearance of their home, after all. Once I really got into the heads and hearts of these people, it was so easy to go in there for a $50 job and walk out with a couple of hundred dollars; all I would have to do was point out a few little things here and there. It's all about learning where you can squeeze those emotional triggers.

People buy stuff that excites them more than they buy stuff that they just need. But it's important to point out that they select among the competitors even for those items that they need, and those selections are *still* made for emotional reasons. That's why your message — your offer of a free or inexpensive trial — is important. Now they're getting something for nothing.

Setting Up the Systems

Let's talk a little bit about setting up your own front-end and back-end systems. What I'd like you to do is take out a piece of paper and make three different columns on it. Make one column for low-cost items — typically something that's free or up to about $20-25. The middle column is for items in the $100 range. Make the last column for big-ticket stuff — $500-1000. For every business, you should be able to come up with different ideas about what you can offer in each of these categories, and as I go on, I'll give you examples of brick-and-mortar businesses and how this relates to them.

Next, **start brainstorming ideas for different types of products** that you put in each one of those columns — because if you set up the system with the back-end *before* you set up the front-end, you'll end up with a continuous flow of products. Once you've got new customers in, you don't have to scramble around trying to figure out something for the back-end. In the beginning, focus on free or low-cost items. The Video Professor example I mentioned earlier is a great one; it's a free CD with information on it — though it does cost $6.95 for shipping and handling. But even though they have to pay shipping and handling, the customer still sees that as a free product. So your front-end offering, at least in the beginning, should be a free or

MARKETING SECRET #21

People want "The MAGIC Bullet":

- The one product/service that is going to make everything okay.

- It's going to solve some major problem.

- Or give them a miracle cure!

- An instant solution!

- And an on-going solution.

If they believe you can give this to them — you will get their money.

low-cost item that's very easy for you to deliver. You don't want to get into something that's complicated to deliver, because that will just eat away at your profit margin.

The second thing you want to **focus on is something that's of very high value to your prospect or customer.** Look at information — maybe insider information. I discussed the usefulness of memberships earlier: about how valuable it is to make people feel important that they're insiders, that they're really part of something, maybe even a part of history. Give them information that can change their business.

I want to make it clear that this isn't the place to give away junk — say, something that wasn't selling very well, or that you couldn't even give away. If new customers start receiving junk, they'll assume that the rest what you have to offer is junk, and that they shouldn't pay any more for whatever else you have. **Your front-end could be some part of a high-end product that you're going to give away,** like the first chapter of a book, or the first few tele-seminars in the beginning of a course. Offers like these really lead people to buy the higher-end product.

After you brainstorm all of these categories, you can start crafting different offers. How can these items work together? What would the flow of one to the other to the next be like? The last step, of course, is finding other businesses that offer your type of product, and studying them for pointers.

Let me give you just a couple of examples of good front-end/back-end systems I've heard of recently. A local library offered a summer reading program for kids, and if the kids read so many books they got a free cookie at a place called the Great Harvest Bread Company. Since the librarian tells kids that they get this free cookie if they read books, they not only read the books, but they become a pain in the butt to their parents to go get that free cookie. When the parents take their kids to go to get this free cookie, they can't just walk into the Great Harvest Bread Company and ask for a free cookie. They have to buy a loaf of bread, too. The bread is $3.50, so suddenly that "free" cookie has cost them $3.50. And if the Great Harvest Bread Company took their names and addresses at that point, they could continue to offer the parents different products by mailings — and the parents might listen. After all, they know where the store is; they've been there before. The people there were nice to their kids — they gave them free cookies — so the parents will probably continue to go back.

Here's how the front-end/back-end worked in this example. First they got the customer in with free cookies, then they upsold to the $3.50 bread. Now it's time to move up to the mid-category, the $100 range. That may be something like a year's supply of bread that the customer pays for at the beginning of a 12-month period. Maybe it's a membership — a "Bread of the Month" Club. There may also be other things they can try to get that customer to give them more and more money, as a result of their initial "free cookies for kids" program.

As you can see, **there are many different things out there that businesses can do to generate business.** If you start mapping out, in the beginning, some of the low-cost, mid-cost, and high-end things that you as a business owner can offer people, you can quickly create a good, step-by-step path from beginning to end, so you're not trying to come up with something all of a sudden later.

Here's a handy tip: **be sure to get it all down on paper.** So many times we try to internalize these things and juggle them in our minds, when really the best thing is to document it all. Create a flow chart of how the different elements of the system are interconnected. What makes one work? What makes it work better? Then you can see the flow of money. If you're constantly creating value, you're constantly going to be getting maximum income from each of your customers.

Here's another thing. Unless we put something on paper, it may be that everything I'm saying here just sounds like a great idea.

FREE GIFT! Go to www.RuthlessMarketing.com/freegift

You're going to read this chapter, it's all going to be somewhat entertaining to you, and then you're just going to forget about it. For this to work, you have to document your strategies and implement them. My best advice for implementation is to do what I've been trying to do for a number of years: get up every morning and try to focus on your business before all the workaday interruptions get started, before all the distractions get in the way. **Try to think these things through, to develop a plan. Use these very clear, step-by-step strategies to do it, and for goodness sake, write it all down!** That's the best piece of advice I can give you.

A Backup Back-End

One of the most useful things about mapping things out in detail and documenting them is the fact that you can include a plan for those people who won't take you up on that first offer — a backup back-end offer, if you will. Maybe it's a lower price; maybe it's got more bonuses or more value than your other offer; maybe it's something related, but in a sub-category in a different direction. In a week or two, after you've seen whether your customers have responded or not, **you can take those same people who raised their hands in the first place and give them another shot at doing business with you. You know they're going to want to do business with you, because they're pleased with what you over-delivered for the $10 or $20 they gave you to start out with.** You don't want to let them sit too long and forget who you are. I think it's a good idea to make sure your plan branches out. Make contingencies. If they *do* buy your backup back-end offer, do you then send them a higher-end offer, and when? If they don't buy that, do you send them another offer that's going to move them into the funnel better? More to the point, if you have multiple items in your low-cost and mid-cost categories and one isn't working, you can try another.

In any case, **it's important to keep going after them.** You might think it's a pain to keep getting postcards from the same realtor, over and over, month after month — but when you're ready to sell the house you're living in, who are you going to call? Probably the agent who sent you 25 or 30 postcards over the years. So don't give up. Keep sending; stay in touch with your customers, because the more you stay in touch with them, the more likely they are going to respond to you if you have something they want. And make them specific offers every time. You're not just staying in touch with them, asking them to call you for no reason; **you're telling them** *exactly* **what you want them to do. You're telling them** *exactly* **what's in it for them. When they do respond to you, they're doing it for a very clear and compelling reason.**

The best part about all this is that once you've got them with your front-end offer, it doesn't matter if you're not the best copywriter in the world. At that point **your copy doesn't have to be perfect,** because you already know they're interested in what you have. Chances are, they're going to want more of it — they're going to be asking, "What's next?" So don't worry about being a world-class copywriter; just whip out a sales letter talking about your next product and send it to them, because you've already broken the ice with that front-end offer. I've said it before and I'll probably say it again: good enough is good enough.

The Sum of Its Parts

There's an old marketing question

every business owner should ask himself: "Am I in the business of making sales?" And the answer is: No, **you're in the business of building relationships with customers.** When you develop that relationship, you'll have a pool of customers ready and eager to buy whatever it is you have to sell. Isn't that worth developing a front-end system?

The answer is yes. Earlier, I mentioned the fact that a lot of business people are lazy. Well, if you're lazy — and we all have that streak in us — then you should be excited about what I've gone over in this chapter, because doing well in this business is really about developing relationships. The front-end — the things you do to attract the best prospects, those who are most likely to end up doing business with you in the future — is just the beginning. It's a necessary evil, and it's a lot of hard work. But then comes the real business of making money: the back-end business, where you're building relationships. **For those of us who are lazy, this is the easiest money you'll ever make** because all you're doing is being a friend. People will do things for their friends that they won't do for anybody else; when somebody has a relationship with you, there's a trust built up there. They'll do whatever you ask them to do, as long as they trust you enough and as long as they believe in you enough. Really, that's all this is about. It's the easiest money you'll ever make in your life.

MARKETING SECRET #23

MARKETING MAXIM: You can tell everything about a person — by simply paying attention to what they spend their money on.

- People reveal their true selves — by the way they spend their money.

- "It is where a man spends his money that shows where his heart lies." (A. Edwin Keigurn)

- This is why 2-Step marketing is so powerful.

SECRET FOUR:

Harnessing the Power of Direct-Mail Marketing

It's time, now, to let you in on the secrets of Direct-Mail Marketing — and there are a lot of them. If you think you already know all about Direct-Mail, you're probably wrong! You'll need to pay close attention to what I'm going to share with you in this chapter, because **Direct-Mail is something that can make your business obscene amounts of profit — and most people don't understand it at all.** If they're using it, they're using it in the wrong ways. Therefore, by practicing the methods and strategies I'm going to reveal in this chapter, you can quickly rise to the top to the heap, because you're going to know things of which none of your competitors have ever heard. Among other things, this chapter is going to teach you how to formulate a good Direct-Mail piece and how to come up with good, moneymaking ideas for this format.

First of all, what *is* Direct-Mail Marketing? As the name suggests, it's a form of Direct-Response Marketing, that super-effective marketing tool I discussed in detail in Chapter 2. It's very important for any business, especially since you can't communicate on a personal level, with every client or prospect with which you're doing business. One thing about Direct-Mail that you should really take to heart is the fact that if you send a letter to somebody, it cuts through all the advertising clutter with which they're faced. **It puts your message directly in front of the right prospect at the right time, unlike any other medium out there.** Direct-Mail then, is a personal medium that really gives you the ability to go out there and communicate one-on-one with your client.

One of the biggest advantages of Direct-Mail is that it's

targeted. You use it to communicate directly with people who have an interest in your product, many of whom have been your customers in the past. When you're doing the latter, **you're talking to people without dealing with the waste you have to face when you use most forms of advertising.** What you've done is filter out all the extraneous advertising that people are hit with; if they're reading your ad, they're not seeing the undirected ads sent out by all your competitors. It's not in a publication, surrounded by similar offers that could beat you in terms of price or some other aspect. Direct-Mail puts your message directly in the hands of someone who has the capability and the interest to buy your product.

Here's another thing that makes Direct-Mail so useful: **the amount of control you have.** In most businesses, the advertising you do is really broad: you put an ad in a local newspaper or the Yellow Pages, so anyone can see it — *if* they're looking. That's not targeted at all. With Direct-Mail, you have the ability to control exactly who sees your offer and when they see it; what time of the year they see it and, in some cases, what day of the week they see it. I think **that level of control makes Direct-Mail one of the most useful tools in the serious marketer's arsenal.** Plus, most TV, radio, and even newspaper advertising is superficial. You can only use a certain number of words to get your message across. But with Direct-Mail, you can use several pages, you can go into detail, and you can present all the benefits of your services and products. Largely for that reason, **it's low-rejection marketing.**

Nobody likes rejection. When you're doing face-to-face selling or working with someone on the phone, you take the chance that they're not going to accept your offer, whatever it is. Even if it's the best offer for them, it may not be the right time for them to purchase that product or service. Even so, it's a very personal rejection. Whereas with Direct-Mail, you can stamp a few thousand envelopes, send them out in the mail, and only the ones who want to do business with you respond. So it's really a positive feeling; instead of suffering through 99 rejections for every time you get a person to buy, **you hear only from the people who want what**

you've got.

Direct-Mail also gives you the ability to multiply your effort, in terms of selling. You don't want to base your marketing initiatives entirely on face-to-face or one-on-one selling, if only because you can reach just a small percentage of your potential customers in person or by phone. With Direct-Mail, you have the ability to sell to 1,000 people at a time, or 10,000, or even 100,000. And you always let that sales piece — your Direct-Mail letter — do the selling for you. The best thing about that is your sales piece never has a bad day, unlike a real, live person: it's your best employee every single time someone reads it, and it can go out to the perfect people and give the perfect sales pitch thousands of times in a very short period. **A good Direct-Mail offer is nothing more than a salesman in an envelope.**

Think about that last statement for a moment: a good Direct-Mail offer is nothing more than a salesman in an envelope. With Direct-Mail, you can have thousands of little salesmen working for you every single day — and it's the rare company that can afford thousands of flesh-and-blood salesmen. Your sales piece never needs to eat, sleep, take off sick, or get a pay raise. That typifies the power of Direct-Mail, because they're like little genies in a bottle out there, popping up and grabbing the customer's attention and provoking them to do what you want them to do, which is buy from you.

Direct-Mail is a proven and time-tested method of marketing; it's been used for decades, if not longer. Recently, my colleague Chris Lakey was doing some research for one of his projects, and he came across a book on Direct-Mail that was written in 1952. Amazingly, that book discusses many of the same marketing theories we use today — particularly the psychological and emotional reasons that people buy. The book is 55 years old, but it tells you all the same stuff you hear today! Obviously, Direct-Mail worked well then, and it still works well now. Oh, and did I mention the money potential of Direct-Mail? With this medium, **you can get your sales letter in the mail and have money coming**

in in as little as 48 hours. Most other methods of advertising are slow, or they're for brand awareness only — that is, you're just running ads to get people to recognize your name or stop into your store next time they happen to need whatever you offer.

Here's how effective a good Direct-Mail piece is. If you'll take a few minutes to think of the top three salespeople you know — the best ones you've personally met and spent time with — and make a list of all the qualities those three salespeople have, you'll get a good indication of what a good Direct-Mail sales package is all about. Just looking at all the qualities you listed will teach you more about Direct-Mail than most people know. Most business people think they can throw anything in the mail and get results, but then most business people don't understand that it really *is* all about salesmanship.

Getting Your Feet Wet in the Direct-Mail Ocean

It's fairly easy to understand what Direct-Mail is. We all get it in our mailboxes (physical and electronic) just about every day, so we understand the forms it takes. But understanding how to get started, how to put together a good Direct-Mail piece — well, that's a trade secret, and I'm going to reveal it to you here.

Developing a decent Direct-Mail sales piece is all about preparing and

planning — something that many business people don't bother with. Too many people start developing their sales pieces before they ever know what they should be writing, and that lack of preparation is the reason that most of them fail in their Direct-Mail efforts. Therefore, let's start with what you do before you even put pen to paper.

First off is problem hunting, an exercise you can perform for any business, regardless of what business you're in. **In order to be a good problem hunter, you've got to become an expert on your customers, so you can get inside of their minds and hearts. Just immerse yourself in your knowledge of your customer base, and think about everything that your target audience wants and desires — all the biggest problems in their lives.** What you're going to do is identify their irritations and their frustrations and, more to the point, their *pain*. What's really the thorn in their side that makes it hard for them to do business? What can you help them do that will make them more successful, and make them really want to do business with you?

Not only do you have to know how you're going to solve that problem, but you have to know how you're going to package what you're offering so that it's attractive. **You're essentially going to be asking people to give you their money in return for your solution, so you want to make certain that you create a solution that's much more attractive to them than what they get by holding onto their money.** They've got to be willing to give up what they buy in order to have what you're offering. Sure, that's really simplistic, on the face of it — but the truth is, most of us don't think that way when we're constructing an offer. We think of "offer" as, "Gee, what kind of price? If I sold it for $100 before, and I'm offering it for $50 now; that's a hell of an offer!" But that may not, necessarily, be the offer. The degree of pain that you're going to solve for your customers and the benefits they're going to get may be more important than the price.

Often there are multiple problems available for you to tackle,

---

but you want to handle one at a time. Therefore, it's a good idea to focus your attention on one big problem per offer, though sometimes you can do a combination if you handle it carefully. One of the things about which I need to caution you — and this is big! — is that you have to make certain that it's not just a problem in your mind; that is, be sure your customers actually see the problem as a problem. A good way to do that would be to contact a few of your customers and ask them if the problem you perceive is something that's really a concern to them, because you don't want to spend time writing copy that's not going to make you any money. Once you've confirmed the problem these customers are all having, you can go through a relatively straightforward process when you're developing and constructing your Direct-Mail piece.

Develop Your Empathy

First off, you need to **take the time to understand your customer — to understand what they're going through, what they're feeling, what they want, need, and desire.** Once you've done that, take all that you've gathered, and *then* start to put the offer together. Many people who go out there and try to make money in Direct-Mail, and in their heads, hearts, and souls, they're thinking, "This is a great deal!" when actually they didn't spend the time to look at the market and understand their potential customer base.

The trick to really succeeding with Direct-Mail — and, really, with most aspects of your marketing — is to **know your customers and prospects more intimately than they know themselves,** because often they're buying things at a deep emotional level. This is the problem with focus groups: in real life, **people buy for all kinds of weird emotional reasons that defy logic, and those aren't things you can capture in a focus group.** Some marketplaces tend to be much more emotionally driven than others, so it's up to you to try to get a handle on who your best customers are, and what they're all about. For years I kept a running list of all of the qualities of my customers in a three-ring

FREE GIFT! Go to www.RuthlessMarketing.com/freegift

binder, until I filled up the whole thing. It's all color-coded and pretty thick, and I still have it.

This type of customer understanding is vitally important, because most business owners believe that people are coming in to buy a certain product; so whenever they create any type of marketing, they sell the product itself. They say, "This product looks like this and it's got this many pages, or it kills this many bugs, or it makes your lawn this much greener." But **if you have a real understanding of your target market, you'll understand that customers aren't really buying the product; they could care less about the product itself. What they really want are** *results***.** People have a problem, and the result they want is the eradication of that problem. They want that problem gone.

You're going to be ahead of all your competitors if you can really understand their pain at an emotional level, and understand that your product has to hit the hot button of dissolving that pain in their lives. In the text of your copy, **you're actually going to spend most of the time talking not about your product, but about how it gives the user the result they want — how it eradicates their pain, or maybe even gives them pleasure in the fastest, quickest, easiest way possible.** Sometimes that's difficult for business owners to do, because they're so bonded to their product. But you have to move past that and understand that you're not just in business to make yourself happy; you're not in business to shine your product and stock your shelves. No, you're in business to make money. If making money means that **you're delivering what your customers want,** then that needs to be your focus — **not falling in love with your product.**

An important step in developing this kind of understanding is asking some of your customers and prospects about their problems. Many business owners take their customers for granted; they don't ask people walking through their store for their feedback. If you do, you may be able to get ahead of your customers, at least in regard to what they really want. They may even help you tailor your offer even better than what you'd originally anticipated.

Feeling Their Pain

Never Fear Objections.

- Don't hide! Be upfront about the skepticism you know they feel... Bring up the biggest objections yourself. Then overcome them one by one. You'll win their trust and respect — and you'll get their money.

- The best prospects have major objections that must be faced head-on and not skated around.

The first thing to do with your sales letter is to state the problem, and make sure your customers or prospects feel it. You need to bring the pain to the surface — so really rub it in, but in a nice way. You don't want to get out there and go, "Ha ha ha! This is your big problem!" You want to make sure you do it using language with which your customers are familiar, presented in a nice, conservative fashion... **but make them feel the pain, because then you're going to sell them the solution.** Keep in mind that people will typically do more to avoid pain than they will to gain pleasure. So if you can bring that pain to the surface — make them feel it in your presentation to them — you're going to grab the attention of a lot of people. This is where the *ruthless* part comes in. You twist the knife and make it hurt, make them really feel it, and make them focus on their problem so you can offer them a solution.

Every time you come up with a new piece, just make sure you go back and **focus on the big problem.** Before you get started with anything, look at what your product is and think about all of the problems it solves. If you're still searching for a product, understand your audience and develop your product to overcome or

FREE GIFT! Go to www.RuthlessMarketing.com/freegift

provide a solution for them. In either case, focus your Direct-Mail message around the problem you've found, and make sure your prospects are really experiencing that problem.

Sharpening your Salesmanship

Another thing you need to do is **make sure you understand how to sell your product before you sit down and write the piece.** If you've got people on the phones selling and interacting with your customer, find your best salesperson, the one who's really good at addressing these problems. Chances are, if they're really good at what they do, they're really good at identifying the customer's problems. Record their presentation to a customer, and take that presentation and use it as a basis for starting your sales letter. If you don't have anybody selling your products, you could always call some customers on your list or in your target audience and try preselling to them first, and find out how they respond. Then go with whatever worked best on the phone as your starting point for your sales material.

This goes right back to what I talked about in the introduction to this chapter: **it's all about salesmanship.** That's what the heart and soul of Direct-Mail is all about: **persuading people to give up their money in exchange for something that they perceive is worth more than that money.** If you're one of those people who can't sell things, you need help. You need to find the best salesman in your company or hire someone who knows what they're doing, or else you won't succeed in Direct-Mail — or in marketing in general.

Choosing Your Target

Before you actually create your Direct-Mail piece, you have to know exactly to whom it's going, because that knowledge will be informative on how you put your offer together. The primary question you'll need to ask yourself is this: "What mailing list should I use?" If you're going to rent an outside list, it had better be of people that you *know* are interested in your services or products. If it's your own list — **which is the best mailing list you can use, of course** — then you know they're interested in what you're selling (at least to some degree). Now, in conjunction with that big question of "What mailing list should I use?" **you've got to ask yourself several associated questions**:

- "Who are my prospects?"

- "Is this list going to go right to them?"

- "Does this list include the people that we have to reach for this offer?"

Once you've set up your target, you have to start thinking conceptually. Ask yourself, "What motivates these people to want what I'm selling?" As I've said before, **you've got to go beyond the obvious.** They're not simply looking for your products and services; they're looking for the solutions to their problems, or they're looking for the anticipation of getting something of value that they want. So consider that, and then start thinking about the most important benefits of your services and products.

Jumping in Head First

Your Direct-Mail piece is a letter to your prospect, and it needs to begin with a headline. I believe in **writing the headline before you even do the sales letter, because it will guide you as you write the sales piece.** A good way to look for the right headline, if you're not an accomplished copywriter, is to consider the "how to" approach. Here's a good one: "How to eat more and weigh less." I honestly don't know how or if that works, but it's a good headline. Here are some others:

- "How to win friends and influence people" (the old Dale Carnegie approach).

- "How to make yourself judgment-proof."

- "How to fire your boss."

All these are great headlines that you can emulate. You don't want to use them verbatim, of course, but follow their lead. You'll be able to take the "how to" approach and then put in your details that pertain to your own products or services.

When you finish doing that, you can go into your letter and start listing the benefits, because it's the benefits that make people buy. **Exactly what action do you want the reader to take? Make it very specific.** Then it's a good idea, too, to look at your competition and see what they're doing. If you have a really good competitor who's using sales letters, get ahold of one of their sales letters. **Don't copy them word-for-word, but** *do* **look that piece over and see how you can create a letter that's every bit as good or better than what they have.** This is an approach that will get you started right.

Okay, so you're thinking about the headline, which will have a big benefit in it. You're mailing to the right people, and you're testing. Even if you plan to mail it to 5,000 people, it would be smart to mail 500 first to see the response. **Most of us don't do enough testing, and I can't emphasize its importance enough. Testing is what separates the winners from the losers.** You can make subtle changes if something isn't working, or you can increase the volume of outgoing mail when it *is* working. These are just some of the things you need to think about when creating your sales letter.

Some people will say, "I could never write a sales letter." But the truth is, if **you can write a good, emotional letter to a friend or to a loved one, you can write a sales letter.** Put your love in the letter. Don't get gushy with your customers, but convey the message that, "I have something here very important that can help you, and here's why it can help you." Then list all the different reasons why it can, and make both the sincerity and empathy you feel obvious. That's a very important part of the whole process.

Never, never, never, never delegate your marketing to someone else.

- It's far too important. And nobody is ever going to care as much about it as you do — or be willing to sacrifice as much as you are.

They'll use the information you give them to decide if it's important to them, or if it can really help them.

Here's another fact about sales letters, and I think it's one that a lot of people don't realize. Maybe there are some copywriters out there who can do it differently, **but most sales letters are written in pieces over a period of time.** My first sales letter took me three months to write. It's not at all uncommon to spend three solid days or even a week writing a letter; you just do them a piece at a time, though you're never trying to give people the impression you're doing that. You try to make it look like you did it all from start to finish, even if it actually took a lot of time and was done patchwork quilt style. Of course, it probably doesn't take a week to get the words on paper; but you get them on paper once, and then the next day you look at them and you say, "Well, maybe this belongs here, and maybe this word would be better than that word," and you play with the text until you're happy with what you've got.

When you're done you think, "How could I have ever put in a week on this?" Sometimes, when you look at a letter after it's been re-written several times, to the naked eye it may not look a whole lot different than it was three or four days ago, when you looked at it before. But the devil's in the details, as they say. **It's all in the minutia: the little things that you do**

and tweak differently that have the biggest impact. It's not necessarily that it looks a whole lot different than it did before. The real difference is in the fine art of tweaking, and going back over it again and again, **looking for little details that need to be changed. This comes with experience.** Even if you can't tell a big difference in a quick scan of the letter, those changes can make a huge difference in sales.

Another key is **reading your letter aloud.** I've found that if you read your letter out loud, **you'll find gaps where the text doesn't quite fit together, it doesn't flow,** or it doesn't really progress the way you want them to — and you can easily make changes. Sometimes, you'll come to a point in a letter where the words just don't roll off your lips, or the rhythm changes, or there's some indefinable awkwardness there. You may not know why necessarily, **but simply changing one word here or adding a word there can help.** It may be that it needs three adjectives instead of two, or vice versa. You'll feel a rhythm when you say it out loud that you'll never detect if you're reading it silently. This is important, because you have to remember that your customers and prospects aren't going to see your letter the same way you are. Most of time, when you're reading a book or reading an offer yourself, it's like you're saying it out loud in your head while you're reading. If a customer is reading your offer, they're going to stumble on those same points that you stumbled on when you read it aloud. Anytime you have a spot that you stumble on that doesn't seem real clear — one that makes you stop and say it again, because it was confusing — that's a point you need to work on polishing out, because when your customer is reading your offer they're likely to have the same problem.

The bottom line is, a sales letter is a piece of art. It's a challenge, and that's the fun of it. That said, don't let the challenge of producing a work of art keep you from sitting down and actually putting pen to paper. One of the things you've got to remember is that while you're crafting the ultimate salesman by making this sales letter, **you're probably not going to get it perfect the first**

time. If you do, you're a genius, and that's great — but you should always at least have a shoddy salesman out there. Get something down on paper and send it out. Test it. If it doesn't sell as well as you'd like, sit down and rewrite it. Don't be scared. Just because you've created a sales letter and it's out there in the world doesn't mean that it's written in stone. You can always change it, reapply yourself to it, and tweak it until you get it to the point where it's performing optimally. Then go back out there and do more mailings with it. Here's a truism you should take to heart: *You're never going to make sales with a sales letter if you don't have it in the mail.*

Facing Your Fear

I'll be the first to tell you that I understand there's a certain amount of fear involved in creating any sales product. You want to get things right, you want to make money, and most of all you don't want to look like an idiot. I've got a newsflash for you: this nervousness, this fear, never goes away entirely. I've been doing this now since 1988, and in the process I've created sales letters that have earned more than $100 million. I've done hundreds of promotions, but still, on a big promotion, **I always go through a period of total confusion.** Now, of course, it's become so common that it doesn't bother me anymore. It's not nearly as painful, because I expect it and I realize that I'll get beyond it. But **there's always a period of frustration and uncertainty** I experience when I'm developing something new, and that part is not so easy to deal with. Those are the times when I'm trying to figure out all the answers, and things aren't coming together very well. But that's a hump that you get over, and it gets easier after that. Many times, if I spend three days working on a sales letter, I'll get more done in the last day than I did the previous two days together. The last day is like coasting downhill; it all just starts to flow.

It takes work and effort to make things come together the way you want them to. According to my friend Jeff Gardner, he usually finds that when it gets to be very difficult, he's over-thinking it. He's so focused on getting it right that he's paralyzed, and I've felt that myself. But **you can't let indecision, uncertainty, or the need to get everything just right keep you from doing anything.** Let that feeling go; tell yourself, "Okay, look, I know what the product is. That's not a problem. I know what the results are. I know my target market. What I need to do is just sit down and connect with the customer."

Even though you may know all that intellectually, there's still that point where it's all frustrating; it's difficult, and it's a real challenge. But if you work through that, believe me, it does get easier. It probably won't be easy right out of the gate, but if you stick with it, you're going to be successful. This attitude gives you the ability to ease up on yourself. Sure, you should understand that it's going to be a difficult situation each time; but you should also understand that **if you go past that and get through all those things that keep other people from writing great copy, you're going to be able to make a lot of money.** You're not alone; a lot of copywriters at all levels go through those same type of struggles, and if they can make gobs of money, why can't you?

Naturally, there are some people for whom this all comes easy, and you might find that you're one of them. I admire and I'm envious of people who can whip out sales copy in no time, because it can be extremely difficult — and writer's block is no laughing matter. But once you get in the flow, you can make tremendous amounts of profits, profits that your competitors will never even *begin* to make, just by mastering this skill. This is because **a thousand sales letters, if they're done correctly, are like a thousand salespeople going around knocking on doors.** Just like any great salesperson, they're enthusiastic; there's a tremendous belief in the product or service being sold, so they can do a powerful job of selling. That being the case, it's worth all the extra effort you put into it!

The Personal Touch

Here's something that I always keep in mind while writing a

"Getting a new customer is like riding a bicycle uphill on a hot summer day. Doing more business with an established customer is like coasting that same bike downhill." — Jay Abraham

- Re-sell to your existing customers more often.

- Sell more stuff — to more customers more often!

sales letter, and I know that many of my colleagues do too. **Try to make the letter as personal as you can.** If you're writing to 1,000 people or 10,000 people, **the key to success is to make it look like you're writing to *one* person.** Always think of one customer, not 500 or 5,000: that's the key to success when writing Direct-Mail copy. You want to address this person with passion; you want to convince this person that they need whatever it is you're selling them, and ideally you should explain why. **The passion in a good salesman's voice has to come through on paper** just as if you were saying it to someone — one of your best friends, or your parents, or one of your children. You don't necessarily have to follow perfect grammar rules; you just have to **talk to the prospect as if you're talking to them in person, and you'll get through to them.**

Avoiding the Blank Page

For some of us who struggle with writing, the problem's not so much being unable to communicate, it's dealing with that blank page. **Some people are born writers, but others are born talkers —** and I'm one of them. I can communicate something in speech much better than I can in print, and if you're like me, you might find it hard to get started when you're faced with that blank page (or these days, that blinking cursor). It can be overwhelming to think of writing a long-form sales letter when you have to start with that blank page.

Technology can come to your rescue here. If you struggle with actually getting something written down, then why not **grab a tape recorder and record your sales letter on audio?** Once that's done, you can let someone else transcribe it and get it into print, and then all you have to do is some judicious editing. Recording your sales letter is one way to hit that tone where it seems that you're speaking directly to your customer, communicating one-on-one. You don't even have to record the whole letter; maybe it's just the headlines, or good benefit-driven bits and pieces of a letter, that you get out of your mind and onto tape. Maybe you record your headline and then rattle off a bunch of benefits off the top of your head, **as if you're telling a customer, face-to-face, about what makes your product so special. Then you talk about the offer and the price.** Once it's transcribed and on paper, you'll end up with pages worth of good copy that you can shape into a sales letter — and you never have to worry about staring at that blank page.

Here's another good option, and I suspect it's one that most copywriters employ: **use another sales letter as a template for your new one. Basically, you just keep writing the same sales letter again and again.** So if you had a seminar for your customers last year and you're getting ready for this year's seminar, just pull up last year's copy and change the titles, dates, and some of the offers to come up with *this* year's copy. That way, you're not dealing with a blank screen or page, ever. Just keep files of those previous promotions that you did, and you can easily pull them up, change the name of the file, and rewrite a new offer.

Elements of Style

One of the reasons that copywriting can be so difficult is that you have to grab your prospect's interest from the word go. The first page is crucial, because it's where you hook them. If the first page doesn't work, all the good stuff later is useless. Some writers rewrite and polish that first page as much as possible before moving on, and they find that the rest of the letter flows more smoothly as a result. Once you have your beginning and you know your ending, the letter can flow between those two points.

Here's something to avoid on that first page. Amateur copywriters writing their first sales letters often start out by talking a lot about themselves, about their business, how old Grandfather Jed started it all back in 1901. Don't overindulge in that kind of writing, because the prospect really doesn't care. You can touch on some of that stuff, but what you really need to do is **get as many benefits as you can on the first page.** If you're sending a six-page letter, some people will make a decision within a matter of seconds about whether they're going to continue to read it. You'd better be talking about benefits for *them*, not the fact that Grandfather Jed had this vision and started the company in 1901.

Beyond Page One

By now, some of you are probably horrified, if only because you came into this chapter thinking that a sales letter was a one-page document. Remember though, we're speaking in terms of a Direct-Mail letter, and that's often much more than a single page. There are long-form sales letters and short-form letters, and **long-form letters can be surprisingly effective.** Obviously, if you can tell your entire story on a single page, that's fine. But in most cases, if you're trying to make a sale, it's going to take a lot more information than that.

People considering Direct-Mail for the first time are often flabbergasted to learn that serious marketers regularly send out 15- or 16-page letters. They think that no one is going to take the time to read a 16-page letter; **but if you're trying to make a large sale and it takes 16 pages for you to tell your story, then a 16-page letter is what you need to write.** If you've targeted your prospect right, he'll probably read that 16-page letter. In fact, if it's written well and tells him the benefits of a product or service that will fill his needs and fix whatever problems he's facing, he'll probably read a 30-page letter. That may seem a little extreme, but it works if you set it up right.

The Sincerest Form of Flattery

If you're new at the game and don't have any old copy of your own to use as a template, one way to learn what works is to study the masters. Find yourself some really good sales letters, then sit down and write those sales letters down, in longhand, word-for-word. Rewrite them too, if you can. **This can get you into the mind of the copywriter,** so that you can see how they went about identifying and bringing out the benefits of whatever it was they were selling. **It's a very powerful method, because it can help you see the different elements that are flowing through a letter.** If this sounds a lot like homework — well, it is. Writing a sales letter word-for-word can help you understand how the whole letter is set up. You could never use that letter to sell to clients — that would be plagiarism — but the practice will help you understand how the copywriter who wrote it was truly thinking.

This is one way you can pick **up the language of good salesmanship in print,** and you have to be careful when you do it; you can take it too far, and lose what makes your own copy special. You can even take special classes to learn how to write the perfect sales letter; I know a famous marketer who teaches copywriting seminars, and he has a loyal following of people that he's instructed. He gives his students all kinds of formulas for writing copy, and yes, I've seen a lot of the work done by his students. If there's one big criticism I have, it's the fact that **everybody follows the formula to the point where their copy is too homogenized.** Not only does it lack any scintilla of their personality, it's too perfect overall. It looks too pretty; it looks too clean; it looks too neat. In other words, **it's not human enough!** There's no life to their copy; it's too bland.

When you look at a good Direct-Mail package, one that really inspires and motivates you, **there's a humanness to it. It's raw. It's real. It's just like a salesperson.** The best salespeople I know aren't necessarily attractive people physically, but they do have overbearing personalities. They will not be denied, and they believe

- Believe so deeply in your ability to give your market what they truly want — that failure is not an option! Develop a missionary zeal for what you do! Then communicate your intense passion to your prospects!

in their product or service very strongly. They may be hairy and ugly looking, but who cares? They're passionate, and they're real. They inspire trust. They inspire confidence. They have total believability in what they're doing. You cannot help but be moved by these people. They're hitting your buttons; **you're getting pumped up, so excited by their pitch that you can't wait to send back an order or get to that store.** And that's *exactly* what you, as a marketer, want to accomplish.

The Value of a Deadline

Copywriting deadlines can help you in two ways. First of all, you should set one for yourself. Rewriting is important in copywriting, since the right changes can increase your profits tremendously; the only problem is, you've got to stop at some point. I'm convinced that you can overwork your copy if you go too far. There comes a time when you can actually screw it up if you don't step back and accept that what you've got is good enough. You need a deadline to keep you from doing that. If you set a date that the letter has to be finished by, you can rework it all you want — but when you get to that deadline, it's done and you're ready to mail.

Don't forget to **add a deadline for the prospect or customer as well.** *Always* give them a deadline when they should act; **never send out a sales piece that just lets them decide, at their own leisure, when** they're going to take advantage of your service or product. Make your deadline ten or twenty days from the time you mail it; make it clear that they have to take action *right now* to get what you're offering at this special price.

The Seven Steps to Super-Profitable Direct-Mail Copywriting

By now, you've probably gotten the point that with Direct-Mail, it's all about salesmanship: getting to know your customer, explaining the offer in a clear, beneficial way, and carefully crafting what you're going to send out and do. **This all takes a lot of learning and experience to get just right, but I've boiled it down to seven steps that anyone can handle.** Most of them I've mentioned before in this chapter, but I want to take this opportunity to re-emphasize them by summarizing them in easy-to-swallow morsels (this is the teaching method also known in some circles as Pounding It Into Your Head). Without further ado then, the Seven Steps to Super-Profitable Direct-Mail Copywriting are:

- Research
- Prewriting
- Writing
- Rewriting
- Mailing the Offer
- Studying the Results
- Testing

In the following sections, I'll talk about each of the Seven Steps in more detail.

Research

The first step is research, and researching your copy involves several different elements, all of which have to happen before you take any further action. First of all, you have to know your prospect: you have to know who they are, how they think, and what their hot buttons are psychologically. I won't belabor that point here, since I covered it extensively in earlier sections of this chapter. You also have to know your offer inside and out, before you even sit down to write. **Be clear on your offer's biggest benefits. Then take some time to study your swipe file.**

That last suggestion may have you a little confused, since you might not even know what a swipe file is. Remember how I suggested earlier that you should emulate successful copywriters, at least at the beginning? One way you can start doing that is by building a swipe file. At its most basic, **a swipe file is just a collection of winning ads, sales letters and offers that have been proven to work.** Of course, you'll want copy that sells products and services similar to your own to similar prospects. Send off for offers, collect the Direct-Mail that comes to you, clip out well-done ads in magazines and papers, and put those together in a swipe file so you can research what's been working in the marketplace.

Prewriting

Before you sit down and actually write a sales letter, you should list, on paper, all the benefits, selling points, bullets, and other items that you're going to need to include in your offer. Also list all the other "must have" elements — how to order, the action you want your prospects to take, and any questions and answers that you feel you need to include. Basically, **you're creating an outline of how you want the sales copy to flow.**

Writing the Offer

Once you have your outline together, it's time to actually start writing the offer. This is arguably the hardest part, though some copywriters will say that it's easier than the research phase. In any case, start with the headline. If you don't have a good headline, you're not going to be able to draw people into your offer and get them to read anything else in your sales letter. Use words that sell. I could go on for chapters and chapters about how the words that sell, like *you* and *free* and *new* and all the others, are so important, but that'll have to wait for another book! At the very least, be sure to use the word *you* a lot, so you can make it personal: remember, you need to **write this as if you're talking to your prospect one-on-one.** Talk about *them*; don't talk about all your customers in general, and don't make broad statements about whom you're trying to sell to. *Speak to your prospect specifically.*

While you're at it, **make strong, even outrageous guarantees.** If you can't guarantee your product, then you shouldn't be selling it. You've got to have some kind of guarantee; that's a given. Be sure to **carry the main theme from the sales copy to the order form.** Order forms — where you tell people to order and let people order from you — are a great place to restate your offer and your guarantee. Some copywriters actually do the order form first. Now, that's a big pet peeve of mine: I think those people are boxing themselves in. A better formula I've adapted is to write the sales letter first and then work on the order form, because you never quite know where you're going to go with your letter when you're in the thick of it.

In addition to using the personal touch and offering solid guarantees, use testimonials if possible. Scientists like to make a big deal about how anecdotal evidence isn't worth squat, and maybe that's true in scientific research — but it's gold in marketing copy. **People want to hear from other people like them about how your product made their lives better.** Some of your current customers will be willing to give you testimonials about your products, and if you can include their names and a little bit of a description about who they are, that's good. If you can include their picture, it's ten times better.

Nobody likes to make a decision all on their own. If the customer knows that people have made these decisions before, or

There's a lot of competition for your customers' money. Never forget this. If you can't answer the question — "Why should I give it to you and not your competitor?" then you don't deserve to be in business.

- Just like in sports: the team who wants it more than the other team — wins!

that people are actually using the product and seeing these results, that's something they can use to help them make their own decision. The best part is, the power of testimonials works no matter if you're selling to an individual consumer or to a corporation. You see, **people don't do business with companies; they do business with people, and Direct-Mail is all about one-to-one communication.** It's the next best thing to going up to somebody, looking them straight in the eye, giving them one of those great big Bill Clinton handshakes where you use two hands instead of one, even slapping them on the back a little like every good salesperson does. **It's all about that human element.** Make the customer feel important — learn the names of their kids, and their birthdays if you can.

You need to realize that people all want to feel special. They want to feel like they're loved, appreciated, respected and admired — and they're usually surrounded by a whole bunch of people who are sick and tired of them. They go to their mailbox, and if we do a good job — and this works especially well in niche markets — **we can build bonds with customers in which we give them all the things they're lacking in their regular life.** You see this a lot in women's business groups, where they get together for just those social events. Mary Kay Cosmetics has done this for years with their conferences. The average consultant doesn't make a whole lot with Mary Kay, but they have this incredible social environment. They're made to feel important, they get medals, and they get to wear different colored blazers if they get to a certain level. They can even get a pink Cadillac if they work hard enough. It's a social network that makes a group of women happy; it's their way to feel important. With a little skillful copywriting, you can do the same for your customers.

Rewriting

Ask just about any writer, and he'll tell you that **writing is mostly *re*writing.** Very rarely are you going to get something just right the first time through. Take a little time between your first draft and the rewrite; put the copy in a drawer for a few days, and go on to something else. Fresh eyes always give you a new angle; often, something strikes you that you didn't catch the first time. **You may discover that half of what you've written during your writing phase may be total crap, while the other half may be brilliant. You don't try to decide what's right and what's wrong when you're in the thick of it; you just throw it all out there, and then you start the rewriting.** The rewrite phase is where you weed out all the bad stuff and save all the good stuff — just like you boil down a good gravy.

As you're going over the text, make sure all your benefits and selling points from the research and prewriting phases are included, that you didn't leave something out. Pay close attention to the headline and closing. Just like in golf, you drive for show and putt for dough. **Your money in sales copy is generally made on the headline and the first page — where you draw them in — and on the last page, where you make your closing arguments.** As you're rewriting, revise any areas that focus too much on you and your company, because, like I've already said more than once, your prospects really don't care about that. They prefer that you focus more on them, and the benefits of your product or service that relate to them.

As you're looking for any of those areas to polish over, be sure to read the copy aloud so you can catch any snags that aren't obvious in print. Here's an especially important point: be sure you **mention the offer *at least* three times.** Most people aren't going to read your entire sales letter from first to last word; they're going to skim and scan it, and you may miss giving them a good reason to buy if you don't mention your offer over and over again, and in various formats throughout your letter.

Mailing the Offer

There are many routes you can take when you're mailing out a Direct-Mail piece. You can go totally commercial, where the piece is plastered all over with benefits and sales copy, or totally personal, where you send it in a generic, bland envelope, and make it look like it was written by their cousin or their nephew or their brother. **There are all kinds of tricks and strategies you can use when putting that offer in the mail, in order to make it rise about all the background noise.**

The list of people to whom you're sending is one of the most important things in this entire series of Seven Steps, and this takes us back to the research stage. Knowing your prospect is crucial; if you don't know to whom you're mailing, then what you mail doesn't really matter. **You could have the greatest offer in the world for basket weaving, but if you're sending it to people who could care less about basket weaving, you'll never make a dime. That's the reason you should capture the names and addresses of every single person with whom you do business. Most businesses don't bother to do this,** and as a result they have no real idea who their customers are. People come in the door, they buy something, and they go out the door. Even if they write a check, which has their name, address, and phone number printed on it, most businesses won't bother to record that. Well, you'd better start!

The most important point — and I can't emphasize this enough — is that **you've got to get that offer in the mail!** You can't make any money at all if your salesmen aren't selling. As I've said before, your copy doesn't have to be the best in the world, though it should certainly be the best you can do. But you can even learn this skill poorly and have a competitive advantage, because most businesses just don't mail out copy. So even if you put something out there that you might not think is the best of the best, but it still hits all the customer's hot buttons and you're talking to them on a personal level, and you really pour it on right from your heart — you're going to have a huge competitive advantage, even if your copy's not perfect.

Studying the Results

One part of becoming a good marketer is learning from your mistakes. It's crucially important, after you mail an offer, to take a close look at the results of the mailing. You may make money hand-over-fist, and by that you'll know you've done it right. On the other hand, you may make just a little money or you may not make any money at all, and that tells you that you have to retool, look at a new market, and even look at new products altogether.

Testing

The seventh and final step is testing. **Once you know what works, your next goal is to try to find something else that beats it and works *better*. You do that by testing.** From that moment forward, every time you mail an offer, you can split the mailing equally in half and run the one you already mailed versus something new. However, you should never test more than one thing at a time. If you try to test more than one thing, you'll have no way to easily quantify the results.

Keep testing new things: the headline, the price, the offer, the letter length — even the color of the outside envelope of your package can be tested. Sometimes the changes that work best can be as subtle as the way you sign off the letter. That alone could be the one little change that makes a difference between a mediocre letter and one that makes millions. So, yes, the **testing is a continuous, ongoing process, but it's worth the effort when the money comes flooding in.**

* * * * *

And there you have it: the Seven Steps to Super-Profitable Direct-Mail Copy-writing. Of course, I have to admit that my colleagues and I don't necessarily follow all the steps every time. Often, we just sit down and write our letters and don't follow a particular formula point-by-point. But I'm not being a hypocrite here by telling you to do these things while I don't; because I can guarantee that by the time I'm done, the copy I've produced *does* fit these guidelines. You see, it all comes with experience. When you're just getting started in the business and you're just beginning to write sales copy, it's best and easiest to follow these steps.

It all sounds like a lot of work, doesn't it? I can assure you, it is — but it's probably the most valuable thing you'll ever do in your business. You may sit down and work like a demon for a week or two, but in the end, mail that sales letter out for five or ten years or more, and in the process, generate millions of dollars in income. That's a pretty good return on your investment: one week of strenuous mental work for millions of dollars. Works for me!

FREE GIFT! Go to www.RuthlessMarketing.com/freegift

Getting in the Groove

One thing that I want to point out is that for me, and for most of my colleagues, copywriting is as much a labor of love as it is hard work. You have to remember this: 99% of your competition won't bother to do this at all. They'll just put a sign in the window that says they're open for business. This is one way to get a competitive advantage over your competitors, and very quickly, too — and why is that? Because as my favorite quote has it, "In the land of the blind, the one-eyed man is king!" Read this book, and you'll be the one-eyed man in a marketplace full of blind businessmen, who have little or no understanding about anything I'm telling you here.

You may not think that you have the time to work on your copywriting, but in most businesses — especially the information business — you can't afford *not* to write consistently, day after day. Like I've said, **your copywriting will eventually become your most profitable activity.** Even if you're cruising along with a workable offer, talking on the phone or working with current clients, you're not growing; your income level probably won't change much. So if you just **make it part of your daily routine** to sit down and write, say, one paragraph of a sales letter, or look over something that you've already written, and edit a little section or something, you can start to make progress. You don't have to do it for two hours at a time; start with 20 minutes, and see how that works for you. You're going to find out your business is going to grow exponentially because you're talking to many more people, a lot of whom will become new clients. Here's a bit of incentive: according to one Direct-Marketing guru, every word that he writes generates another $20,000 for him. Imagine that! So if instead of spending an hour watching TV one night, he writes a paragraph or so — or even a couple of good sentences — he stands to make hundreds of thousands of dollars.

This might not happen to you right away, but if you'll just write a paragraph or two every day, eventually you'll have a whole sales letter with which to work. **Over time, as you gain experience, you'll find that every word you write is going to generate dollars for you — and you'll get to the point to where you'll feel guilty if you don't write.** After all, the money you want to come in next month has got to come from somewhere, and Direct-Mail is a good way to get it. It's an addicting kind of marketing, too, once you get in the groove. Once you have some successful promotions that pull in big bucks, you'll be addicted for the rest of your life, and **it won't be work anymore.**

In Summation

In this chapter, I've talked about selling to people using the Direct-Mail method of Direct-Response Marketing. Selling of any kind is an emotional, human undertaking, and it works best whenever you're able to connect with the people to whom you're selling. I have a favorite Mexican restaurant that I take all my out-of-town friends to whenever they come and visit. My wife and I have been going there since they opened. They have hundreds of loyal customers, and they know all their best customers by name. They come out and cook special things for you; they make you special desserts; and they do things that make you feel guilty as hell if you don't go there on a regular basis!

Ultimately, it's all about treating people well. Every salesperson knows that instinctively. **What we're talking about is a powerful marketing method where you're able to translate the best of the best of what physical, one-on-one salesmanship is all about into print, so you can stick it in an envelope.** That way, you end up with a whole bunch of the best salespeople out there. They never call in sick; they never go smoke dope at lunchtime; they never quit to go to work for your competitor down the street, or quit to start another company. **They're salespeople that you control in every way,** and it's worth learning to be an expert copywriter in order to get them.

SECRET FIVE:

Take-Away Selling Made Easy

In this chapter, I'm going to share another powerful marketing principle that can lead to tremendous profits for your business, *if* you're willing to master the techniques involved. This one's called "take-away selling," and I'm not talking about fast food here. I'll be frank: **you may find take-away selling a little disagreeable at first, because it's not just one of the most powerful marketing techniques you can use, it's also one of the most ruthless.** That said, take-away selling is a legitimate part of marketing, though naturally you'll always want to err on the side of the ethical — and you'll always want to avoid using it cruelly.

The thing is, even if you're being perfectly ethical, take-away selling *feels* cruel — and it should, if you do it right. That's why it's such a ruthless technique. Basically, it involves putting an offer before your prospect that's so desirable that they desperately want it. You get them to the point where they feel the desire, the *need*, to absolutely have it, and then you put a roadblock or a barrier in their way — some caveat that removes the satisfaction of obtaining what you've just built that desire for, at least until they reach another goal or meet another step. Consequently, although it seems to go against the grain of logic, you can actually double or triple the desire for what you're offering, making them ready to buy even faster. **That sounds a little perverse, but human nature being what it is, that's how things are.**

Here's a quick idea of how take-away works. Say you walk into a department store and check out some new shoes you're interested in. Because you don't see any in your size, you ask the sales representative if some are available. They go into the back room and emerge a few moments later saying, "I found a pair in your size, and it's the only one we have left in stock." Now, how much more do you want those shoes?

Faced with a choice like this, some prospects will just get irritated and walk away. But that's okay; you can use this reaction to your advantage. One of the good things about take-away selling is that once you're in a position where you can pick and choose customers, you can use the method to get rid of those customers who are more trouble than they're worth. Now, that may sound like a horrible thing for any businessman to say, but while **80% of your profits are going to come from about 20% of your customers,** the same's true of your problems — though ideally, it's a different 20% who bug you. Take-away selling allows you to get rid of that bottom tier of customers who are giving you the most problems and ultimately, raise your profits by not having to spend so much money on that group. We'll talk more about that later.

What it comes down to is this: **take-away selling is a lot like taking a starving man to a restaurant, closing the door before he's fed, and telling him he's got to wait until morning to get the food. It creates urgency and scarcity, and it makes people want your product that much more.**

Take-Away Selling in Action

To show you how take-away selling works in practice, I'm going to use an example provided by my friend and colleague, marketing genius Alan Bechtold. In early 2006, Alan launched an E-Publishing Marketing Mastermind, a small group of people he gathered together who were willing to pay a substantial sum of money to work with him personally, and with the rest of the group, utilizing the Mastermind Principle. Each member was guaranteed that by the time he or she finished the group, they'd create an original eBook, launch an original eZine, and tie the two together into a marketing system that works every time.

Now, that's a pretty sweet offer. Alan was asking $4,000 per seat for this Mastermind Group, and he limited it to 120 participants, maximum, by the launch date. Do a little arithmetic, and you can see the profit potential. He took it a step further, though; **instead of selling those $4,000 seats right off the bat,** he announced that he was also shooting for the highest success rate for this kind of Mastermind in the history of Internet marketing — **so every potential participant had to _apply_ for a position**.

In other words, when prospects visited the sales website, read the material, and clicked the "APPLY NOW" button, they found that this didn't mean that they could order. What they could do was fill out a fairly extensive application so that they would be considered for joining Alan's group. The application was his Take-Away #1. It set the prospects up for the fact that even though they might have $4,000, even though they might be willing and able to spend it to join Alan's Mastermind, they _still_ might not be accepted in the group, and so might not get all the benefits as a result. What's really cool is, the information he gathered about each applicant in **that application form allowed him to cherry-pick the best applicants — to actually stack the deck to increase his success rate.** But even with those he rejected, he got some useful, detailed information about what they wanted in the future, and what they were willing to spend to get it.

But he went one _more_ step further. He also recorded the entire six-month process that he went through with this Mastermind. Every weekly call, and every minute of the hands-on live workshop he held for the members, went into a course he's putting together. He recently test-marketed the course with a special pre-publication sale, and he used take-away marketing extensively for this sale.

First, he sent a series of five emails to his mailing lists. The emails, which went out over an entire month leading up to the sale date, first pointed people to the original sales website that his Mastermind prospects had read. **Only now, when they clicked "APPLY," all they got was, "Sorry, this Mastermind is closed."**

The greatest get-rich ideas come from a consistent state of activity. You'll never get them by sitting on your butt. They only come when you are moving forward. The best ideas come when you are buried deeply in a blur of many different activities, projects, and actions.

- Focus on serving your customers.

- Focus on the road ahead.

- Keep looking for winning combinations and concepts.

He stressed in the emails that you couldn't join because the Mastermind was already underway; enrollment was closed; you missed it. But, for a very limited time (one day, actually), you could order the entire recorded Mastermind, notebooks and course in advance. On that day, on the last day possible, he sent those people to a site where they could order it all.

This ended up being a great example of a successful failure. Alan set a goal that he didn't hit with that one-day sale: he wanted to make a million bucks. He didn't, but he still generated over $50,000 in sales *in one day* with this technique. Now, that's a good month by anyone's standards! The point is, despite not making the money he wanted off this offer, he did what he said he'd do, and pulled it after one day. He'll still be able to roll this course out later, but it'll cost a lot more, and everybody who came around the first time and didn't take advantage of that special offer will know that he meant what he said. That's classic take-away selling.

Take-away is, in general, scarcity marketing. Alan calls it "scarcity marketing with a knife," because it's really scarcity on steroids. **You offer something, make people want it, make then actually ready to order it, put it within their grasp — and then you yank it away.** Putting up a roadblock to their satisfaction only makes them want it all the more.

Here's another example. Recently Randy Charach, another savvy marketer with whom I work, was telling me a story of a client who had just bought one of his courses. The client had received the course three days earlier — and he was calling to complain that he hadn't made any money yet! Randy's employee put him on hold and said, "Boss, what do I do with someone like this?" And Randy told him: "Insist that we give him a refund. Tell him to send it back, and we'll refund him right away." No surprise there, because none of us wants to deal with an irrational client like that. Of course, as soon as was told that, the light bulb went on in the client's head, and it was impossible to convince this person to return the course. Immediately, the customer came to realize that he was being ridiculous, and all but begged Randy to let him keep it.

What Randy did is something that most business people are scared to death to do. We're trained that it's the worst kind of sin to give up money that could be and should be ours — but thinking like that can hurt you. In the business world, you have all kinds of competitors who are willing to do anything and everything to get business. I call them **business whores.** They carry their cell phones with them constantly; while they're in the bathroom, they're talking on the phone to their clients. They even give their clients their home phone numbers! They're too accessible, and you know what? **People tend to value what they have to work hard to get.** Sometimes, in order to make the real money, you've got to make people jump through some hoops.

First of all, you've got to qualify them, in order to make sure they're the right kind of person. You do things to get them to raise their hands, to show their interest by taking some action. **The bigger the action they have to take, the more they reveal how interested and serious they are; and the more you can take control over the entire selling process.** You get them to start chasing *you* instead of you chasing *them*. In Alan's case, he started getting all kinds of calls after he let those applications sit there for a few days. "Well, did I get accepted? Am I in yet? Man, I'm really sitting on pins and needles here." They were hoping Alan would accept their $4,000, and that made him appreciate them all the more. He treated them special from the beginning, and after he'd converted them from applicants to prospects to surefire customers, he kept treating them that way. **He wasn't treating them like every other client that comes in the door: he made them do things. He made them participate. He made them *interact*.**

In so doing, he also controlled the relationship. The process of qualifying them made them feel privileged to be a part of the group, and privileged to give Alan their money. At the same time, it created greater value in their minds, and took them to a higher level. I like the fact that when Alan's organization called to accept them into the Mastermind, they weren't calling to sell them anything; they were calling to give them the good news that they could write Alan a check for $4,000.

You see, **most people don't like to be "sold"; but often they really want to buy, especially if they feel there's a scarcity of what they're after.** With take-away selling, your goal is to let your customers feel like they made the buying decision themselves. It's really just psychological manipulation; or, to put it more bluntly, it's a kind of head game you play with the customer. You get inside their minds and take them step-by-step to the point where they're actually asking you to let them buy.

It has to be done correctly, of course. **In the hands of a beginner, the savvy consumer will see right through this tactic.** You have to mean it, too. If you tell your customers that you're not going to take everyone, or that the offer will go away if they don't act soon enough, that really does have to happen. In Alan's case, he followed through with his threat and didn't accept more than half the applicants. Of the 150 or 180 who applied, he only ended up taking 75 of them. Of course, when you do this, you have to tell your customers you've done it, because most won't know until you make it a part of your marketing message.

If you get a reputation for making it difficult to do business with you, all of a sudden the word gets out amongst the best prospects that there really must *be* something here! The building isn't just one of those movie props with 2 x 4s behind it; it's a genuine offer, genuinely limited. The word spreads. That kind of message — that kind of seriousness — just blows some people away, because they're used to hearing, "You must respond in ten days or the promotion is going to be over!" When they hear that, they just roll their eyes and say, "Bull! You're lying to me! That's not true!" and most of the time, they're right. **When you actually do things like this, you shock these people. Now you've gotten their attention, and they're sitting up and taking you seriously.**

You have to be a real hard-ass to perform take-away selling well. But a reputation for being hard to do business with — a reputation for meaning what you say, for being unwilling to prostitute yourself for a quick buck — can help you in this business. There's this guy most of us in the business know; I won't mention his name here, but he's famous for doing all kinds of Joint Venture deals. But he's also famous for suing people! He's sued enough people who were former Joint Venture partners that nobody would ever cross him — he's got a huge reputation for that. But everyone wants to do business with him, because first of all, he's got a huge customer base, and you can make a ton of money by partnering with him — as long as you don't get crosswise with him. **He demands respect.** From the very first moment you start seriously considering a Joint Venture with him, you're doing it on his terms, not yours. He's got your respect right from the start, because you know he's sued a dozen different past partners. I see that as a good analogy with take-away selling, because **what you're really doing is separating yourself from all your competitors by letting your best prospects know that you really are completely different than the rest.**

Sure, I'll Buy It... Tomorrow

Take-away selling is all about overcoming procrastination. Even if the product or service you're offering someone is exactly

---

True power is knowing your strengths and weaknesses.

- Don't lie to yourself about these two areas. Most people tend to overestimate their chances of success and underestimate their chances of failure. You must become stronger in the areas you are already strong — and delegate (not abdicate) your weakest areas.

what they need or want, they may not buy unless they're given a gentle, friendly ultimatum: "Hey, you can do this now or never. Buy now, or forever hold your peace."

Take-away selling, in the simplest terms, is a way to limit the supply of a product or service in order to increase its scarcity. It's a proven fact that scarcity sells, based on that age-old law of supply and demand: the less the supply, the greater the demand. People don't know how much they want something until it's about to be taken away from them. It's just human nature.

The great marketer Jim Rohn once said, "Without a sense of urgency, desire loses its value." Why? Because procrastination is the biggest killer of sales. This is particularly the case online, where the chances of a prospect staying on or returning to your website in today's click-happy world are minimal. **You really need to grab that person's attention and cut through those natural tendencies to procrastinate — to get them to take action now, right away. You do this by shaping your offer, not just your product and services, but your whole offer.** Many of its elements should be time-sensitive or quantity-bound, and you shouldn't hesitate to turn people away when the time's up or the quantity's exceeded. Of course, you have to provide a reasonably logical explanation to justify your qualification.

And you've got to follow through. That's critical.

But Take-Away Selling Won't Work for My Business... Will It?

If you take the attitude that take-away selling won't work for your kind of business, then you're sunk before you've even gotten started. The fact is, take-away selling can work for absolutely any business. Here's an extreme example: Randy Charach, who started out as a professional magician. That's right: hocus-pocus and abracadabra. He was very, very good at it, and he started it at a very early age; we're talking younger than ten years old here. At one point, when he was doing his magic shows as a youngster, he started getting double-booked. This happened by accident. Say, he'd have a booking for Saturday, March 5th at 2:00 p.m. for some kid's birthday party, then he'd get another call from someone who wanted him at the same time. All of a sudden, they weren't asking him how much he charged; instead they were saying things like, "Oh, gee... can we book you for next year, then? Because we can't change the time of our party."

So now Randy's getting booked up a year in advance, and he's thinking, "Well, maybe I should charge a little bit more," which was another form of take-away selling. Other people were charging $5, so he started charging $6. And then, when they started charging $10, he went to $25. And then they came up to $25, so he raised his own price to $50. Soon he was far more desirable, because now he was the most premium-priced magician out there. He continued performing right up until a few years ago; by then he was demanding a cool $10,000 per booking, and getting it. He's not doing it anymore because his marketing business is more interesting and more lucrative, and hey, he just doesn't feel like it. He has a family now that he doesn't want to leave to go off and do these shows.

Basically, Randy charged $6 for his first show, and it quickly went up from there when he realized that other guys were getting more. By then end of his magic career, he was a top non-celebrity performer; not a household name like David Copperfield or David Blaine, but well known within the corporate market in which he was performing. He was getting top dollar, where other people were charging $1,500 or $2,500. Did his clients get good value? Absolutely! His show was as good as, or better than, anybody else's. In fact, there were other people in that price range who weren't as good as Randy, so Randy's clients were definitely getting good value. They knew he'd show up, he'd do a great job, and that he was 100% consistent.

Now, I'm not suggesting that you should overcharge, but **by having this premium, it's clear that you're in demand. When your product or service is in demand, people want you more.** It comes back to my earlier example about Randy, when he first started to get rolling. When he wasn't available, price was no longer an issue — and all of a sudden he was booked a year in advance! That was something that Randy learned fairly quickly, and that's one of the reasons he was able to become a millionaire as a magician, and do over 5,000 shows during his twenty years as a professional entertainer. That's the essence of take-away selling.

About ten years ago, Randy spent a year as a business broker, just because he wanted to learn more about business in general. All the other business brokers he worked with were going out and begging for listings, and taking them on and paying for advertising themselves, and going after small businesses at the beginning. Well, Randy knew a little more about take-away selling than they did, so he started off with Direct-Marketing in the business magazines. This way he attracted people to *him*, rather than cold-calling them. He also didn't list any businesses under a million, which is really unusual. So is the fact that he charged a fee for advertising upfront, which none of the other agents did. He ended up being in great demand as a business broker, and turned out to be very successful — but he didn't really enjoy it, so he moved on to other things. Now he's become successful again as a marketer. The point here is that he was able to take the take-away selling principles he learned as a magician, apply them to vastly different fields, and *still* make a lot of money. If he can, then you can too. I firmly believe that.

Take-Away Options

There **are three basic specific types of take-aways you can use for your products and services, whatever they may be.** You can mix and match all three in various combinations, of course, but I'll go over each individually. Here they are:

- Limiting the time.
- Limiting the quantity.
- Limiting the offer.

The first option is *limiting the time*. That's done by adding a deadline to the offer; I talked about the value of deadlines in Chapter Four. You've also read a few real-life examples about how to apply time limits here in this chapter, too, so you can take the principals that Alan and Randy used and apply them to your own situation.

We've all seen the websites and ads that have date stamps on them, saying you're going to miss out if you don't ACT NOW. Then you go back the next day, or see the ad in the next issue, and it hasn't changed. It still says you've got to ACT NOW. Well, we've all fallen for that; it's an acceptable strategy, but **its value gets diluted if you overuse it.** The words "LIMITED OFFER" and those date stamps stop meaning anything if you don't mean it. What you really want to do is employ true time sensitivity, and stick to your guns.

Time sensitivity may simply be a result of the way you prefer to do business. Every marketer in the information business knows people who sell a limited quantity of their product, and then move on to the next product, because they don't want to do that product

Testimonials sell!

- What you say about yourself is not nearly as important as what others say about you.

- "Any fact is better established by two, or three good testimonies than by a thousand arguments." — *Emmons*

anymore. In their mind, they're moving at light-speed, and they've got all these other products they want to create and bring to the marketplace. Even though a product might still be selling, their emphasis — the time and effort that they put into it — is limited. Therefore, there's an urgency in marketing that particular product. Yes, they might have created the urgency; but it's there.

Next: *limiting the quantity.* You can limit the number of units available, assuming it's stock or inventory, or openings if it's a service offer. Again, consider Alan's Mastermind offer, and Randy's schedule as an entertainer. Here's another case, offered by my friend Mike Lamb. He limited the quantity of his product, his coaching services, the same way Randy did: by raising his rates. Last year, he started charging $2,500 for ten hours of his time. Before that, he was charging $95 an hour and was only doing it one hour at a time — and it was costing him a lot of time and effort. He was putting a lot of time into the marketing without a lot of great results, and he spent a limited amount of time with his clients, so they didn't see the kind of results that they would have if they'd spent a longer period of time together. So one day he decided that there are only so many hours in the day, and he only wanted to work with so many clients at a time. To really make this work, he had to raise his rates. That was it, and he let people know the specifics right up front. For the customers who really mattered, money was not an issue.

Later on, he raised his rates again: from $2,500 for ten hours to $5,000 for fifteen hours. He actually gets more people coming to him now, and he has to turn away business. He gets a better quality of client, too, because if somebody is willing to spend $5,000 up front, then he knows that they're serious enough to spend the time they need to with him, and do the assignments and all the other things he wants them to do.

The last — and arguably the most useful — way to create scarcity is by *limiting the offer*. You do this by limiting elements that are part of the offer, such as the guarantee, the bonuses, the premiums, or the price. I'm not suggesting you should offer a discount, but you can use something like an imminent price increase after a certain time, perhaps to cover the extra cost in dealing with more customers, or for something logical like the packaging. Maybe, since the product is bundled with other products or components, it won't be available after "X" number is sold. You can limit the extras, too, as in free support, free installation, or free shipping, and so on. I've noticed that Dell Computers is really good at this, offering limited-time extras like an extra two years of support, or free shipping, or discounted shipping. **There are so many different variables that you can play with in limiting the offer.**

Strategic Pricing

One of the things I want to drive home to you about take-away selling is something I mentioned earlier — because it's the key advantage to practicing this principle. That's the fact that **you can raise your prices, and *still* get a whole bunch of people who want your goods or services!** Remember my story about Randy Charach? He ended up charging $10,000 per show, and people were willing to pay that because he was so good at it. Similarly, Mike Lamb went from charging $95 per hour to $5,000 for fifteen hours for his coaching services, over the course of a couple of years. I can't think of a better advantage than being able to raise, and raise, and raise your prices, because that means more profitability in the end. It means **you can have fewer customers, so you can do a better job of taking good care of your best customers — and since birds of a feather flock together, that can help you attract more of the best types of customers.** You can charge more money, have more enjoyment, get rid of all those deadbeats I was alluding to earlier, the "price whores" who just want the lowest price, no matter the quality. You can clean out all that sludge, work with the best people, and charge premium prices.

Remember: one of the most important things about **take-away selling is that it's based on a proven economic principle of supply and demand.** I've got a story here that's probably going to make you a little mad, but there's no better example of supply and demand in action. My friend and colleague Chris Hollinger was recently speaking with a client who plays golf with a major oil company executive. Now, I think we can see the effects of supply and demand every time we go to the gas pumps nowadays. The conversation Chris' client relayed to him was this: the oil executive told him, "Over the last two years I've been instructed to close three of the refineries I oversee." The client was surprised. He said, "What? Why are you guys closing refineries? We have a shortage of refined gasoline here, and it's driving the price up!" And the executive said, "Exactly."

There might be thousands of reasons why the oil company would want to close those particular refineries, but if you think about supply and demand, I believe you'll see the real reason right away. Now, that seems sinister, and I don't want to be conspiratorial here — but if they dry up the supply, what happens to the price? It's supply and demand in action. We've all seen prices going up, and it's always blamed on various things — but all it comes down to is a lack of refined fuel.

Randy Charach tells me that when he was in the magic business, other magicians used to ask him all the time: "Should I raise my prices? I'm afraid to raise my prices because if I raise my prices, I might be out of work." His own experience was that **every time he raised his prices, people wanted him more.** But don't be too eager with this tactic: the thing to do is to gradually increase that price. Let everyone know, for example, that after 30 days, you're going to increase it a certain amount. Then in 30 more days you can always say, "I've got to raise my price again. But before I do, you'd better get in now — because on this date, it goes up again. I've got to do it." And do so.

I know of one marketer who raises his price with every offer he sends out the door. He once had an eBook for sale, and it started out at something like a dollar — but then it went up a dollar every sale. All it took was a nice, automated script on his website, and the 500th guy who bought the book was paying $500 for the same book that the guy who acted first got for a dollar. Not a bad deal, eh? There comes a point where you have to level it off, of course, but it was a way to sell a whole bunch of his eBooks right away. You can get some testimonials, it's fun, it's interesting, and it's just plain good marketing.

I think this indicates that **raising your prices on a regular basis can be very effective in not only gaining you more money, but also in drawing in better qualified prospects.** Now, there's a limit to this. You need to make sure that in your heart, you have a genuine feeling that you're worth it: that you're offering great value with what you're presenting. Because ultimately, if you just raise your prices over and over, and you don't feel like you're offering good value, it'll come back to haunt you. If you don't have the goods, that's a great recipe for putting yourself out of business very quickly. You always have to have the goods, and you have to be able to deliver and over-deliver the value, no matter what. Frankly, I think a lot of goods and products and services are undervalued out there, so it's not hard to raise the bar.

Here's an example of how to do that. **One of the best ways I know of to increase the value of what you're offering is to make yourself a celebrity in your marketplace.** Celebrities — at least

In lead generation, the more you tell — the less you sell!

- Just give them enough information to get them interested and excited! Make them an irresistible promise and get them to send for more information.

the most famous ones — represent what take-away selling is all about, because there's such a tremendous demand for them. These people can't even go to the bathroom without being followed by reporters and people wanting their autograph. They sometimes need a tremendous herd of bodyguards and entourage to go before them, just so they can live something approximating a normal life.

You can become a celebrity in your marketplace. Some businesses lend themselves more to this than others, but **there are definite things you can do to break out of whatever crowd in which you find yourself** — whether it's having your own local radio show, or a local-access TV program, or doing seminars or workshops, or writing books, or creating information products. There's something that you *can* do to rise above everyone else and make yourself an expert in your marketplace, where people just naturally see you as somebody who really knows their stuff. And then, all of a sudden, everybody just goes crazy over you! You position yourself in a way that your competitors don't even think they *can* position themselves. By positioning yourself in that way, you're offering yourself so that your clients automatically believe that there's far more value there than they can ever afford. It does more for your credibility than you can imagine. It also gives you a tremendous power, in the sense that **it suddenly makes clients start** coming to you, rather than you having to go out and constantly attract them.

Marketing as Sexuality

There's an old marketing joke that goes like this: "What's the difference between a $25 street prostitute and a $1,000-an-hour call girl?" The answer? Marketing. That may seem crude, but in reality, it's the only difference. They're selling (ahem) the same product, but they do different things. You're never going to see a $1000 call girl out on the street trying to flag down traffic, like a street prostitute would. Same product, different presentation.

The same thing is true in business. We're all trying to find ways to differentiate ourselves from our competitors, but **sometimes there's really not a lot you can do.** That's why you have to be a smart marketer and do things to make yourself an expert in your marketplace, to gain celebrity status, and to do things like limiting the supply of the product — or at least to limit the *perception* of supply — and to **increase the demand by being as different as you can from everybody else who does this.**

I think take-away selling lends itself more to sexual metaphors than most marketing principals, because, again, it's all about supply and demand. I did a program years ago on Internet dating. It was called "The Secret of Internet Dating." We produced something like six audio cassette tapes, and we brought in experts to reveal the secrets. There was one principle that's written in stone when it comes to online dating, and it also applies to business. And that is: Never, never, *never* answer another person's ad. Never be the guy who goes out and answers all the girls' ads on the Internet, or a girl who answers all the guys' ads. You run your own ads, and you let the lonely-hearts come to you, because **there's a difference in the whole relationship when it's them chasing you.**

Something changes when the prospects feel they're coming to you, rather than having you seek them out. That's part of the perception you're trying to get with take-away selling. You see, it's the old strategy of "playing hard to get." That's why it's so natural and easy to fall into this. Just remember that old rule of playing hard to get — the way every girl was raised by their Mom, where they were taught that you don't go after the guy. You play hard to get. You bat your eyes, and then you disappear into the crowd. You don't give them your phone number; you make them beg for it!

That's another reason that marketing-as-sexuality is such a natural analogy for take-away selling. It fits so well. In marketing you do the same thing as when you're playing the field, and you do it **by the way you build your persona.** That's the whole idea of **making yourself less available, making yourself more scarce.** You can do it with each of your product offerings: limiting the quantity, limiting the time frame, limiting the pricing. Combine those, and you've got a power-punch that just won't fail.

The Guru Principle; or Nothing Succeeds Like Success

If you don't like the idea of marketing as sexuality, think of it as being like the guru at the top of the mountain. One way or the other, you'll do best when you make your prospects chase you. There's no question that you can dominate your market, have a competitive edge, and have an unfair advantage over all your competition if you understand how to properly execute take-away selling. But to do that, you've got to understand the principle that **no one goes to the bottom of the mountain looking for the guru;** they want to find the guy who's sitting on top of the mountain, the guy who's successful, who's making money, who's doing something with his life.

Keep that in mind. Psychologists have proven, over the years, that **people often want what they can't have.** Using take-away selling in offers makes people want to get that service or own that product even more. It creates a sense of urgency. You've got to understand people: how they think, how they reason, how they *feel*. If you do that effectively, you'll be able to use take-away selling to produce bigger profits and more sales.

As I noted in the previous section, take-away selling helps eliminate problems and increase profits. It gives you, as a business owner, a proven and profitable way to a) get rid of your problem customers, b) leverage off those customers who are bringing you the most profits. One way to do both is simply to contact your customers using Direct-Mail, email, or even the telephone. Tell them, "Hey, thanks. I appreciate your business, but here's a situation that's developed. In the last few weeks we've found the demand for this product has increased so dramatically that we're going to have to cut back on supplying it, except to a very select group of our customers." **If you do that, you'll create a sense of urgency, a demand for the product that might not have existed originally. Now, understand that when you do that, you're really benefiting your client, as well as yourself, because the value of what you sell only increases more and more when your clients think they can't get it easily. It's all about accessibility.**

It's just like the guru on the top of the mountain: everybody wants access to him. People want access to you and your product, if they feel it's being withheld from them. This gets people to take action immediately. The thing we all hate as marketers are those folks who, when they're reading our sales copy, are saying, "Well, let me think about this." Take-away selling gets them to stop thinking about it and do something. In their own minds, they've raised the demand for your product, just because you've told them the supply is limited. Why is it limited? Because it's selling like hotcakes! You're a hit, and people want to do business with successful businesses. They want the guru at the top of the mountain. **If you seem like you're desperate for business, or desperate to make that sale, then you probably *won't* make the sale** — because your prospects will think, "Well, maybe nobody really likes this guy, or he doesn't have a product that's really worth owning."

If you're not quite there yet, then you just have to **"fake it til you make it."** Believe it or not, you can buy tapes that make it sound like you're in the middle of a busy office. If you're a solo operator working at home, you can play the tape in the background when you're on the phone with someone, and it's got all kinds of office noises in the background, with people slamming file cabinets and all that sort of thing. It makes you sound like you're part of some busy organization, instead of at home in your underwear. You see, it's not that different from the salesman who dons a new, really fine designer suit and hops in his nice new Lincoln to go close sales — even if it's the first sales call he's made at his new job, and he's flat broke. You don't want to look flat broke, because success breeds success. That's the one thing to remember. People equate you being at the top of the mountain, or you being a success, with your accessibility.

Limited accessibility indicates a scarcity of time. If that scarcity is there — if they've increased the demand for that product, at least in their own mind — then they want to do business with you. When you take away the accessibility to that product, they'll find a hundred different reasons why they've simply got to have it. Limiting an offer creates urgency because it creates scarcity in your prospect's mind.

My colleague Michael Penland has a tale about what he calls "another lifetime"

— back when he was selling franchises for a travel company in New York. One of the things they did was have people fill out an application prior to an interview, to see if they qualified to own that franchise. There were 32 questions on the application, but the most important one was Question 15: "Do you have the money to invest?" As far as Michael and the people selling the franchises were concerned, that's really what qualified them; but in the prospect's own mind, there were 32 points on which they had to qualify, so the questionnaire created a sense of scarcity, and it created a sense of an elite group of individuals who could possess this franchise.

You've got to make the customer want you. You've got to make them become afraid that they're going to lose out on something. You've got to create that sense of urgency, because urgency helps people to buy *now*. **Customers respect you more, you have more value in their own eyes, and you provide more value to them. They feel privileged, and that allows them to buy.** It gives them a good feeling, and it keeps you and your product at the top of the mountain — because remember, with take-away selling nobody's going to the bottom of the mountain looking for gurus down there. They all want what's on top of the mountain. They want to buy from successful people, and successful people are often short on the product or service they're offering simply because they're so good at selling it, and it's so useful to those who receive it. So make that product non-accessible unless they qualify. Get them to jump through the hoops, and take-away selling will work for your business well.

A Sense of Belonging

Looking for a new way to connect with your customers? Try sharing some of your success with them. It's easy, because we all want to feel special. These days, a lot of marketers don't call their customers *customers*. Some call them *clients*, but the smart ones call them *members,* and **they create membership-type opportunities within their company. Then they have a way of**

identifying each level. For instance, a lot of marketers now have Silver, Gold, and Platinum levels among their memberships. Some marketers find even more ways to break it out: so you'll have Silver-plus, Gold-plus, Platinum-plus. Each level costs the member more money, but it also represents more value: there are very specific kinds of products, services and benefits that are attached to each level.

With each level the purpose is to turn all your Silvers into Golds, to turn all of your Golds into Platinums; and marketers who use these schemes do things to increase the scarcity of what they're offering, particularly at the highest levels of their membership. The very topmost slots may be limited to only 18 or 19 members — and that's it. **So what happens is, you get a waiting list of people who are ready to fill one of those 18 or 19 slots, just as soon as one becomes available.** The price points for those slots are right there in the sales material, so they know how much you're charging. It's no secret, no surprise. You may have thousands of members down at the lowest level, and they know all about the structure that moves them on up the ladder. Scarcity is up at the top, in terms of limited quantity and increased price, so you're helping to educate them. If you do it right, some of the customers just can't wait to get to that next level, so they keep moving right up the ladder. This brings to mind a quote I once heard: **"A satisfied customer is apathetic. But a loyal customer — one that you've really developed a relationship with — is your advocate."** If this member has a connection with you and your product or your service, they're willing to go that extra mile and become a Platinum or Platinum-plus member.

Membership has its privileges; that's been the slogan for American Express for years. Your customers want to feel special; they want to belong to a special community, and they all want something that no one else has, or at least something that most people don't have. Our ability to manipulate this desire to belong cuts at the heart of take-away selling. It really pokes into their psyche, if you will, and pulls out that behavior that you want them

FREE GIFT! Go to www.RuthlessMarketing.com/freegift

to exhibit, at a time when you want them to be part of what you're doing.

Making Your Offer Very, Very Clear

You've probably gotten the point, by now, that when you're the guru on the mountaintop, you can set your prices higher. But you have to be very clear, from the outset, that you're doing this. I know a guy in Las Vegas who sells $10,000 biz-ops; he's very famous within our industry. I got a chance to spend some good, quality time with him a few years ago in Jacksonville, and I learned that his whole marketing strategy was very simple. He was using lead-generation TV commercials that got people to call a toll-free number that gave them a recorded message. Three times within that recorded message — three different times — he told the caller that this was a $10,000 investment. Does this sound familiar? Back in Chapter 4, I told you that when you're writing sales copy, you should always mention your offer several times within the text. That's exactly what this guy was doing with his sales pitch. By the time the listener left their name and address so they could get more information, they already knew that he was going to hit them up for ten grand.

I think that's so smart! **It's a form of take-away selling, because it's a form of qualification. That's what we're really talking about here: ways to separate out the best prospects from the worst, and then making the best prospects come to you rather than you chasing them.** You do this by limiting the supply and increasing the demand. Making it clear that you're charging a lot for the privilege is one way to do that, and it's an up-front way of doing it. You're getting rid of the cheapskates, the complainers, and the people who can't afford what you're offering from the very beginning — and there go most of your future problems. Doing business this way becomes an excellent time-management tool, because **it weeds out the undesirable and the disinterested, so you're not spending any time marketing to the people who aren't serious.**

Keep your cash flow flowing!

- Keep your money in motion! Always moving! Always flowing back into the plans, systems, marketing, and promotions that sell the largest number of products/services to the largest number of people — for the largest profit!

When you make your price very clear for the outset, and people raise their hands anyway, what they're really saying is, "Sure, I've got ten grand to spend." You can use that against them later, in the closing process. You could go to a prospect and say, "Look now, you came to me. I didn't come to you. We told you very clearly that if you didn't have ten grand to invest, then you shouldn't waste our time or yours." At that point they'll either go away, or write you a check.

Fire Those Suckers!

Take-away selling helps you add a little sanity to the often maddening marketing world. You can't be all things to all people, and the concept of supply and demand is absolutely key. Your time is what's mostly in demand, and it's incredibly valuable when it starts getting split between everything that you have going on with customers, with your business, with your family and friends, and everything else. As I've already mentioned several times, while take-away selling is a great way to help you build urgency for your goods and services, it's also ideal for helping you rid yourself of your problem customers. It's a sad fact that not all of your customers add value to your company, and in this section, I'll go into more detail on how you can fire those suckers.

Take-away selling demands respect. It also allows for increased margins. **With**

more money coming in, you're essentially doing less work, so you're able to focus more productively on building a relationship with those customers who bring you the most money. That means you can fire the worst of your customers, the ones who generate most of your problems. Now, how to you do this? Among other things, you can do it simply by telling them you're going to have to raise prices; or you simply don't offer them the incentives you'd offer someone you want to keep. Most of them will take care of themselves by walking away. Will they be disgusted by what you've done? Probably, but what do you care? **Think about all the money you'll save, not having to deal with that worst segment of your customers.** Meanwhile, your current clients feel privileged. They feel good about being your customer, and feel you're bringing them a great deal of value.

As I've said before, **a lot of business owners are customer whores; they'll go out there and do anything to get customers.** We've all done it, because we want to build our businesses. But this absolutely kills you when you're dealing with a value-draining customer. At some point you realize, "My God! This customer is draining me — not just financially, but mentally and emotionally — just from trying to keep them happy!" Sometimes they're not worth it, so the cost of serving them is too high. By using take-away selling, you automatically eliminate those people.

Rotten to the Core

One of the best ways I know of to handle customers is by being rotten. I'm not talking about pelting them with old tomatoes or cussing at them: by *rotten*, I really mean ROTten, with a capital "R", a capital "O", and a capital "T." That's Relationship Over Transaction. I want to have a relationship that I control with every one of my customers, one in which I'm continually evaluating them. An easy way to do this is by using surveys so your customers can let you know exactly what they're thinking. That way, you can give your customers what they want, when they want it, at exactly the right time that they want it. Most businesses want to be able to do that. But you can also use these surveys to identify your demon customers — those customers who just gobble up too much of your time, your emotional energy, and your money. You want to get rid of them, and you can do that by developing those relationships and having the mechanisms in place whereby you can grab that the information you need at a moment's notice.

It's not simply technology, though that's part of it; you also have to know how to measure the right things. Look at the information you've gained from your customers; determine which are your best and which are your worst, then go through the process of getting rid of your lowest 20%. If you're ROTten to your customers, then you'll be able to do that. The process that helps you to do that is take-away selling.

Once again, this boils down to time management, and it's simply a by-product that you get with the best take-away selling. **Who do you want to spend your time with: some guy who's spending a few dollars and whining about it, or someone who's spending thousands of dollars with you?** The latter's a better investment, time-wise, and I think that's pretty obvious to anyone. If you have to, put some extra steps in a potential prospect's way to see if they're worth spending time on. Tell them, "Look, you don't qualify unless you do this, this, and this." Once they perform those steps, you can happily take their money. It was a good management of your time, and actually elevated the value, in their mind, of what you had to offer. **If they're not willing to take those steps, fine: they'll go away, and it'll be obvious they weren't worth wasting your time on.** Pretty soon there'll be another person with whom you can try again.

It's important, too, to point out that you don't have to wait until you're booked up to use this technique to your advantage. You don't even have to lie about the numbers. You can simply say, "My time is valuable. So is yours. I want to make absolutely certain we're a good match. Therefore, you must first do this, then do this and this." Act busy, and you'll *be* busy. **Remember the guru on** the mountain? If people think you're really successful, and your time is limited, then they'll want you more — and those who would waste your time will generally just melt away.

Setting the Limits

Everyone should fire customers when they can, if for no other reason than it'll make you feel better, more in control of your business. This is especially important for those of us who have service attitudes. Our hearts are in the right place; we want so much to give, give, and give some more, because giving and receiving are opposite sides of the same coin. We all want to serve customers, and we want to help people. But take-away selling is just like a woman who says: "Look, I'll be with you for the rest of my life and I'll be supportive of you and I'll love you... but if you ever screw around on me or hit me, I'm going to leave you so fast you're not going to know what hit *you*." She sets a precedent, and you need to do that with your customers. In doing so, **you train people on how you want them to treat you.**

Right away, you let your best customers know that you're not going to be abused. Only do this with the best customers; forget the rest of them. Take it to the point of even firing some of them, if you have to — but then be sure to let the rest of your customers know that you've done it. You should *never* do anything like this unless you make it a part of your marketing, so that all customers know the story. Do it, and you command respect. People know they can't push you around; they become more respectful of your time and end up treating you better, and the business becomes more enjoyable.

Your customers have to understand that, and you have to make that attitude clear. Tell them, **"You've got to qualify to do business with me.** It's not just something you can walk in here and do. There are certain criteria, a certain standard, that I'm looking for in a client." It's important to stress, too, that this can work for anybody; I know I'm mostly using examples Direct-Marketing, but the truth is that take-away selling works in all businesses. Sometimes, exclusivity is nine-tenths of it making a business work; it works for shoe stores, and it works for boutiques (by the way, guys, a boutique is a dress shop that made itself more exclusive and harder to reach — and therefore more expensive).

Rewire Your Thinking

The hardest thing to get over (and you *must* get over this) is to stop thinking the way *you* think about the price of things. This can hamper you severely, just because you're thinking: "Well, I wouldn't pay that much for this! I know how much it cost me." But as I pointed out in Chapter One, being the cheapest is *not* the best way to make the most money. I started out in business by being a cheap date. The only thing I had going for me was my low prices, and that's what I made my USP. But since then, I've found out something very, very important: **the best prospects don't want cheap stuff. What they really want is the best stuff for the lowest price.** They want value: as much as they can get for the best price. They want expensive stuff for good prices more than they want cheap stuff. Let's say they're after a nice air purifier. There are some models that can be had for $100 or less, but they're not the best there is; and maybe quality and value are what the customer's really looking for, rather than economy. Money may not be an option. A lot of people equate most expensive with best; sometimes it's true, sometimes it's not. In any case, they may not want to take a chance on their health and the health of their employees, if what they're after is clean air — so it's better to try to sell them the $1000 air purifier first.

What the heck do you want with the customer who only wants the cheapest price, anyway? Those are the best customers in the world to pass on to your competitors! One of the coolest ways of firing your problem customers is to whip out your Rolodex and give them some other numbers to call — preferably those of your competitors! But here's an important caveat: you have to realize that new prospects aren't always looking for the cheapest price, even if that's what they ask about first. Sometimes they don't know what other questions to ask, so don't get defensive right away and give them to your competitors. You want to use scarcity, but you don't want to scare them. Do this in a tactful way; you still want to be compassionate and kind and fair with all your customers.

That said, the best customers are the ones who, when they want something, are willing to pay top dollar for it. Those are the members of your customer base you really want to cultivate. **You need to decide right away what quality of customer you want.** If you're going to be somebody who wants to do massive volume and sell cheap, I don't think you need to be reading this book — though hopefully, I've already changed your mind on that.

Run Away!

Here's an example of the kind of customer from whom you want to run away — though in the end, he was practically begging for what was being offered. Randy Charach tells a story about a client who bought one of his products with resell rights, for a price tag of about $3,000. Not long after that, the client sent Randy this huge five-page fax that Randy describes as "passive-aggressive and kind of nuts." Right then and there, Randy decided he didn't want to have to deal with this guy as a customer, so he just told one of his employees, "Go ahead and refund him and send him a fax." Now, the client wasn't complaining or asking for a refund; he was just weird, or at least that's how Randy perceived him. Of course, the client very quickly sent back another fax, basically saying, "No, I don't want a refund. Please."

That's take-away selling for you. **Randy simply didn't want him as a client, and he could afford to say no. That's quite liberating!** It gets into that time management idea I've already brought up: Randy perceived that his customer was going to eat up much more of his time than was warranted, even at the price point they were paying. He wasn't going to be a customer who played nice — so Randy didn't. He took the initiative and got rid of him. It's even smart to get rid of people like this as you're building your business. You have to ask yourself, "Am I better off spending additional hours dealing with this customer, or building my business?" Isn't it worth giving back the $3,000 so that you can go about finding more customers that fit into that profitable 20%?

I'm not suggesting that you should necessarily get rid of your clients if they become needy. It all depends on where they're coming from; do they seem like logical, sound people you can truly help, or are they just plain wacko? If they are, get rid of them; you don't even have to be rude about it. You can be nice as pie and still be firm, like Randy was. Or even better, combine firing your customer with being ruthless with your competitors. At M.O.R.E., Inc. we do that all the time! We put our worst customers on a list, and we seed our list as we put it out on the market for other companies, who use it as part of their new customer acquisition programs. They always get our worst customers — but hey, that's one of the reasons why I call it ruthless marketing!

But honestly, this isn't necessarily as mean as it sounds, either for the customer or for your competitor. It may simply be that **the customer was a bad fit for you, so you're doing them a favor by handing them off to someone else.** Suppose, if you're performing a service such as coaching, that your client is at a self-imposed roadblock — a boundary they just won't cross over. Instead of spending your time and their money beating them up, trying to get them to move to the next phase when they're not ready, just give up. They may be ready down the road, but at this point, you've done all you can for them. You have to politely say, "This is where we have to end this relationship," and hope the relationship ends on a positive note.

Avoid Power Plays

Here's a theory for you to consider when it comes to your worst customers. I honestly believe that in most cases, their complaining, their nastiness, their five-page faxes — **it's all about power. These people want to dominate you; they don't want an equal partnership, where you both profit.** I realize that there are exceptions to this, but when you're in a relationship with somebody you really care about, someone you've got a bond with, you don't treat them like dirt all the time. Some of these customers are treating us badly, and it's up to us to make sure that doesn't happen — and to then send that signal very strongly by sending the message out to the rest of your customers.

Take-Away Selling in a Nutshell

I could probably write an entire book about take-away selling alone, but I think this chapter covers the basics very well. I realize that some of what I've outlined here is subjective, and that I've used lots of metaphors in trying to explain it. Some people may find the whole concept of take-away selling to be distasteful — but it's one of the most effective tools in the marketer's toolbox. **Yes, I'll admit that it's somewhat manipulative; but before you let that put you off, remember that *all* selling is somewhat manipulative. Don't think about it in a bad way. The advantages are these: you can charge higher prices, work with fewer customers, deliver higher-quality products and services, and have a lot fewer headaches and a lot more time to do the things you love.** With all of those as the advantages, it's worth

The purpose of a business is to find and keep customers.

- You must do all kinds of things to get them to come and keep coming to you, instead of your competitors.

- What is your competitive advantage?

thinking deeply about how and where you can use the principles of take-away selling in your business. I encourage you to read this chapter several times, take notes, and then ask yourself the tough question: "How can I start using this powerful marketing principle to dominate my competition and gain an unfair advantage in the marketplace?"

SECRET SIX:

Lead Generation

In this chapter, I'm going to focus on the power of lead generation. This is an important subject about which most businesspeople just don't spend enough time thinking and strategizing. For that reason, they're constantly attracting the wrong customers — if they attract any customers at all. My purpose with this chapter is to share some of the great secrets of lead generation, so be sure to keep an open mind and read it very closely. I'm going to cover a lot of small details that you've probably never thought of before.

A Brief Explanation of Lead Generation

Ask a dozen marketers what lead generation is, and you'll get a dozen different (but related) answers. In this chapter, I'm going to offer you several different perspectives on the subject. One thing that they all share, however, is the conviction that lead generation is absolutely the lifeblood of any business.

No matter how you handle lead generation, you have to start with a list of prospects. You have to have customers coming in the door, or at least prospects you can convince to *become* your customers, even if you're already making money hand over fist. That's because you'll always suffer some attrition. **I don't care how well you treat your customers or what kind of offers you make to them, you'll see the numbers dwindle eventually. They lose interest; they change their allegiance to another company; they get divorced; they move away; they may even die.** With attrition, you can start out with a huge list and, if you do nothing, eventually end up with few, if any, prospects for your offers.

That's why lead generation is the lifeblood of a business. It keeps new prospects coming in the door, raising their hands, saying, "We're interested, and we may want to buy what you have, and we may become your customers." **That's all you're looking for: people who'll raise their hands and show their sincere interest in what you've got to offer,** whether it's used books or a new way to win at blackjack. With no leads, there's no business, so you need to find people interested in what you have. Lead generation — the process of locating, targeting, seducing, and then nurturing that prospect until they hunger for your product or your service — is how you do that.

Of course, **customer retention (reselling to the same customers over and over again) is vitally important to the success of any business. But it simply won't happen unless you bring in a lot of leads and turn them into customers.** So good marketers use free offers and low price offers to get people in the door, and then do everything possible to keep them as customers. I've mentioned before how vital it is to develop relationships with your customers. Well, lead generation is the very first step in creating a relationship with a potential customer.

One last point before I get into the meat of the chapter. Too often, businesspeople tell themselves, "My product is for everybody." My friend Kris Solie-Johnson, President of the American Institute of Small Business, calls that the "kiss of death" — because it means the people running those businesses don't understand lead generation. They don't know how to focus in on the people who are going to be worth their time and money to go after. **They have no idea who their prime targets are, the people they need to hit in a lead generation campaign in order to make their business as profitable as possible in the long term.** With this chapter, I'm hoping to change that for you.

The World Wide Web as a Lead Generator

My pal Alan Bechtold pioneered the use of the World Wide Web for lead generation, and he's been doing it for more than 21 years now. That's longer than most people have even been aware of the existence of the Internet — in fact, he's been active online since the Web was mostly just a bunch of bulletin board services linked by shamefully slow phone modems. He loves the Web as a lead generation tool, and there's a reason you should too. You see, **lead generation on the Web is fast and cheap; in fact, there are many ways to do it absolutely free of charge.** I can't think of any better way for any small business — local, regional, or worldwide — to find the right leads, with the least amount of risk, than by using the Web.

Alan's favorite way to build a list of leads for any business is easy, and it's basically free of charge. First, **start an online newsletter.** This isn't as difficult as it sounds; it can be as simple as a few paragraphs a week, telling people what you've learned. If you can write a letter to a friend or a family member, you can write a newsletter to your customers. In fact, it's best if what you write does sound like it was written to a friend or family member; after all, you want your leads to become your friends, and open their wallets. What you want to do is put up a simple Web page, which you can have any web designer do dirt-cheap. If you've got any skills with HTML or one of the web-page creation programs like FrontPage or Dreamweaver, you can do it yourself for $5.95 a month; all you have to do is use a search engine to find a low-cost web service. Some of these services offer website-building tools right online, tools that are so easy that they tell you exactly where to cut, paste, and point to create your own sites.

What you want this simple web page to do is tell people why they would want your newsletter, and what they'll get by subscribing. Here's where you get a little bit ruthless with your technique. Explain that the newsletter is $29.95 per year — or $79.95 per year, on sale for $29.95. And they can pay that, if they like. Give them a place online to fill out an order form and give you their email address, and a way to pay you $29.95 a year, and they'll receive every weekly issue. Or, for a very limited time, they can enter their full name, their email address, and mailing address, or answer a brief survey — and hey, they can receive your newsletter free of charge. Obviously, what you're doing here is capturing their personal information for your house list. What you shouldn't do is ask right away for their phone number. That seems to be a real response killer on the Web, at least until people get to know who you are and what they can expect from you.

But the act of having them take the time to fill out a form with a name, address, phone number, and email address is about the same as the old two-step approach to any Direct-Mail lead generation system — like asking for five or ten dollars for a free Special Report. You're asking people to stop, as they hop around on the Web, and fill out a form. If they go to that much trouble, they're targeted: they're interested in what you have to offer, and they're well worth your time.

Then you want to go to your favorite search engine and type in "ezine directory" or "e-zine directory." Try it both ways, and you'll find hundreds and hundreds of them. You can list your newsletter, now that you have one, for free on all of them. List them there, and you'll start seeing people come in. It'll be a trickle at first, and then they'll pick up. **Offer free subscriptions to other marketers who have lists of prospective clients you would like to use to attract to your business; they can add your newsletter to their list of bonuses with**

other products and services they offer. This will allow you to effectively tap into other marketers' lists.

The same thing can be done with a free eBook or a free report. But here, you have an added advantage because it's free information either way; people love free information. Here, you create a simple Web page selling people on downloading and reading your book or report. Do it the same way as I suggested for a newsletter. Charge, say, $14.95 or $24.95 for your book or report. Or, in return for their mailing address and full name and email address, give it to them for free. Either way, never allow that book to be downloaded directly from the site. Always send it to their email address. That way, you're going to at least get their email address so you can reach them again. Or you can offer your item free, as a bonus to other marketers. List them in eBook directories on the Web. There are those, too, by the hundreds. Advertise it with free classifieds. **This way, you *will* build a list of qualified, targeted leads that just keeps growing and growing and growing... even while you sleep.**

With your newsletter — and especially with your book — you've got the perfect landing page going, and you can feed it with pay-per-click (PPC) advertising. That's the hottest proven way to pay for leads on the Web, for very reasonable rates. With Google or MSN or Yahoo PPC advertising, you can pay as much or as little as you want for each person visiting your site, depending on the keywords you choose. Those are the words people type into the search engines, looking for what you have to offer. The cost depends on which of those keywords you select, and how much you're willing to bid for each person who sees your ad and clicks to visit your site. You only pay when someone clicks, so it's a great deal; and I've got to tell you, free information is what most people are searching for on the Web today. Even better, you can start getting responses to PPC ads in minutes!

You can also set a daily limit on how much you want to spend each day, so that you can ease your way into this process, and test it to your satisfaction. You can set up two or three different campaigns, using the same keywords, and then change the ad that displays to get people to click, or drive people to a slightly different website where they click. **This allows you to test market your lead generation campaigns in days instead of the weeks and months Direct-Mail and print ads require.** Test it. Tweak it. You can find yourself getting tons of qualified, targeted leads signing up for your newsletter or downloading your book or report in just a few days, at a cost of as little as a nickel or a dime per lead.

Brick-and-Mortar Options

Don't fool yourself into thinking that online marketing, especially PPC ads, won't work for you just because you have a brick-and-mortar business. Even if you're just looking for customers within a ten- or twenty-mile radius of your shop, it's an excellent way to drive business to your store. As far as PPC goes, Google offers a special option at the moment, one I'm sure that the other major search engines will soon mimic. You can literally say, "OK, I only want to pay for people who click within X miles of this zip code." That way, you can narrow it down so that you ONLY get leads from your area. It's still a powerful marketing method, even when limited to the local region.

If you've got an offer of a newsletter or book that people can download on the Web, start out by adding that Internet address to all the traditional advertising you do for your business — the Yellow Pages, the newspaper, your business cards. You can drop cards in every sack that goes out the door that say, "Hey, go to this website. Sign up for my free newsletter!" Now you can reach those customers, so they'll hear about new specials, new sales you've got, or new stock that just came in.

Even a small, local business can use an online newsletter. In some cases, depending on the customer profile, you might even want to pay for an ink newsletter, as well as an online one. If you have a bookstore or a music store, you can review books and music for people; people are interested in this. You can have a kitchen products store, and hand out recipes, as well as information about the new kitchen products you're selling. If you're a financial planner or an insurance provider, you can keep folks up-to-date on financial news that they're interested in and, of course, tell them more about your products. **No matter what type of brick-and-mortar business you have, there's a way to use a newsletter to capture more customers.**

Let's say you're a regular guy or gal who owns a carpet cleaning business, like I used to. You can still benefit greatly from the Internet. All you need to do is ask everybody you come in contact with for their email address. It could be as simple as saying, when they phone in to order carpet cleaning, "We'd like to add you to our special announcement list. We have different specials on carpet cleaning we can offer you when we get your email address." You can also do this when you arrive to clean their carpet. Once you have enough email addresses, you start a regular eZine newsletter that offers them different things. If you keep track of the date they subscribe, and you know how often people generally want their carpets cleaned, then you can set up an auto-responder to automatically send them that newsletter at pre-determined intervals so you can catch their interest at exactly the right time. **An auto-responder is simply an online mechanism that lets you preload messages in text and/or HTML, so you can send them out at specific times.** I suggest using text. HTML looks pretty and all, but with some people it just messes up their computer. Another reason to use text is that it gets through the "spam" filters a lot better than HTML.

So if you're a carpet cleaner, send them a simple text message with some tips for keeping their carpets clean on Day 90, if that's about the time when you figure they're going to want their carpets cleaned. All it has to say is something like this: "It's been three months since you last had your carpets cleaned, and we'd like to offer you a special. We'll clean your carpets again within the next ten days if you respond to this offer, and we'll give you a 20% discount or do an extra room for free." That's how can utilize the Internet in your local area through a simple email auto-responder. You can find a good auto-responder at http://www.mybizkit.com. It's very inexpensive; just for auto-responders, I think it's around $20 or so a month, for unlimited messages and unlimited auto-responders both.

I would add, too, that many towns around the country are struggling to keep their downtown areas alive. With the Internet, in combination with delivery systems like FedEx and UPS, downtown businesses can advertise globally and help keep their businesses alive that way. If they can expand their businesses using the Internet, they don't have to rely on their immediate location to make some bigger dollars. Bill Gates once said, "If you're not on the Internet, you're not in business." Similarly, Dennis Waitley, the motivational speaker says, "If you're not online you're going to be in the bread line." That doesn't just apply to the biggest businesses — it's as valid for Mom-and-Pop shops, too. In fact, I think this principle particularly holds true for small, local businesses. They have to compete with all these global businesses trying to sell their customers products that obviously take money out of their hands and out of the local marketplace. **I think that** *anybody* **who's in business — whether they're online or brick-and-mortar —** *has* **to use the Internet with a** local flavor and a local appeal to continue to build their share of the marketplace and fight off the competitors. More and more people are viewing businesses that way. In fact, about 80% of business buyers are now researching the Internet before making their buying decisions. You really need that online presence to credentialize yourself and add credibility to their business.

Establishing Your Credibility

Personally, I like the idea of giving away something of value — particularly information — to establish your credibility, and to prove that you're the person who has the information for which your prospects are looking. The newsletter or free book is a great tool to locate the most intelligent prospects. There are all kinds of free deals you can use to try to lure people in. But a word of caution here: **you need to be very careful about the type of lure you use in your lead generation campaign, because if you use the wrong one — well, you can get a whole lot of people to raise their hands, but the only reason they're raising their hands is because they want the free calculator or whatever it is that you're offering.** If you give away the wrong gift you're going to attract the wrong kind of people, and you don't want to spend too much time or money attracting tire kickers — even if you happen to be selling tires.

Even if you do offer the right giveaway, it can backfire on you a bit. Here's an example from Kris Solie-Johnson that didn't work out the way that she thought it would. At the American Institute of Small Business, she ran a grant program in which they'd give away free money out of their bottom line to a small business owner if they applied online. There wasn't an application fee or anything — it was free for them to apply. What she attracted were people without any money to spend on anything else. It was like she was trying to attract deer and put out cheese, and didn't get what she was looking for. So you do have to be careful about the kind of free offer is that you put out there; you want to attract the right people. In a way, **it's kind of like going fishing.** They could be biting like crazy, but if they're not fish you can eat, then you're wasting your time and bait.

Here's another example, this time from Russ von Hoelscher, one of my mentors. He once ran a business opportunity ad in *Parade* magazine, which goes to 30,000,000 Sunday newspapers around the nation. But it was the *wrong offer*. He offered a free booklet, had 11,500 people send for it, and thought, "My goodness! We're going to get rich with this one little listing in *Parade!*" **But then he found that 99.99% of the people who raised their hands wouldn't** *buy* **anything regarding a business opportunity. They just sent for a free book because it was free.** I can't emphasize enough that your free offer must go to the right people, and you want to attract only the right people.

I want to make a confession here about one of my worst mistakes I've even made. If you've been paying attention, by now you know that my best friend has a pest control business. Once upon a time, I tried to help her get more business. Here I thought I really knew a lot about Direct-Response Marketing. I thought I was just going to come in there and help her triple her business in no time flat, and I was going to be a big hero and they were going to write songs about me. Anyway, I thought I was so damn smart... so I did this elaborate Direct-Mail campaign that was highly targeted to only the very best prospects. I was using a model of a Direct-Mail package that I knew was making tens of millions of dollars a month for Omaha Steaks, the company out of Omaha, Nebraska. I was using their letter as a model.

But the big mistake that I made — and I can only say this now, after four years of thinking it through — was that **I used the wrong premium!** I was looking for people to raise their hands, and we were trying to sell them a termite control package for $2,000-4,000, maybe as much as $10,000 in some cases. **I offered them a gift that had absolutely nothing to do with the termite thing.** It was a beautiful atlas I was giving away, and it was more than just a regular atlas, because it had a bunch of special features. It was fancy. It was nice. I had a lot of people raise their hands and send back those cards. I just knew — like Russ did with the *Parade* magazine ad — that I was going to be a hero! And then it turned out that we were able to close very, very few of the leads.

In hindsight, we should have offered to give away a free newsletter subscription on how to protect your home forever from termite damage, without ever having to worry about your investment property getting eaten up by these little tiny insects! Granted, that's a boring premium; we would have had so few leads compared to the big avalanche of leads that we actually got. But the salespeople could have then put all of their focus onto that smaller group of leads, and we would have closed a greater percentage of those people. I think a lot of businesspeople make the same mistake, and I shouldn't have: by then, I had already been in Direct-Response Marketing for a decade and a half. Here's what I learned: **I'd much rather have one or two leads a day that are closeable, from people realistically interested in what I have to offer, than 10,000 that aren't going to respond.**

Once you've picked the right offer, the next step is to help people appreciate what you're giving them. You've got to make its inherent value clear in their minds. There has to be a reason for you to give that particular item to them, because otherwise it's just a freebie that they'll put very little value on, so you get the reverse of what you're trying to accomplish. If your offer is valueless, it makes your business seem valueless. **You want to be sure they understand the inherent value of what you're offering them, why you're doing that, and what they need to do to qualify for that free gift — whether it's a newsletter or a discount coupon in your store.**

You do have to be careful. I want to stress that the cool thing about the Internet is that you're going to get a lot of responses very quickly — but you'll get a lower-quality group if you give something away absolutely free. People expect to be charged

Selling and marketing is the ultimate game!

- Show me any game or sport without ten tons of obstacles and challenges — and I'll show you one boring game! The only game worth playing is the one that lets you test your skills on a daily basis.

- Entrepreneurs thrive on challenges! We welcome the adversity. We need the problems, challenges, and obstacles. Without these things, the game is pretty boring.

something for anything that's truly valuable. Also, make sure what you're giving them is highly targeted. That way, the only people who would ever say, "Go ahead and send me that for free," are people who really want what you have to offer in the worst kind of way. That's a great way of qualifying people.

When it comes to lead generation, qualification is the most important thing. And if you're giving them something free that's delivered electronically, even if they *aren't* targeted, at least it didn't cost you anything to deliver it. You could use a more complex process of qualification, too. **You can get people to raise their hands, but then you take that big group and whittle it down through a series of steps that continue to qualify them even more.**

Getting More Information

Up 'til now, I've been talking about getting names and email addresses, but it's also great if you can get even more information from your prospects. You can give them a choice: they can pay you a certain amount of money to get what you're offering, or they can give you more information or fill out a survey to get your product for free. If you ask someone to stop and give you their email address, name, and mailing address these days, that's about the equivalent of asking them to pay you $5.00 or $10.00 for something. Another way to do it is offer them a free physical product, like a tape or a printed report (something not digital) that has to get mailed to them, to encourage them to give you their mailing address. Now, I don't consider myself an Internet marketer *per se*; I consider myself an information producer, and I use different media to generate leads, including the Internet. I also use snail mail in all sorts of different ways to get leads, to build traffic, and to get customers. If I can get more information, if I can have every *bit* of information, all the better. **When people call our office to order something, we always ask them, "Can we get your email address? Your fax number?" We want everything, so we can contact them various ways. People respond differently to different types of offers, presented through different forms of media.**

Keep on Plugging — Yourself

One way to help generate leads for your business is to plug yourself whenever you can. My friend Randy Charach often introduces himself this way: "Hi, I'm Randy Charach from 123smg.com." See what he just did? Whether he's doing a presentation, asking a question in an online chat room, attending a tele-seminar as a listener or participant, or attending an event, he puts up his hand and leads with, "Hi, this is Randy Charach from 123smg.com..." He gives them his name and Web address, and right away he's generating leads.

Now, if you go to 123smg.com, you'll find a website that has one purpose and one purpose only: to capture your name and your email address. It has a headline, it has bullets; it's a fairly long page, a hardworking sales letter. It's a chance to get people to pay money for a product Randy's offering. There's a value there: it says, "Soon we'll be charging $197.00 for these exact same secrets," and that's not a lie. It won't be at this site, and it won't be in this form, but Randy's going to be taking these 1,054 secrets and putting them into a different product, which will sell for $197.00. But here you get that information, one week at a time, for 100 weeks — that is, around two years. Nothing here is misleading. All the information is true. There's a nice cover of the design of the book *Synergy Success E-Zine* — again, just as if it were a real product. This may be what the cover of the book that sells for $197.00 will look like, so a lot of the work is already done. There are many, many different offers there, each one the same: "Enter your name and your email address and join *Synergy Success*." This particular site is Randy's focal site to capture email addresses.

The question is, how does Randy get people to that site? There are many different ways, of course. One is by introducing himself the way he does: "This is Randy Charach from 123smg.com." Another way Randy does it is by providing testimonials for other products; people look for them, because he has a name on the Internet as a marketer. If you don't get asked for testimonials, you can volunteer them. When you give a testimonial, it's fair enough to include your Web address at the bottom. If you're an expert, the person who wants to use your testimonial will want to display that on the site, because it adds credibility to the notion that he's not a made-up person.

Establish Yourself as an Expert

If you can get the word out that you're an expert on a particular product or service, you can really draw in the leads. Kris Solie-Johnson tells me that at the Small Business Administration Awards in 2005 in Minnesota, there were three young brothers — all under the age of twenty — who had started a company that gives away free screensavers. They could really target the market they were getting into, because they knew a lot about it. So they began giving away these free screensavers for the computer, and then they started letting advertisers buy into their list. These three young men were doing about $40 million a year this way. So when you find out enough about your market, giving away something for free — whether it's a screensaver or a free report — can really expand your business.

Let's go back to my friend's pest control service. Suppose

---

we'd decided to hand out free screensavers instead of atlases. Those screensavers might display close-up images of different pests, with facts about their lifecycles and ways to keep them out of your home. **One of the best ways in the world to sell anything to a list, and to build that list of prospects, is to tell them** *exactly* **how to do what it is you can do for them. Tell them in excruciating detail, so they could take care of it if they wanted to... but make it clear that it's going to be such a hassle that it's not worth it. Now, you obviously know how it's done; you just told them. But they won't want to bother with it, so you give them your phone number so they don't have to.**

We see copywriters doing this all the time, because establishing yourself as an expert is one of the best ways there is to generate leads. **There's nothing that works better than making yourself out as the one that has all the answers.** If I were looking for Internet marketing stuff and I heard a guy like Randy Charach give his presentation, I would immediately know that this was a guy who really knows what the heck he's talking about, and I'd be willing to give him whatever he asked for information-wise, especially if he could it put together without me having to do any work. Like I've said before, when you use this technique you need to get as many different contacts as possible — their fax number, their email address, their home phone, their business phone — because that gives you more ammunition for reaching them in a variety of different ways.

When Randy does this, he doesn't just put his leads into an auto-responder. Sure, they'll get an email, but they'll also get a phone blast — a one-minute recording giving his pitch. You record this message, reminding them to do something, or making an offer, then send it to your list based on the day they subscribed. You can also send messages by regular mail and fax machine. So: email, phone, mail, and fax. Get it all set up sequentially, automatically, and you only have to do it once. You can't do all this using the mybizkit.com site (that's only for autoresponders), but you can get it done if you carefully integrate several different systems that are available on the Internet. It might cost you a pretty penny to get it all set up, but remember, these are very qualified clients you're sending to, people who have truly offered that information to you, knowing exactly why they're giving it out. They're worth spending a little money to market to, as I've made clear in other chapters. They're going to receive these messages, and the sales and responses will shoot through the roof.

So once you get the leads, pounce on them; don't ever give up. Keep the pressure on them in a nice way, with a message of altruism, that you're there to help them. You're not just trying to shake them upside down until all the money falls out of their pockets. You're trying to do things that let them know you really have what they want, that you can help them in the areas they need help in, that you can provide the solution to their problems. Then you're making them specific offers, so there's never any question about what you want them to do in exchange for the money you're asking them to give you.

It all starts with this expert positioning. Good marketers constantly offer free information, with only sporadic pitches salted between the tips. This pulls leads in, using the funnel system. Picture the funnel — wide at the top, narrow at the bottom. We bring as many leads as we can into that funnel, as quickly and as cheaply as possible, using a free or inexpensive offer. As they come in and work their way through the funnel, their numbers decrease, and ones that are left are starting to spend more and more money with us and, of course, the trust is building, and the value is increasing, and the types of offers are changing.

Infect the Web with Viral Marketing

Another way to plug yourself and your business is to include your web address and contact information in online articles, which is one form of what we call "viral marketing." I'm going to talk about this specifically in relationship to the tips that are sent out to an auto-responder, starting automatically on the day the person subscribes and then going out every seven days afterward. This goes on, say, for a hundred weeks. Now, in addition to receiving those tips, you can give your subscribers the permission to reprint those tips — which is another benefit that can get people to subscribe. They can get free reprint rights from you, and then they can take those tips and do exactly what you've done, by loading them into an auto-responder for weekly distribution. Or they can put them into whatever form they want — heck, they could even compile them into a book. The catch is this: **they have to include your tag line at the bottom of the tip, so you get the credit for writing it, and they also have to include a link to your site, plus an email address. As long as these are included at the bottom of each tip, they can give them away.**

That's fair, right? They don't have to write these tips; they don't have to pay anyone to write them. They can use them to attract people to their site. They can use them as bonuses or whatever they want, as long as they include your tag line. That's the viral part: **soon they're sending them out all over the Web, and they've got your name on them. So it's win-win for everybody! Other people get to benefit from the information, and you get to build more and more people into your list of leads.**

This can also be done, by the way, through eBooks. It works the same way as the tips: you can give away this eBook for free, as long as you fix it so that they can't change any of the links in there — and the links, of course, go back to your site, which generates free traffic, which generates leads. **Another way to generate a lot of leads is by using a landing page prior to any sales page that you may have.** This isn't always done, of course; it depends on the product. Here's how it works: before you can even read the sales letter, there's a landing page, which basically says, "To get this information, please enter your name and email address here." Once they do that, they're sent to the page with the sales letter. **The landing page is also referred to as a "squeeze page," because that's how you squeeze their contact info out of them.** Now, you may be thinking, "Well, that's going to turn off a lot of people who won't even see my sales message. Maybe it'll cost me some sales, because the people who won't even put in their email or name aren't going to end up buying from me anyway." But it's been tested; it works.

Smart marketers don't do this on every web site, because it could be seen as disrespectful in joint venture relationships. If you have another marketer who's willing to send traffic to your website as an affiliate so they can make money on the product, you don't want to be scooping up all the traffic leads that are sent to you from them. They may not appreciate it. Just ask; you'll find that some won't mind. If that's the case, then great: you can build all these leads and get all this traffic and have them filter in through your landing page.

There's a special kind of viral marketing called "buzz marketing." My friend Alan Bechtold calls buzz marketing "viral marketing on steroids." You can create a little inspirational message, cartoon or joke related to your business, with a tag line at the bottom that gives the readers your Web address as an illustration. You can do this with a simple email with a "Tip of the Day," or a really cool unknown fact. How many of you get those cartoons and jokes that people pass around? **You could use one of those with a tag line at the bottom to visit your site, especially if it's tied in to what you sell — and watch it spread all over**

the world without you spending a dime. Here's an example: There's a guy out there that my friend Mike Lamb interviewed several years ago on his radio show by the name of Stanford Wallace — a real whiz of a marketer. He decided to go proactive and build a permission-based list; last I heard, he had 27,000,000 people that he emails to on a somewhat regular basis with offers... and he makes ungodly amounts of money. That's one of the things he started doing early on when he went proactive: he created a website that allowed you to pass along the latest Internet joke, or the latest Internet flash movie, or the latest whimsical thing about the President, or some comical or topical item. I still don't see that being done a lot. I think you really need to focus on what niche you're in and do that within your niche, because it's a very workable solution for creating a list.

Postcards: the Fabulous Offline Option

I realize that not all of you out there are into online marketing, whether you should be or not; but you can still plug yourself and your business offline in an effective way. Here's one way that generates a lot of leads: postcards. **Work hard to capture the names and addresses of all your customers, and occasionally send then simple postcards.** Even if you're not an Internet guru, or you're unable to write books or reports or newsletters, you can send out a simple postcard that either tells people your current offers or gives them a special deal if they come in within the next few days — and this can work like magic. It's a very cheap way to contact people, and you can rent lists or acquire lists through joint ventures. When I say, "rent lists," I'm talking about lists of magazine subscribers, organizational memberships, and the like — there are all sorts of lists you can rent. Once you've got those lists, **you send a postcard out with an 800 number, with a free 24-hour recorded message.** They can call anytime; they don't have to speak to anybody. It takes away that sort of pressure, where they're thinking, "I don't want to call, because somebody's going to try to sell me something." **If they're interested, they leave their information, and then you follow-up by mailing them a product or a report.**

You can also put on the postcard, "Or, respond by email or by visiting my website." Include a combination of any one, two, three of those.

Referrals, Online or Off

Another way to capture great leads is to get people to make referrals to you. From the Internet side, you could ask your current client base to send you referrals of their friends. If you're sending them an email newsletter — say, about how to get that stain out of your carpet — you can include a coupon for 15% off of their next carpet cleaning. Sweeten the pot with a reward for passing the message on, and you end up with a piece of viral marketing. The message gets passed from one person to the next, and you just never know where the offer will end up, or when some of those messages will bring in business. The same thing is true with postcards; give them an easy message with a good deal that they can pass on to their friends, and you end up with a very easy viral marketing piece that can keep the money rolling in.

Lead Generation and the Relationship Game

Lead generation is really about establishing relationships with your prospective customers — and some of the most effective ways of doing this are the methods we've all been using for years. Now, let me qualify that a little: people have been using these methods for years, but they're not necessarily using them to their full potential.

First of all, let's talk about business cards. Probably **80% of the business cards I get are blank on the reverse side. I think that's truly a missed opportunity.** In some cases, you can buy full-color, front-and-back business cards for $200 or so and get 5,000 cards. Here's another tip: vary your cards for different purposes. Sometimes people use the same business card for years and years; but Bob Poppick, who is a business card expert, teaches that **you should have multiple business cards for multiple objectives.** One of the objectives you can use a business card for is building your list. So what you should do is have the business card information — all your generic content information, call to action, and that sort of thing — on one side of the card. **Then, when they turn the card over, it's got a call to action to go to the website** — to go to your list — and basically get that free report or that free list of tips or whatever the case may be. It's a remarkable way to build a list with people you give your business card to, or that you put your business card in front of.

Many people just hand out business cards; they don't do much else. That's a great idea, of course, **but you can also leave business cards wherever you go, and drop them wherever you can.** Leave one with the tip at a restaurant. Staple your business card to the invoices that you send to your electric company, your phone company, your gas company, your insurance company, your finance company — whatever the case may be. At some point, **some of those people are going to take your business card, look at it, turn it over, and go to your website and start receiving information from you because they're on your list.** If you don't have an online list, or if you're only working with a brick-and-mortar store, on the backside you could simply tell people, "Return this card to me for a 20% discount next time you come into the store." That's a great way of utilizing that lost space.

Business cards and postcards are in the same boat. You've got an offer on one side; you've got an opportunity to join your list on the other. There's a lot of different ways you can use business cards and postcards, but those are two very effective ways that I know of. I think the most important thing to consider when choosing a lead generation technique is how your audience is going to react to it. **Networking, knocking on doors, talking to people, meeting new people, building relationships, is like learning to drive or learning to type. It's always a bit uncomfortable at first, but how long does this feeling really last? Sooner or later you're going to feel comfortable about what you're doing:** you get behind the keyboard of your word processor or get behind the wheel of your car and just go. The more things that you can do to generate leads, the better your business is going to be, and the more money you're going to make.

Mike Lamb interviewed someone interesting on his radio show several years ago. What she did was go online and answer questions on the discussion boards — especially questions that other people weren't answering. If she came upon a discussion thread and there was one person there who didn't have an answer to their question, she would make sure that her answer would be there. Then she'd invite that person to do various things. In an eight-month period she sold 10,000 copies of an eBook at $24.95, just off the leads she generated from that discussion concept. It wasn't theory. She looked at discussion boards and saw what other people were doing, and she saw a great opportunity and decided to generate leads from the answers she posted on these discussion boards. There are many discussion boards online, and many ways to interject yourself into those. For her it worked out really well.

I think existing clients, and other professional contacts you have with family and friends and the people you hang out with at sports clubs and social clubs and health clubs — those people have an enormous amount of influence over the people they know. The people in those groups can be the fuel to help market and generate leads for your business. You can also pool your resources with other people, whether you work in an office or whether you have a hobby group or a group of people with whom you hang out otherwise. Those people offer a really good opportunity to build and create more value in your lead generating database. You should see every invitation that lands on your desk, everything that comes in the mail, anything where somebody is trying to contact you or build a relationship with you, as an opportunity for lead generation. Say to yourself, "Oh, another chance to meet a new contact! Another possible new sale! Another way to increase my fees!"

Mailing business letters sometimes seems very time-consuming, but many times you can send out a very simple letter to somebody, or scribble something on a note and stick it in an envelope and send it out, and people will actually react to those more than they do a big, long, drawn-out sales letter. You don't need any special graphics or anything much; you just need to have a note saying why you're contacting them. Believe it or not, you can practically put a Post-It note on the lip of an envelope, send it to somebody, and make money. I've done this and I've gotten good reactions from people, because it's unique; it's something that not everybody does.

Also, you want to follow-up on anything that you send out. Did they see it? Find out what their needs are. The tone is important: what you actually say and how you say it. You're there to help. You're there to provide information. You're there to be a resource.

I think we miss opportunities so many times in finding new customers and generating leads. Every group you associate with has someone in it who's a potential customer. **You've got to make sure that you're not just throwing things into the wind, hoping the wind is going to catch something and blow it back to you.** There are almost limitless numbers of methods for generating leads. I've talked about the Web; one of the most effective ways to contact people and generate leads online is to build an email list. But many people have a huge email list to which they never mail. Maybe they're intimidated, because they think the next time the email goes out, a bunch of people are going to want to get off their list. That happens, and it sometimes hurts, but that also tells you those people aren't interested in what you have.

You want to make sure that you follow-up with the people you do come in contact with, and that you have something valuable and important to say when you're saying it to them — whether it's in an email, a letter, a postcard, or whatever it is you're doing. Make sure that the relationship is the most important thing in building lead generation, because it is the relationship you develop with these people over time that's going to make your business truly successful. **A lot of people say it's a numbers game, but the truth is, it's more of a relationships game.**

I've already mentioned surveying your clients and prospects. This is important, because you want to find out what it is you can give them. Find out what they need, and let the relationship build that way. If not, you'll never know who it is on the other side of the computer screen, or on the other side of the mail, or on the other side of the phone. You don't know what those people need, and you don't know how much money they have. **I think a lot of people online (and just in business in general) are wondering how they can get new business, how they can make more money from an existing customer. Well, often all you have to do is ask.** Find out what it is

MARKETING SECRET #44

Major success in life comes from our ability to communicate to others in the most powerful way possible.

- Everything we want in life MUST come from other people. And communicating to their hearts — minds — and emotions is the secret to getting them to happily give us whatever we ask for!

they're actually interested in, and let that be part of your relationship-building process.

Here's some ideas from Russ von Hoelscher in the San Diego area, which might help some people elsewhere. Russ worked with a chiropractor in Pacific Beach a few years ago whose business wasn't what it should be. She was very reluctant to use lead generation, but Russ finally convinced her to do it, and **she started to offer a free examination worth $75 just to get people to her office — and she was flooded with business!** Then there's the realty company in East San Diego County that does free property appraisals. They tell you in their ads there's no obligation; you don't have to list your property with them. But if you're getting a free appraisal, you're probably thinking about selling your property, and you may feel a bond to the person who gives you a $200 property appraisal for free. Now, someone who works for Russ showed up at his office some time ago with a little penlight keychain that came from China. It probably cost a quarter, but Russ liked it. He said, "Where'd you get that?" and his employee said, "It's free! There's a hardware store just three blocks away that gives them away free for just walking in the door." Russ liked it so much he went there a couple of days later. He got the little keychain with the light on it, but he also bought some merchandise that he normally would have bought at Home Depot. See how that promotion worked for the hardware store?

These are just some of the things you can do **to lure people in.** Russ's local El Cajon Video and DVD store has a huge ad that says, "Thousands of DVDs and videos for 69 cents each — three day rentals!" He goes there quite often, and they've got the whole back wall and part of the right-hand wall full of thousands of these older DVDs or videos that you can rent for 69 cents — but if you want the newer stuff you pay the premium price. Russ said to the guy there, "Look, you're doing something very smart. You're probably not making any money with these DVDs rentals at this price, but you're getting people in the store and they buy other things." He said, "Russ, since we started running this three months ago, we've actually turned our old movies — which we had a hard time renting — into a big profit center." So **some of the things you can do for lead generation can be quite profitable, since you're giving away free things that don't cost that much anyway to get people there to spend money on other things you have.**

Another way is to find complimentary businesses and do a reciprocal agreement where "X" business says to "Y" business, "Look, your people need my service, and my people need your service. So let's give away each other's services with every order." This works best offline, of course, but it's another great way you can boost businesses by developing relationships.

Get Off Your Duff

In order to make your relationships work for you, **you should do something to generate leads *every single day*. If you go to bed at night and can honestly say that you didn't do something proactive to generate appropriate leads, then you've just wasted your whole day.** So every day of every week, you'd better ask yourself what you did to generate leads, and well in advance of that day, you should have a strategy! A lot of these ideas we've talked about are low-cost, so you can't use the excuse of, "I'm broke. I don't have enough money to do this or that." **As long as you're doing something every day to develop the highest-quality leads possible, and you've got a system for selling and converting those leads, then you *never* have to worry about going out of business.** So many people are going out of business these days, and it's their own fault. If you're doing something proactive every single day — like the suggestions I've been giving you in this chapter — it will never ever have to happen to you.

It's amazing to me how many times somebody tells me they're not getting new business, or their cash flow is down, and I ask them, "What are you doing?" They say, "Well, I don't have enough money to do marketing." Most of the things we're talking about, for the most part, are cheap. Yeah, okay, so you spend a couple of hundred dollars on business cards: well, that's five thousand potential new customers. Let's say you can start some kind of automated relationship with ten or twenty percent of the people to whom you give a business card. That's a pretty good percentage. Admittedly, it takes time, and it takes the belief that it's going to work. You've got to open yourself to abundance. You've got to say, "Money will come to me." You have to believe it, and then you just have to move your own story forward.

If you do that — if you move forward and you start doing some of the things I'm talking about here— you can't help but have money come to you. You can't help but make sales. In the years I've been in business, I've had the same thing happen to me that happens to everybody else. You get beat up. You get depressed. Things don't work. I've failed more times than I've been successful. So have most of my friends and colleagues. But now I'm open to money. Now I'm feeling abundance, and doing the things I need to do in growing my business and building new relationships. It's almost to the point, now, where I'm drowning in what I'm doing because there's so much coming at me.

The secret is to be proactive. To get people to come into your store, to call your business, to write you, or whatever means you want them to take — to get that, you've got to take action. Sitting back with a sign that says, "Open for Business" won't get the job done. If you're proactive and you're constantly thinking of low-cost and *no*-cost ways to promote your business, if you give out flyers and cards and you get even a two or three percent response, these schemes will pay for themselves over and over again.

Sometimes it's the simplest things that work the best. The very first sales job I ever had was right outside Fort Carson, Colorado, and I worked in a place that sold everything from TVs to furniture and appliances to military people who were coming out of Fort Carson. We had the dumbest little marketing thing going, but it brought in so much business to our store that it kept four salespeople busy full-time, about 14 hours a day. And here's all it was: every time we made a sale to a customer, we gave them a whole book of little slips. Sometimes they'd come back to get more. We'd sell them a TV, or a stereo, or fill their house full of all kinds of over-priced crap; then they would go out and tell their friends, and they'd hand their friends these little slips, and every time their friends came in with one of those little slips we paid the person who referred them $10.

You might think $10 is no big deal — and it isn't, unless you've ever worked for the military. They don't pay much. For some of these guys, $10 was a couple of six packs on a Friday night. It really, truly worked. **It was like we had salespeople working for our company that we didn't have to pay any money to unless they made a deal — and these guys were bringing in business like crazy!** A dumb little idea like that brought in tens of thousands of dollars a month for that one company.

Metrics, Expertise, and Low-Cost Leads

When generating leads and building relationships with your prospects, it's important to know your metrics. If you know the lifetime value of your customer, and if you break it down into different promotions and such, you can know how much you can afford to spend for a particular lead. Of course, you want to be able to structure your business in such a way that the cost of the lead is no object; that way, you can spend more than other people for leads. Let's go back to my earlier example of pay-per-click (PPC) advertising. It's a very fast way of getting leads for a few cents each if you're online, but the same principle applies offline, no matter what you're doing. Admittedly, it's a tough thing to do and make money at, unless you know how much you can spend. **Fortunately, you can make a lot of mistakes and not know your numbers and still make a ton of money, especially if you know it's going to take very little to make money on a promotion. Nonetheless, if you want to get smart about it, then you want to know what you can afford per lead.**

PPC advertising is ideal for businesses that are entirely online, but I'll be honest with you: if you've got a brick-and-mortar business — a Laundromat, a dry cleaning business, a sandwich shop, a little hardware store — you may not want to get involved with it, even if you're limiting clicks to the local area. **You've got to think of other low-cost ways to promote your business,** with cards and flyers and little ads in the right publications, through trading flyers with your fellow businesspeople, and things like that.

Let's look a little more closely at that Laundromat I mentioned earlier. While Internet advertising might not be the best thing for a place like that, you don't see near enough Laundromats using the simple tactic of putting a sign in their window with a special offer for new customers. Something like this: "New customer offer... bring in your shirts for the first time! Two shirts cleaned for the price of one!" **It boggles my mind how many of these businesses just sit there and wait for you to come in, or count on the customers they've got.** Once you get them in, you should always take their names. A lot of people joke and complain about Radio Shack, because they won't open the register till they have your phone number, to check to see if they have you in the database. And why do you think they've survived with the advent of all these big box stores like Circuit City and Best Buy? First of all, they're a little bit specialized, though they've started to get more generalized lately.

But the real reason is that they have a huge list to which they continue to make offers. Even for a local business, you can do a lot with just a business card and the right signage in the window.

In a way, you can go overboard with this. Mike Lamb was telling me about a Laundromat owner who does more to promote *outside* interests in the Laundromat — multilevel marketing programs and various Affiliate Programs — than she promotes the Laundromat itself. She's got all these different things on the table when you walk in the door, so you can pick up a piece of paper on this, or this card on that, or a brochure on another thing. That doesn't really fall under lead generation; but in a way, it is. If you want new leads, and you've got to get the word out — and **sometimes it's as simple as doing something outrageous in your store, something nutty that will get the attention of the press.** What about trying to wash the biggest sheet ever washed and dried in a single cycle, or a laundrython, where you're going to do laundry for 48 hours straight? You just get nuts and throw a big party around it, and invite everybody to invite everybody, and you give away little samples and free gifts, and you're handing out your card, and *collecting names while they're there*!

Keep one thing in mind: if you're proactive and you're constantly looking for ways to get new customers in, you're going to be successful, because 95% of your competition will do *none of these things*. **The mindset with most business owners is basically to get a location downtown or in a strip mall or wherever, and just be open for business — and that's all they'll do. Some of them are successful only because they have the right location where there's heavy traffic. But they could double and triple their profits if they do just some little things on a regular basis — like set up an automatic system for generating leads.** In the words of Nike, "Just do it." But I'd add this: constantly do it and never stop doing it, and you'll beat your competition, because they're probably doing very little or nothing.

Regarding that business that's doing very well because

they've got a great location: I'd say that's temporary rather than long-term. **If another competitor comes in with the same type of business, if they're doing better marketing, that good location will soon be a good location to go out of business.** Even if your business is doing well, you must have a lead generation program, because competition is especially prone to popping up when you're doing well. When you least expect it, someone is planning to take over your customers, using some of the tactics and strategies that I'm talking about here.

Here's a great example, courtesy of my friend Kris Solie-Johnson. There was a bead store in her local area that was making $300,000 a year, just by selling those little, tiny beads used for making jewelry. Pretty good, right? Well, now there's so much competition in the Twin Cities that they're barely surviving, and one of the companies that came in captured all their customers' names and addresses. This new competitor is continually mailing out to their list, and they have big events because they can contact their customers, and they're doing ten times better than the bead shop that didn't capture customer information from the beginning.

What I'm trying to say here is this: **you've got to become the competitor that you most fear. You've got to find a way to build a wall around your customers so people can't penetrate it.** One of the ways to do that is something I've been talking about all along here: you become a real expert, somebody who stands head and shoulders above all the other competitors in your area. **When you're a recognized expert, not only can you play on that to draw people in, but you come up with all kinds of workshops and party-type events where you bring your customers together.** You've got newsletters, you've got business cards, you've got all kinds of deals that really build those relationships with your prospects and customers. **When you've got a relationship that's built up solidly enough with somebody, they're going to value you and appreciate you and honor you — and they're not going to go give their business to somebody else, unless your competitor is doing a really great job.**

The Value of Your List

Earlier, I mentioned Radio Shack. Randy Charach tells me that in Canada, Radio Shack is now called "The Source." I don't know if the company still has the same owners, or if they were bought out; but whatever the case, it reminds my that by building your list — online, offline, or both — not only will that increase your business, but it's going to increase the *value* of your business. In the Radio Shack example, let's just say hypothetically that this other company, The Source, bought them out. If that's the case, then I'm sure the shareholders of Radio Shack received a lot more money for their business *with* a customer list than they would have without it. Your business is worth a lot more with your list, no matter what business you're in. In fact, it may be that the only value you'll have in your business, if you go to sell it, will be your list.

Here's a good example of that from Kris Solie-Johnson. She worked with a woman who owned a software company, and it was basically a consulting company. How do you sell a consulting company if it's based almost entirely off your skills? Well, she had a customer list. She went out and hired a valuation consultant who interviewed all of her clients and asked how much they would spend over the next year in services. She could actually go out and prove what the cash flow would be in her consulting business. This isn't like a retail business, where you're buying equipments, fixtures, and whatever it is the store sells. In a business like hers, if you don't have the client list, you've got to build that client list from ground zero. **It's much more valuable if you keep the list when you're buying a business, especially if it's a service-based business. You're purchasing the goodwill value. Often, the goodwill is more valuable in dollars than the business's assets themselves.**

In fact, let me put it this way: I wouldn't want to buy a company without a good list of existing customers. Otherwise, I'd just start my own company. You see, **it will change your life once you start appreciating the value of a list and the relationship associated with it.** I've heard a story about a restaurant that burned down to the ground, and it took nine months or so to get the new location built (because they built it on the ashes of the previous restaurant). But during those nine months they did all kinds of things to stay in touch with their customers: they had parties, put up tents in the parking lot, even went and rented other places. When they re-opened, they were stronger than ever. The other cool thing is they were actually taking reservations in advance for the restaurant on the anticipated opening date, months in advance. They were selling a year's worth of meals for a discounted price, which continued the cash flow that allowed them to continue to build.

And let's not forget the power of free publicity. Free publicity is free advertising, and it's a lead generator. Russ von Hoelscher was telling me that he read, recently, that in Los Angeles, some very wealthy people were getting married and this bakery built what they called the "world's largest wedding cake." It was right there on the *L. A. Times* — there was a big splash on it. And then there's a store in San Diego that sells lighting and furniture. They advertise, "If it's not American made, we don't carry it," and they show a big American flag right in the window of their store. They've gotten a lot of free publicity. They say, "We've got to keep the money and the manufacturing here in America," even when that's not a popular sentiment. So **anything that you can do — and there's a *lot* that you can do — to get free publicity will**

also help generate leads and build your business. Creativity is key in that, because you want to be something new and unique.

But you'll also need a certain amount of aggressiveness, and a hunger for it all. I think, also, you have to intimately know who your best customers are. Until you internalize all the characteristics of that perfect customer, you should take notes. For years I kept a notebook, which I've mentioned once or twice before. I haven't read it for a long time, because I've internalized what I need to know about my best customers. But in the old days, **every time I came up with any impression about our customers, I wrote it down and I kept it in this huge, overflowing three-ring binder.** I wanted to know my best customers better than they knew themselves, and so I just take notes — like a good General in an army does, or a good football coach. **The way to attract more "best" customers is to know the best customers you have now.**

Use that notebook in conjunction with your list, but be sure you have that list handy. If your place of business catches on fire, what are you going to grab first? If you can only grab one thing, make it your list, because that's where the value is. Always have a daily backup of your list available, at least in electronic format.

Wrapping It Up

When it comes to developing and maintaining leads, **it's all about creating good, value-driven, long-term relationships with your customers. Do everything you can to build that. Why? Simply because it gives you the dominant competitive advantage in your marketplace, because most people are doing** *nothing* **in regard to lead generation.**

I hope that you'll go back through this chapter and reread it several times. I've given you many ideas here; some may apply to you, while some don't. Take what you like and leave the rest. It's kind of like a smorgasbord in that sense, but I do believe that you have to go through this chapter several times and really process what I'm sharing with you here. I sincerely hope you'll do it!

SECRET SEVEN:

The Importance of Internet Marketing

In this chapter, I'll focus on just how critical Internet marketing is to today's marketer. In my opinion, it's something every business in the world should use. As I pointed out in the last chapter, motivational speaker Dennis Waitley has a saying: "If you're not online, you're going to be in the bread line." I thoroughly believe that, which is why I intend to spend a whole chapter talking specifically about all the ways online marketing can be a vital part of any modern business.

Why You Should Be Marketing on the Internet

One of the biggest advantages of online marketing is that you can address a much larger audience than you could if you were just dealing with your local area. If you're a brick-and-mortar company selling books or records, for example, the ability to do that nationally, through the Internet, is very important. You can expand your reach exponentially in this way. Also, **the ability to communicate back and forth with your customers is heightened on the Internet.** When you get right down to it, it's a very interactive type of advertising. It gives you a much more dynamic, two-way communication "street" with your clients, which translates into much better profit margins if you handle it professionally. That's what we're all in business to do, after all — to make as much money as possible. Well, **the Internet is the key to expanding your business well beyond what you can do just from your brick-and-mortar locations.**

Even for a smaller business — *especially* for a small business — Internet marketing should be an important part of your total advertising mix. It adds interaction, color, and all sorts of communication accelerators that the average small business can't afford in their normal advertising. Now, I'll admit that it may not be as important to some businesses as it is others; but whenever possible, it should definitely be included as part of a typical business media blitz, which includes everything from the Yellow Pages to classified ads to business cards and flyers.

In addition to giving you the ability to reach a larger group of people — never something to be sneezed at — the Internet is also a big money-saver. It doesn't just make it easy for prospects to communicate with and purchase from you; **it helps bring in income when they use it for, say, Frequently Asked Questions (FAQ) sessions on your website, for online support, for customer service, for company news, or for publicity. If you're a Web-savvy marketer, you can make all these things readily available to the mass public just by putting them on your website.** Major corporations save a lot of money by using this method, and it can save money for small companies as well. It saves on staffing, for example; if you have an FAQ page on your website, that'll cover a lot of common questions and save a lot of manpower. On top of that, you're increasing customer support and bringing in more sales.

These are just a few of the reasons why I believe that *every* business needs to be on the Internet. These days that's the only way some people market, and for good reason. There are incredible advantages to marketing on the Internet, especially when you're delivering information products — but let's extend this to any business, doing anything. **One fact you'd better face is that people are going to the Internet today just to find you.** Case in point: one day, my friend and colleague Ted Ciuba walked out his front door and found he had a nail in his tire. He told his secretary, "Get on the horn and find me a shop where I can get this tire repaired." What does she do? She doesn't get on the phone, which is what Ted was actually thinking; she gets on the Internet and finds a tire repair shop in the neighborhood. You see? If that repair place hadn't been on the Internet, they probably wouldn't even have had a chance of getting Ted's business.

So yes, being on **the Internet's good even if it's just an extra channel of business.** It's cost effective, because once you've invested a few hundred bucks in the basic infrastructure, you've got your domain name, you've got your Web hosting, you've got your web text and your HTML. It costs next to nothing to put a web page up. And whoa, it's not like some ad you run; it lasts forever, until you change it! Part of the reason it's so cost effective is that it lasts so long — and **these days, people expect an Internet presence. One of the best things about being able to put up a website, especially one with an FAQ page, is that it lets you tell your full story.** If you shell out for billboard, or you put an ad in the newspaper, or you put a sign on the side of your car or flyers on the front of a house, you can't tell the full story there. But on the Internet you *can* — quickly and easily.

A few more cases in point. In Jackson, Tennessee, you can see the home of the famous Casey Jones of railroad fame. One day, Ted Ciuba went to check it out. There was a little shop there selling medieval armor, swords, and costumes. Ted walked in and was asking them about this stuff, because as you might imagine, he was fascinated. He asked them, "Do you have a website?" And they said, "Oh, yeah. We were on the brink of bankruptcy until we put a website up." Here's the whole story. **The place is on Interstate 40, but it was only getting drive-by traffic. Now, all of a sudden, they're getting orders from all over the world.** All they did was get a digital camera, take pictures, and write a few descriptions, and then put it all up on their site. This wasn't even sophisticated or difficult — and suddenly orders were coming in from all over the place. Now they're prosperous, and they're bustling rather than depressing.

Another guy in Atlanta, Georgia, was down to his last $1,500.

MARKETING SECRET #47

The power of pressure: In the midnight hour — when the deadlines are closing in — you are forced to make decisions.

- The walls of indecision begin breaking down.

- And the answers, which were once very muddy, now become clear.

He was also on the verge of bankruptcy, had been going backwards for months at a time, couldn't make it... and finally just said, "What the hell. Fifteen hundred dollars. If I lose it now, it can't make any difference." He went online in a big way, and all of a sudden, in his first nine months, he made $450,000. What did he do? He was selling stained glass doors in the local market, trying to market to construction people, and he didn't do so well. Then he goes online, and all of a sudden, he's in a global market, and it turns out he's getting most of his orders from California — which may not surprise you. But he wasn't marketing to California before, and he certainly wasn't marketing to them for free. Now he's getting orders from Hong Kong and Japan, too. When you get online, you're entering a global marketplace. It's easy to do, and all of a sudden, your customers are looking for *you*.

What the Internet is capable of doing for practically any business just blows me away. I mean, this works for any business at all! Because if you look at it, **Internet Marketing is simply an extension of standard Direct-Response Marketing, multiplied by the power of the Internet. The Internet allows for a greater number and variety of exposures than most marketing efforts, and can save you incredible amounts of money compared to traditional forms of marketing and advertising. Just the money you can save in postage and print alone is sometimes** astounding. Then there's the way you can really build relationships online with your customers.

But if you look at all there is to choose from out there on the Internet, and all the options a business has when it comes to looking at the Internet, you really have to start by asking yourself exactly what it is you want your Internet campaign or website to do. Once you decide, go and find those tools you need to perform that task. With the Internet, everything's right there at your fingertips: tools, information, everything. You can find it and apply it to your business in a heartbeat.

You know, I'm so happy to be alive during this time! I'm thanking the universe every single day because of the technology we have available to us, and because good things are happening to me. As I mentioned in Chapter 7, I'm open to money, I'm open to new relationships, and I'm open to abundance. And that, essentially, is what the Internet is. **When you look at the ability to easily create a website with anything on it that you want, and then put it on the Internet with ease, you're looking at a whole new era in marketing. This is effective whether you're a brick-and-mortar business, an Internet business, a Direct-Marketer — or if you're just someone trying to meet someone else.** You can easily put your resume online. You can start building a presence online whether you're a teenager or a senior citizen, and nobody has to know how old you are. That doesn't mean you're going to be out there pretending to be something you're not — but you can be as personal as you need to be. You can be as over-the-top as you need to be. You can be as big as you want to be. Even better, you can change your online personality whenever you wish. **You have the ability to level the playing field. A big company and a small company can look the same on the Internet, or a small company can outshine a bigger one. Then again, if you're a big company and you want to look more Mom-and-Pop, you can do that, too.**

My colleague Mike Lamb tells me that a friend of his, Cheryl

Gonzalez, once said, "With my keyboard, I have the ability to create millions of relationships, right at my fingertips." In many cases, it's an autopilot situation: you're generating revenue over and over and over, sometimes residual revenue where you do the work once and get paid many times, just because you have a significant presence on the Internet.

In relation to that, let me go back to something I mentioned earlier in regards to Ted Ciuba. This is a very important point: **a lot of people use the Internet as a Yellow Pages, to look for a solution to a problem — and you've got to take advantage of their willingness to do so.** I can't tell you how many times I've opened up the Internet and looked for a website, only to discover that I couldn't find a telephone number or an address when I found that site. Or if I did, it was like pulling teeth to go from one link to the next to check each page to see, "Well, maybe they've got their contact info listed on this page." My point is that I like to look at and use a website as, in essence, a Yellow Page ad. You should structure yours that way, too.

The person who's come to your site has obviously landed there because they're looking for a solution to a problem: they want it, and they want it quick. They want to know how to get it. They want to know how to contact you. They want to know that you're real — that you really exist. In my case, I always put my contact info right there, easy to find, on every page — so they know I'm a real person, and they know how to reach me. The bottom line is that you want to use your Internet presence as an extension of Yellow Page advertising, so that you can be the solution to the problem that your prospect has typed into the search engine. It's a simple fact that **millions and millions of people are becoming conditioned to using the Internet on a daily basis. It's just becoming part of their lifestyle.** Every single year that goes by, the Internet is becoming less hype-filled and more a reality — to the point where now, if you're not on the Internet, you're definitely hurting your business.

It amazes me how **the world continues to shrink as technology expands.** Recently, Eric Bechtold introduced us to a company out of Las Vegas with which we wanted to do some business. This is a multimillion-dollar company, and they didn't know who we were, but we got a meeting with the President and CEO of the company. The first thing she said to us was, "I checked you out on the Internet." She Googled us, did some searches, and she found out about us. That can be kind of scary, but it also can be good if you're doing business with integrity. **She already felt like she knew us before we even got together for our initial consultation.**

I love the Internet. My wife has multiple sclerosis. She's not wheelchair-bound or anything yet, but she does an awful lot of online shopping. We're living in the day and age where **you're really missing out on a lot of money that could and should be yours — money that your competition is getting right now — if you don't implement some of the secrets I'm going to share with you in this chapter.**

Lead Generation Revisited

There are so many excellent ways to use the Internet, and it's such a big thing that you could take the marketing in many, many different directions. In this section, I'm going to focus on lead generation. I know I talked about using the Internet for lead generation a good bit in the last chapter, but I think it's so important that some of this data bears repeating. Most of what I'll tell you here is new information, though.

Lead generation is, hands down, the hard part of doing business; it's how you get your customer for the first time. It's one of the costliest and scariest things a marketer can do, since you don't know how your prospects are going to react, and you can end up spending a lot of money on the front-end if you don't do it right. Once you've got a client with whom you're working, it's much easier to keep them spending money on an

ongoing basis.

But the real trick is getting them in, and with the Internet you can use the standard two-step marketing approach, risking as little money upfront as possible to acquire a new customer. Internet lead generation is a very simple idea, but there are a lot of different ways to do it, and a lot of different nuances that you can pull together to marry offline advertising with your website — not only to more effectively communicate with your clients, but to build your database and clientele at the same time.

The Internet's the best way to advertise not just because it's cheap, but also because it gives you the ability to tell the whole story. Instead of spending huge amounts of money for big advertisements in trade magazines, in the newspaper, or on billboards to draw in the customers, you can place very small display advertisement somewhere — maybe a quarter-page ad, even something as small as a one-inch ad — and use that as a teaser to drive people onto your website, so that they can get the entire story and learn more about you. If you have a promotion going, **use small classified ads, small display ads, or some other cost-effective front-end to drive your prospects to your site, so you can start building relationships. Once you acquire that customer and they're spending money with you, you can afford to spend a little bit more money**

FREE GIFT! Go to www.RuthlessMarketing.com/freegift

sending them different packages and information.

This can be done with Direct-Mail, too. Just send out a cheap postcard or letter driving people to a website, so the website can communicate everything you couldn't get into that little letter. You're trying to spend as little money as possible on postage and printing and everything else, to keep your advertising upfront as cost-effective as possible. On the Internet, you've also got those pay-per-click ads I discussed in Chapter 7. You can use all these methods to drive people to your websites, where two important things can happen.

Your goals in getting prospects to your website are 1) to turn them into potential clients, and 2) to grow your database, and you want to do both things as quickly as possible. Basically, you want to use your website to build relationships with your clients as soon as possible, by capturing their names and their information upfront. When you get a prospect on your website for the first time, give them something: an online newsletter or something of value, where they're going to want to sign up and give you their contact information.

What this does for you is this: it allows you to start communicating with these individuals for free. It's not costing you anything, except a little time, to send an email out to these people. You've gotten them in there; now you can start building those relationships that underlie every dollar you'll make as a businessperson. Do it right, and every time they get an email from you, they'll open it up and pay attention to it, and they'll start to connect with you. **You need to give people the strongest and most compelling reasons possible to go to your website.** Too many people know enough to build a website for their business, then don't give prospects near enough good reason to go. Don't fall into that trap yourself.

Get your sales copy on your website, effectively communicating what it is you want to sell. **Here's the great thing** about the Internet: it's interactive. That's something a display ad can't be, something a letter can't be. You can tell your prospects what you need to tell them, and you can give them the ability to contact you — either through email, live online chat, or by telephone. Like I've mentioned before, make that contact method prominent, so they don't have to click through 15 pages to find out how to contact somebody. On the contrary — put your contact information on every single page. Try to spark interest and get your potential client on the phone with you or emailing you right then and there, and convert them from a prospect into a customer. You never know which page a person will land on when they're searching on the Internet to find you. It may not be your home page, or even your order page or contact page, and you don't know what pages they're going to print out to share with others.

Getting Technical

This brings up another important point. How many websites do you go to where the page isn't print-friendly? It's so easy to use a script and put a little picture of the printer up on the page, especially if you either have a long page of text or you have lots of pictures and graphics. A lot of people, these days, are smart enough to know that if they go to print that graphics-intensive web page, they're going to burn up a lot of toner in their cartridge. Most people have one of those small, not-too-expensive printers where the cartridges are twenty, thirty, or forty dollars a pop. **So if you have your pages "printer friendly," you're more apt to have somebody pass along that information.**

Here are a few technical tips you ought to know, courtesy of my friend and fellow marketer Ted Ciuba. This isn't really deep, technical stuff, but it's helpful — especially if you're like 95% of us, and you're creating your web pages using Microsoft FrontPage. There are a couple of other good programs, but FrontPage, which is basically an extension of Microsoft Word, is the standard.

What do you do when you want a modern look? You create

your very first table, one of those little design boxes that all web-savvy people use to create their Web pages. Make it 600 pixels wide; don't go with 80% or 90%, because what you're viewing on your monitor may not be what someone else sees when they look at theirs, and they may not get all the print that's on the page. A 600 pixel-wide table makes the page printer friendly.

I've talked about your address and other contact information: it needs to be on the bottom of every single page. You can do this by creating a template so you'll have a uniform look, color, and feel, along with the same header and footer on every page. At the bottom do an "include" — this is another Microsoft FrontPage function — and attach the "address.html" so it's part of your template. This is just a small document containing your address, and potentially a graphic or some other embellishment. Include your email address so that they can get to you that way, too. Now you've got everything working perfectly on your template. For every page on your website, you just open that up and put in whatever information you need to (say, the FAQ I referred to earlier), add your links, and save it with a different name. Certainly there's your sales page, and there may be an order fulfillment or thank-you page, along with various articles and that sort of stuff. Everything you do should be printer friendly, and have your full address and contact information on it.

Why the Internet Beats the Heck Out of Other Advertising Media

Taking advantage of Yellow Pages advertising is a great way to use a small advertising space to drive people to your website. Over $11 billion were spent on local Yellow Page advertising in 2005. In a medium-to-large sized city, a half-page Yellow Pages ad will run you $1,346 a month, on average. That's a lot of money. **But you can get a one-inch space in the same directory for about $110 a month. What if you take that $110 space and come up with a provocative headline, and you put your website** address on that ad? Then you can drive them to your website to get a report or some other valuable piece of information. For example, "Ten Things You Absolutely Must Know Before You Hire An Exterminator..."

If that ad is done in bold type and drives them to your website, chances are that you can make a great case in that extra space, give your prospects some valuable information, and build some obligation in their minds. By using a tiny ad as a lead generator for your website, you can save a ton of money.

One thing that's particularly in your favor when doing this is the fact that businesses believe in the traditional Yellow Page ad; they've been raised with the Yellow Pages. When it comes time to build their business, they think, "Well, we have to have an ad in the Yellow Pages." **But things are evolving now,** and more people are saying, "Look, now we have to be on the Web." It's gaining widespread recognition with businesses out there. Just like a Yellow Pages ad, you have to have a website — and once you build it, you have to know how to market it.

Do this experiment: open an Internet search engine and type in "lead generation." In a few tenths of a second, you'll get hundreds of thousands of hits. That just gives you an idea of the power of the Internet, of the amount of resources right there at your fingertips. **The major challenge is finding what works for *you*. Because the Internet is so huge, so densely packed with information, sometimes you can't see the trees because of the forest. You absolutely need to spend the time to figure out what works best for you.** You've got to separate yourself from all the other websites, because the reality of too much information out there is a major obstacle hindering all online marketers. Just because there's such a huge forest of it, it makes it more and more difficult for you to compete. **You really do have to think competitively and try to simplify things as much as possible, so that people can more easily find the benefits they're looking for in your product or service.**

Separating Yourself from the Herd

Here's a mantra you'll want to take to heart when building your website, or having someone build one for you: "Sometimes, less is more." Too many business owners have all these grandiose ideas about what they want on a site: Flash presentations, blinking letters, scrolling marquis, the works. **Well, with a website, less really *is* more most of the time, simply because it's much less confusing. You want to get your message out there to sell your product or service; you don't want that message to get clouded in the minutia of a bunch of bells and whistles.** Even more important is the fact that if you overburden your site with Flash (especially a Flash intro), most search engines won't pick you up. They don't like that Flash, and they have filters that won't allow them to grab a Flash intro.

Along those same lines, even if you have a calm, attractive site, you need to know how to get the most out of it. Ted Ciuba tells the story of a time when he obtained a client at an event in Hong Kong, who immediately asked Ted to look at his website. As it turned out, his site was very attractive: it had plenty of photos, and used pleasing colors — and that was it, as far as trying to do anything. It had not one single offer on it! The client happened to be a photographer, and even when he showed some studies that he'd

---

done, it was just like going into an art gallery. When I go into an art gallery, I don't expect to be sold... or do I? I notice that every time I go into an art gallery or a museum, there happens to be a little shop at the side. Now, I know that the in-gallery selling is low-key, and that's okay. But this guy didn't even take that normal real-life instance of having a shop associated with his art gallery; he just had an art gallery. And by golly, you'll never believe this! He told Ted that he'd averaged it out, and month-to-month he was making between one and four dollars a day. **He was actually trying to tell Ted that marketing on the Internet was very difficult — and he knew that was true because he had experience.**

Well, it was a really quick fix. Even in person, Ted could tell there was something was seriously wrong; and when Ted looked at his website, he realized what it was. The site did have eye appeal, but it had nothing on it that related to sales or Direct-Response Marketing at all. There was no mention of the simplest thing: "We do business in Hong Kong. We'll come out and make you happy about your wedding or corporate meeting." All this guy had were displays, with the tiniest bit of corporate info: you know, "We've been doing such and such for this many years…"

If you're in the game to make money, you need to realize that *everything* is secondary to the sale. It's marketing that makes the money, and it's the other departments that deliver the product. Sure, it's the bean counters who keep everything right for the legislators and the banking crowd, but it's the sales force that makes the money. **Your website should always be designed with the concept in mind that you're a salesperson, first and foremost. That should be your dominant purpose if you intend to make money from the Internet.**

This person Ted was telling me about probably **fell victim to a website salesman.** It's just like the newspaper guy stumbling through the front door of your business, wanting to sell you advertising space in their paper. They're in business to sell the space; that's all. **They're not in business to design an ad that's**

going to sell products. The thing about so many of these websites is that they look great and they're impressive visually, but realistically, their only purpose for existing is to get the website sold to the person who's buying it. They're not designed to sell products; they don't have an offer. They're just flashy, glitzy-looking things that really don't do anything. The bad part about that is when somebody spends hundreds (or God forbid, thousands) of dollars to pay somebody to design one of these sites. They do what this person tells them to do with it, despite the fact that, in most cases, the seller and designer doesn't have a background in marketing, does not know how to sell products, and couldn't sell their way out of a paper bag. **So the poor site owner pays all this money and gets this website, and puts it on the Internet, and nothing happens.** This causes them to say, "Well, the Internet doesn't work. It's so difficult. I can't sell on the Internet. That was a total bomb."

This happens way too often. Most people — even business people — just don't realize that the purpose of a website is to sell. It's also to educate, but education is part of the sales process. You need to make people specific offers, and you need to have special sales. **True, some businesses do tend to lend themselves more to Internet marketing than others; there are a few exceptions that can't profit as greatly as most others. The problem is, most people think** *they're* **the exception. They want to take the lazy way out and say, "Oh, well, that's no good for my business."**

Earlier, I discussed using your website in conjunction with your Yellow Page advertising. This works best if you offer something concrete, something specific. There's no better way to qualify a prospect, and really separate the serious ones from the ones who aren't, than to offer a detailed special report like, "Ten Things That You Must Know Right Now, Today, Before You Hire Anybody To Come In Your House And Spray For Bugs," or whatever the case may be. The only person who would go to your website, and then leave their name and email address so that the report can be downloaded to them, is somebody who's truly serious

A new twist on the 80/20 rule:

- Focus your attention on the activities that rank in the top 20% in terms of importance — and you'll get an 80% return on your investment!

- Are you all spread out — or are you focused on the few key areas that can bring you the maximum sum of money?

about that particular subject. Who else is going to spend their time to get something like that? **You constantly have to look for ways, as you go out there with your marketing, to find out who the best prospects are, and how you can separate them out even as you're separating yourself out from the herd. I can't think of a better way than to use specialized reports as a way of both educating and qualifying your prospects.**

Act Globally, Think Locally

Here's something that I've mentioned before and want to repeat. A lot of people think about the Internet as solely a global medium — say you're trying to sell something to somebody in Bangkok, and you're in Florida. If you're using the bound, book format Yellow Pages, on the other hand, you're only targeting people in your local region. But you can do that with the Internet, too! **It's simple to use the Internet to locally drive people in.** Not only can you use pay-per-click advertising on Google to funnel in people from your local area, you can also set up specific keywords that apply specifically to your local area or state. If people want to go to the movie, or they want to get pizza, they type in "Pizza +Belleview" or "Movies +Houston." And don't forget that you're going to show up on the local online Yellow Pages on sites like Google and Yahoo. A lot of places only have their phone number and address there, but if you pay a little extra, they'll throw in your website URL, too. Some venues might even do it for free. **That way, people who go onto their Internet Yellow Pages to find a certain type of business will see yours listed there, big as life, and they can click that link and go to your website and read the whole story.** There are other inexpensive techniques you can use to drive local business to your site; for example, you can mail a postcard with your URL out to everybody in a specific zip code. You can flyer doors. **Think creatively!**

The point is, you really can market locally using the global Internet. **You don't have to think about the Internet as something big and scary** and then say to yourself, "Oh, but I'm a carpet cleaning business and I can only clean within a ten-mile radius." You can still use the Internet by employing the methods about which I've just talked, driving people onto the site to give them more detail or more added value.

Let the Experts Do Their Jobs

Making money with any business is all about generating more profits — that's it. Here's something about which I feel very strongly, though it doesn't apply to everyone. Although the software is making it easier for all of us to build websites and Web pages — even for people like me, who are very non-technical — I'm a firm believer that you should get it done by an expert who does it for a living. I honestly feel that **it's in your best interest to let somebody else build all that stuff. You should spend your time coming up with the ideas, the concepts, the special offers, the special reports, the different things that you're wanting to do promotional-wise. Let these other technical people — in some cases, acne-faced high school kids who are looking for a little bit of Saturday night date money — go out there and do the technical work for you.**

Be careful about that, though. Sometimes you can get a great person who's good at designing websites and making things look and feel really nice on your website — but they don't know anything about marketing. The best combination, of course, is a Web designer who has a strong Direct-Response Marketing background. That's when you're going to get the product that will really work for your business. In fact, I think I'll take that even a little bit further, and say that **you absolutely *must* have someone designing your website who has a marketing and sales-oriented background.**

No offense to real estate agents — because that's not who this comment is intended for — but I've seen so many realtor websites that are just a shrine to the realtor. They show their pictures, say they've done this or that, or they've won these awards. There's no offer, no mention of how quickly they can sell your house, no assurances of how much more money they can get for your house than any of the other agents can, no details about their service. Where's the benefit to the person reading the darn website? Now, that's fine if that's what the purpose of your site is going to be. If you want a shrine to yourself or a monument to your company, go ahead. But if your intent is to sell products — as much of them as possible, as quickly as possible, for the highest profit possible — you absolutely must have someone designing that website who knows what they're doing in terms of marketing.

In short, you need to **stick with what you do best, and defer to the experts.** Let somebody else do that busywork that you *can* do, but at which you're not an expert. When you build a web page, you have certain responsibilities to yourself, and you can get caught up in the forest-for-the-trees syndrome trying to do your own thing. You need to find somebody who's going to design a site for you, you tell them what you want, let them create what you need, and then you're not sitting around nitpicking on all these little things that are going to waste time and, eventually, waste money. You need to do the things that you really enjoy doing, and let somebody else get those other things out of your hair — even if you can do them yourself.

Your strength should always be in marketing. You may not

FREE GIFT! Go to www.RuthlessMarketing.com/freegift

be able to write your own sales letters — though you should work on that — but you should always be an ace marketer. That said, you can't give up responsibility for the rest. You can't just go to someone and say, "Create a website, and create the graphics to go with it." They're going to come back to you and ask you for direction, and you're going to have to follow-up and make sure their work's suitable. It's not like you can delegate and forget; you can delegate all the work, but you need to keep track of everything. **It's like being the General in the Army. The General is responsible for the success or failure of the campaign of his troops. But guess what? He's not the one out there sweating and getting shot at!** He's not the one going out there digging trenches, or giving it to the enemy, and he's surely not the one who has to stand up and take a hill. Those are bad positions to be in. He's the one who's arranging things and telling people to do things, and in the end, he's the one responsible for what happens. He's the one who's moving the pieces, like a chess master. **You've got to realize that you've got to have other people be your soldiers, because you're the General; you've got other, higher-value things to do. At the same time, all the reports come back to you, just as all the decisions emanate from you.**

That's the difference between delegation and avocation. Avocation is where you just throw your hands up in the air and say, "Ah, screw it! You just take care of everything for me!" Delegation is where you think things through very clearly, and then pick personnel who can take care of each of the components of your strategy. I think something else is very important... and maybe this doesn't have anything to do with Internet marketing, but I think it does. **It's absolutely vital to put together a group of people for whom you have a lot of respect, who really know a lot about selling and know a lot about marketing and business, and to just to throw ideas out to those people once in a while. You see, oftentimes we can be so close to the forest and not see through the trees.**

Recently I was talking with my good friend, Randy Charach,

Think bigger! Focus on hitting the ball over the fence — and you can take your time walking around the bases!

- Sometimes you must keep your eyes to the stars and dream big dreams.

- Other times, you must keep your head down and charge forward like a raging bull!

and he threw out one simple idea — and all of a sudden a problem I'd been thinking about for amost six weeks clicked into place. I'd been wracking my brain, been going back and forth with all these different ideas — and then Randy says something and BOOM! There it was — one little idea from one person put everything together in my head. While that may not necessarily have any direct connection Web marketing, it's still **vital to have people who are part of your brain trust, people with whom you can brainstorm.**

I'm not talking about employees here, although a good set of employees is important too. In this case, I'm talking about the **people in your professional circle — friends and associates, other business people.** The people in your professional circle will have different strengths, and may be able to look over something for you as a favor — a reciprocal deal, whatever you work out with them. Sure, you can hire a Web designer who knows marketing, for an all-in-one solution — but you still want to know they're doing what they should be doing. So what you do is get somebody you know and trust in your circle of friends and say, "You know what? You're really good with Web design, and I'm really good with copy. If you need my help to look over some copy or whatever, I'm happy to do it. I'm hiring this Web designer. He comes highly recommended, but doesn't really know much about marketing. Can you help direct with the marketing?"

It's great to be able to take a combination of resources and mix and match and put them together this way. You do what you're strong at and what you want to delegate time to, find people who are really good at what they're doing, and have them help and look over shoulders of others. The more people you have that you can relate to that have a variety of strengths in a similar field of interest, the better. **Like I've said before, sometimes we get so close to our projects that we can't see the forest for the trees.** Our brains are steaming, we're dreaming about it, we're thinking about it, we're pacing the floor trying to figure it out — and it's just too close, and we can't see the obvious right in front of our noses.

One thing about which I want to caution you: if you go to somebody to help you with something like this, be sure that they know what they're doing, that they've got experience, that they've solved these kinds of problems before, that they're already doing what you're wanting to do. The worst thing you can do is ask the dogcatcher or the guy next door what they think about some aspect of your website. You're not likely to get worthwhile input. They might say something like, "Oh, that's interesting," or, "Oh, that's well written." Well that's great and all, but that's not the kind of input you need. When I ask people to look at my copy, I'm looking for a very specific response from them. If they say, "Oh, wow, can I get this?" That's it! That's the only response for which I'm looking. I know I'm probably on the right track, if it can invoke desire in anybody — including associates who are in the business and looking at it from a different perspective. Until I get that reaction, I feel that I don't have a sales letter that's as winning as it could be.

What you should *really* care about is how many sales your website is going to make for you, and you need an expert for that. In the end, though, it's the customer who gives you the correct feedback, because they're the one voting with their credit card.

But on the Other Hand…

While you should be able to delegate everything that you don't do best, **you should always try to know at least a little bit about every part of your business.** You're the General of your business, which means you should have *general* knowledge of every single aspect. You may not be the best person to do web design, but you should definitely know how to do it in a pinch. Take classes if you have to; they're usually not that expensive, especially if you take them at a local college. My friend Randy Charach recently finished a class in keyboarding (which is what they call typing these days). Before he took the class he was a very fast typist, but he was a hunt-and-pecker: hunched over, staring down at the keyboard, watching his fingers. While he doesn't do much of his own writing anymore — he's more likely to record things and have them transcribed, which is a great time-saver — he decided he didn't want to be a hunt-and-pecker anymore. It's slower and more awkward than it needs to be, and it's not the most ergonomic way of typing. Not only that, you can't always record or use voice transcription software in every situation: it's a little awkward, for example, when you're flying. People are really suspicious of stuff like that these days, and it's kind of annoying anyway. In cases like that, you end up typing if you want to get anything done. Plus, it's handy to be able to type when sending the odd email or when chatting online. That's why Randy's going out of the way to do this. It's fun and rewarding, and it's another phase in his quest to become familiar with every element of his business.

Here's another reason why you should know a little something about everything you do. I'll use an automotive analogy here. Suppose you go to five different places to check on what it's going to cost to fix a certain gadget on your car. You're likely to get anything from, "Oh, here, let me just screw this in and that's fine. No problem. No charge," to, "Well, that's going to be $1,800.00, and there's this and that wrong too," and everything in-between. It helps, then, to understand the basics of what's going on with your car. That doesn't mean you need to be able to do a tune-up; **but if** you have a little bit of knowledge, you're in more of a power position, in more control, and you're not going to get ripped off. It's not hard to get a little knowledge on any subject, especially with the Internet out there. Once you've armed yourself, your BS detectors will start going off if you're talking to somebody who's acting like they know what they're talking about, but don't.

Let me reiterate that you *must* be sure that you deal with somebody who knows what they're doing. Well, how do you *know* that they know what they're doing? There are a couple of acid tests you want to use — and one of them is, you should look and see how successful they really are. The best one is to have a little bit of knowledge about the subject, so you can see right through them in the first place.

Consulting the Ultimate Expert: the Customer

In previous chapters — especially Chapter Four — **I've emphasized how important it is to test your offers and marketing copy. This is especially true of websites, and the fact is, it's a lot easier than with most marketing media, because you can keep tweaking it as long as you need to.** Sometimes you're too close to the project, and you just have to let your prospects tell you whether or not what you've come up with is worth a darn. Let's say you've spent two months developing a website and the follow-up campaign linked to it. First you should have your friends and valued customers test out the site. It's kind of like beta testing with computer programs and videogames. Instead of just saying, "Hey, look at my website," talk to your beta testers and say something like, "Go ahead and sign up for my newsletter, and see what you think about the different emails that are coming to you from my auto-responder." Depending on how intricate your website gets and the kind of feedback they return to you, you may spend a month writing follow-up emails, and a lot more time getting the sales copy on your website just right.

At that point you might throw up your hands and say, "Hallelujah, I'm done!" and may not want to not look at it again. But keep an eye on the input, and have your testers go through the whole thing. Then, after you've relaxed and you can actually look at it through a fresh set of eyes, go back through it all yourself, using what they said to you, and retool your website and make it better.

Then it's time for the ultimate testers: the users. Make sure you include a link where they can report errors, typos, and other problems, so that you can improve your site. That's one of the good things about a website: **unlike a print ad, which you can't change once it's published, you can always make a website better.** It's always a work in progress, and every time you get a good piece of criticism, you can change it, especially if you have a working knowledge of how to do web design. You don't have to, though; you can always just pick up the phone, call your web designer, and say, "Hey, on this page on my website, I want the copy to read this way instead of that way," and change stuff and make it better. **That's what's beautiful about the Internet: not only is it a two-way method of communication, but it's also adaptable, and it just gets better if you pay attention to it. You don't have to do anything fancy at any particular time; you can just change a few words or a number on the fly or test out a new price.**

Hiring Web Help

Depending on what you need done and how often changes need to be made, you can either have someone who sits next to you making those changes (assuming you don't do it yourself), or you can hire someone for a one-time job. Randy Charach was recently telling me about something he had on Elance.com — an online freelancer site — where he was getting quotes from $100 to about $750. He's experienced at doing web design, of course; it was just something he wanted to outsource at that moment. So he was looking at it and thinking. "I know what this takes, what needs to be done." In a situation like that, you don't necessarily take the cheapest bid — but you shouldn't be scared of the most expensive one, either. Randy didn't pick the most expensive, because it wasn't a $750 job.

In a similar vein, Mike Lamb had a client who wanted to create this little piece of software. Mike told him about Elance and Rent-A-Coder, and they found a guy in Portugal. A week later they paid him $50 to do the program; he created it, and he did the graphics, too. Mike told his client to spiff him another $50 because of what the coder did. He went out of his way, and down the road he may come back and say, "Is there any other work I can do for you?" Or, he'll be around to make changes from time to time. And that's exactly what happened. **You can always find people to do good work, if you're willing to do a little shopping.**

It's all just a matter of your priorities, resources and talents, and how much you're willing to learn and do yourself, when it comes to harnessing the immense power of the Internet. If you're an HTML whiz and you can whip out a site without it getting in the way of your real business — creating and marketing your products — then go for it. Otherwise, keep it as a sideline. It's like any other aspect of your business. Sure, you can take the day's checks out to the bank every once in a while, if you want to get some fresh air or banter with the tellers; but mostly, you let someone else do that while you create. It's the same with harnessing the

Internet. You don't have to write the code or create that order form or shopping cart — let your employee do that, whether they're a long-term employee or a freelancer. Your job is to direct them and give them input and get your hands dirty when necessary.

Here's the bottom line: even if you don't have the time, the resources, the confidence in yourself, the desire to learn anything at all — even if you don't want to do any of it, or you don't want to know how any of it is done — **you can make money by utilizing other people's talents.** There are many thousands of people out there doing this right now. As long as you have even a little bit of money to hire other people, or something to trade, you can do this — you can even do it with *no* money. You could go out, not know anything, make every mistake in the world, and get people to do some stuff, and not even have a website or a computer. You could get somebody to post something on eBay for you, and you could start making money. On the other end of the scale, you can be the person who does all of the work — everything — and make a ton of money and still not work all that hard. Or, you can do anything in-between. That's the beautiful part in what I'm talking about here.

My friend Don Bice is one of those rare individuals who does it all himself: he writes his own copy, does his own artwork, he does the layouts, he puts up the websites, he even installs the CGI scripts. **He does all that because he enjoys it. He'll be the first to admit that it may not be the best use of his time, but he does it because he really enjoys it: if you took those things out of the business, it would rob him of much of his pleasure.** Now, here's the kicker. A few years back, Don didn't even know what HTML or a CGI script was. He was comfortable with a computer, but he didn't know anything about it; and it was an adventure for him to learn. It was very satisfying to him as a creative outlet. If it's that way for you and you have the time to spend on it, that's fine. Otherwise, farm things out; get help whenever you can. Even Don does this on occasion.

A Four-Part Plan for Succeeding on the Internet

I'm going to end this chapter with a special **four-part plan that can turn the Internet into a goldmine for you.** I'll lay out the four points here before going into more detail on each.

1. **Get straight on the purpose of what you're doing on the Internet, and what your business *really* is.** That business is *to sell*. On the Internet, it's easy and cost-effective to make sales repeatedly, or to offer a number of different opportunities to your prospect at the same time. It's not just a one-time, "we're downtown, it's Saturday night and I'm going to say today or never" kind of deal. On the Internet you can develop long-lasting, profitable relationships.

2. I'm going to lobby for my particular favorite on the Internet — information marketing. I'll run through some of the vast advantages that you have when you go that route.

3. I'm going to hit on some aspects of product creation. If you don't have a product to sell, you don't have anything with which you can make money. That's *the* basis of marketing, and that's a big stumbling point for a lot of people. I can tell you how to solve that one — how to do it technically and, of course, give you ideas.

4. This is where everything comes together: it's all about traffic and marketing.

Number One

Even though you might get occasional traffic, if you're not working properly to build your conversions, just getting traffic to hit your website isn't where it's at. If you have a lousy page and

Direct-Response
marketing takes a
day to learn and a
lifetime to master!

- There are so
  many variables —
  and few
  absolutes. The
  master is
  continually
  learning,
  growing,
  adapting, and
  taking his or her
  skills to a higher
  level.

- It's better to know
  some of the
  questions than all
  of the answers.

you get 1,000 or 10,000 visitors, and you get no sales, or you get no people who opted into your mailing list — then you have *nothing*. Most people think they want sales, but I've already told you that most websites aren't even oriented to sell. First of all, you've got to realize that you're in the *sales* business. **You need to understand that your website is a Direct-Response Marketing piece. The easiest thing to compare it to is a sales letter.** Now, when someone receives, reads, and consumes a sales letter, at the end of that sales letter there's only one thing you can do, and that's buy the product. Of course, the reality is that you can *not* buy the product. You can also put it off and think about it later. But the purpose is to sell the product. Create your website with that in mind.

Now, you have another tremendous advantage with a website, knowing what you know — and nobody can really buck this, because it's a phenomenon. And that is that **80% of all sales are made on the fifth contact or thereafter — meaning, the majority of people who hit your website will *not* buy.** Well, we already know this: from mail, display advertising, from the Internet. **You'll have a vastly larger number of people who *do not* buy than those who do.** In fact, depending on the price of your product and the market of the product (since different markets have different rules of thumb) you can say that from 1-2% is a normal average for buyers.

That means 98-99% of the people are *not* buyers. Well, surprise! If 80% of sales are done on the fifth or thereafter contact, of course most of the people who buy won't buy on that first approach. What you have to do is use the Internet, and use its abilities **to do what you can to make further conversions.** For example, say you've got a simple e-commerce program like autopilotriches.com that will allow you to create a subscriber opt-in box. You can put something on your Web page that says, "Hey, if you'd like to know the seven biggest scams that private investigators want to foist on you when you're looking to hire them, click here for your FREE Report." Now, if someone went to your PI site, that could be important to them. On the other hand, if you have a carpet cleaning site, they're going to want to know, "WARNING: Don't hire any carpet cleaner until you read this Special Report that reveals the 12 questions you need to ask."

I could go on with a million different examples, but you get the point. You can provide an e-course, too. Now, **all these things cost next to nothing, because you put them up with auto-responders, which means that once they opt-in, it's easy.** And as for opt-in, everybody's seen it. "Hey, if you'd like to know how to cook these 12 delicious Chinese recipes with noodles, leave your name and email address here," and you get 'em. It's called an auto-responder because once they opt in, the response goes out automatically. You wrote a few emails, you wrote a brief study course, and now they go out automatically because **your database is working for you.** You're not even having to write the auto-responder emails: they'll be personalized and automatic. You put in a little piece of code and that code just simply says, in brackets, [First Name], and then every time an email goes out to someone who subscribes, it says, "Dear John...", "Dear Sandy...", or "Dear Bubba..." You get it.

Oh, and by the way, if your prospects come to your website through a search engine — and **90-95% of all Internet ventures begin with a search** — they didn't type in your subject matter by accident, now did they? If you're selling videos on Latin dancing, they didn't type that in because they're really interested in buying a LearJet. They typed in your search terms because they're interested in the salsa and tango. **They're self-qualified, but you still have to work to convert them.**

Of course, one of the most basic things — and this is true in every advertising medium — is getting a good headline. But should you just sit there and try to devise the best one you can? No. Most people say you should write a hundred. As a matter of fact, autopilotriches.com has an ad tracker where you can test three different headlines at the same time. By the time you've got 500,000 hits to your website, you're going to clearly see which one's the winner, especially in conversions. Which headline is making you the most money, and how much is it making you per click? You need to be aware of all these things in order to do good, solid scientific marketing.

So get a headline. Test it. Test your price. **You can do a lot of other things that have been proven beyond any shadow of a doubt to increase your conversions**: audio, for example. I've got friends who have done some audio tests and racked up the sales; they saw a 300% sales increase just from putting up audio. This isn't even difficult. You've seen it before; it goes something like this: "Hi, this is T. J. Rohleder. Welcome to my website about self-hypnosis. If you've ever wanted to quit smoking, this is where you can learn it." Video works now too; we had a few years when it didn't, but now it's easy to do. **Recognize that you're a multi-dimensional marketer, and use every trick you can find to draw people in and convert them.**

Then there are testimonials. You can increase the pull and conversion of your websites by double, just by adding a few testimonials when they weren't there before. This is basic, right? People just rave about your product and service, and that gets other people to buy. But whatever you do, don't invent your testimonials out of thin air! Not only is that unethical, if anyone ever finds out, you've absolutely ruined your credibility.

My friend Ted Ciuba has a website up where they make most of their conversions after people have gone to order. This was the result of a brainstorm on Ted's part. One day he was watching TV, and he saw an infomercial for something he was interested in. He said to himself, "Hey, that's pretty good! They're throwing in 12 CDs, they're throwing in this, that, and the other... and it's all for $39.00. I'm going to order it." So he went and made that phone call — and, lo and behold, before he hung up, he'd spent $189.00. Now wait a minute — how did that happen? It's like this. **The advertisers knew that if they'd hit the pitch on TV with $189.00, nobody would have called. So what did they do? They made the pitch at $39.00, and then when people called, they tried to convert them to a higher-priced sale, and so they made more money. It was easy. They were already dealing with interested people who had already raised their hands to show some interest — people they got in at a low level of resistance. Now, though, with a little bit of copy — in this case, a telephone script — they were able to more than quadruple their original sale.**

So Ted thought, "Can we take this to the Internet?" Next thing you know, he's put up a product priced for $27.00. Well, what happened? They had a little button that said, "Click here to order." Of course, they had all their ducks in a row: they had their copy ready, along with all their persuasive stuff — audio, graphics, headlines. And then the prospect clicked to order, and it was a drop-kick. The site didn't immediately go to the shopping cart, you see. It went to a Web page that said, "CONGRATULATIONS! You have decided to order product "X" at $27.00. Would you like this product for free? Well, here's what you need to do…" And then the site talked about an upgrade offer, which gave the buyer a whole lot more value.

Eighty-five percent of the income from this site comes in from the back-end sale that *wasn't even on the front web page*. **That initial offer was a decoy, just as it is with a lot of these infomercials. Sure, it's real enough, but you use it mostly to get committed buyers in at a low price, and then you have the** opportunity to persuade them to buy more. Try that. It's a great way of increasing the revenue from your website.** You don't want to just increase the conversion off the front page, although you do want to max that out. When you can upgrade them, when you can upsell them, when you can increase the money that you can pull out of them — that's important. **Remember, people don't type in keywords to start an Internet search if they're not interested. That holds double-true if they click through to order and you have an upsell.**

Recognize that the purpose of your website is to sell. Do it strategically. Work to increase your conversions, because that's how you increase the revenue from your website.

Number Two

When it comes to Internet marketing, I recommend that you invest in information marketing. There are a lot of reasons, but the best one is that information is different than a widget. Now, a widget could be a refrigerator, an auto part, or a piece of artwork. An information product would be something more on the lines of, "Where To Get The Best Value When You're Looking To Buy A Refrigerator." Or it could be "25 Different Art Markets That You Never Knew Existed, Where Not Only Can You Buy And Enjoy... But That You Can Resell To

Your Friends." This is *information* that you sell. Why do I recommend that? Because you create this stuff yourself. What does it take you to write an eBook of 34 pages? What does it take you to sit down with a microphone and record for an hour and twenty minutes, or to get a few other people to help you record for an hour and twenty minutes? What does it take for you to sit in front of a video camera you already own? You have a fireplace burning in the background and you create an information product. It costs you literally nothing — unlike the refrigerator, unlike the artwork.

Since your marketing cost can be very, very low on the Internet, you're back to the situation where you're not paying much to market, and you're not paying much (if anything) to sell. Did you ever notice that when you deliver an eBook, you deliver it and you've still got it? **You can sell the same eBook (because it's just a file) over and over again.** But you can only sell the same refrigerator or the same widget once, so you've got to go and invest money again to get another one. That's the reason why I recommend information marketing, because when you get it right, **the margins are outrageous!**

Number Three

Number Three is closely related to Number Two. I want to quickly run through a couple of ideas about product creation. I've already referred to all of them. **Product creation can be as simple as getting yourself in front of a microphone, and you've got a product; or calling somebody else on the telephone, and you've got a product because you interview them. Getting a few people to get together to talk about a subject in which they're interested, that they have expertise, guided by you or in freeform, is a product.** There are all kinds of tele-conference service places that will do this for you. They'll even record it and send you the CD. You can put it up online and you've got a product. That's easy. Now, do you think you have to write that eBook? Well, you may want to. But how about that interview that you just recorded? Why don't you just send that off to a transcriptionist? Go to Elance.com, hire a transcriptionist, and have them transcribe it. It comes back, you clean it up a little bit, put the title on it, and maybe put some sub-headers in it because you can't expect them to be creative. But you *can* expect them to be accurate, and they'll break it up into paragraphs — and then you've got an eBook or a manual.

Of course, video is basically the same thing. Most people just put together a brief little outline on a topic; something like a PowerPoint presentation, so that you've got something to guide you. Then you just throw on your tie (if you're so inclined) or just sit there in your t-shirt and cut-offs (if that's how you like to do it), and you talk to the video camera. Click every now and then, and now you've got variety between the talking head and the PowerPoint — not to mention an outline to follow.

This is literally how simple it can be. You want a high-value product? Combine the audio, the eBook, and the video, or combine more than one interview. This is information marketing. This is product creation. It's as simple as it could be.

Number Four

Finally — and this is where the rubber hits the road — start marketing aggressively. Right now, there are a number of different ways to market. They're actually countless. But I'm going to hit on five of them that are all very effective, that you can start making money with immediately, and make what we term "residual income" because that's when you put a sales force out there continuing to work for you. Here they are:

- Google Ad Words
- Affiliate Programs
- Viral Marketing
- Article writing strategies
- Joint Ventures

First off, go to Google.com and start buying Google Ad Words. **You can get traffic to your website, starting in fifteen minutes — really less, but that's how long it takes to start slow.** Remember: you have to contrast this with what it takes to get a magazine ad or even a newspaper ad going. A newspaper ad may take several days, at the minimum. A magazine ad could take several months. Traffic can come in minutes from Google.com. **You only pay when people click through your ad, and they're coming because they're interested.**

When they get there, you've got to have an Affiliate Program available. Why? That's the way it is on the Internet! People know they don't have to do the hard work. They don't have to write the copy. They don't have to create the product. All they have to do, if they have any customers of their own, is join your Affiliate Program, and they can still make 40, 50, 60% on your product (depending on what you set the affiliate commissions on), and they're geared to do that — just like the public at large is now geared to go the Internet to look for information or whatever they want. The way they once used the Yellow Pages exclusively, or the newspaper, now they're using the Internet. Well, marketers are geared to go to the Affiliate Programs. Put an Affiliate Program on your website. If you want more information on how an Affiliate Program works, just go to www.wikipedia.com and type in "Affiliate Marketing." Within 20 minutes, you'll have all the answers you need!

Viral marketing is the most effective tool you can use. It can really let you harness the power of the Internet. What is that power? That power is that it's free, and it's huge! There are hundreds of millions of people on the Internet. Have you ever thought about allowing everybody who wants to to take something of yours for FREE, and to include a brandable link back to you with their Affiliate link to that higher priced product? Which would you rather have — a few hundred sales off your own efforts, or thousand and thousands of sales where you have to give a commission to other people because they spread your name and your fame and multiplied your income? They build your list for you. That's the power of viral marketing.

Another strategy that works very, very well is writing articles in your area of expertise — no matter what that is. Where do you post them? Do a search for article directories and article submission. Any website that's selling anything related to your business or niche is a prospect. Put it up there. **These things last a long time. They establish you as an authority. You're not selling in these articles, so it becomes even more prominent that you're an authority, and you include your resource box — which is information of who you are, and where you can be contacted. Because they last so long, it's a constant, ever-growing source of income.**

Joint Ventures are crucial, and they're a lot like Affiliate Programs. Basically, here's how I separate it in my mind when thinking about a Joint Venture versus an Affiliate Program: they both use the same mechanism, which is the Affiliate Program. But a Joint Venture is like when I get on the phone with someone I know and I say, "Hey, I'm going to offer this program. I think it would be good for your list. I'd give you this percentage... would you market to your list?" In other words, use your personal contacts. It may include even a better profit split than normal. With an Affiliate Program, on the other hand, you just have a link on your Web page: "Click here and earn money now."

The five things I've just encapsulated here are really working like gangbusters today. They're going to help you make money whether you're marketing information products, which happens to be my sweetheart, or any product in the world.

This is the End...

This has been an extremely detailed, lengthy chapter, and I think that this is a good place to wrap it up. Because the Internet is the perfect medium for marketing to massive numbers of people, I believe you need to make yourself an expert in the field. You should be a jack-of-all-trades, but willing to delegate responsibilities to other people in and out of your organization — in fact, I recommend delegating, or you'll soon find yourself snowed under. I think you should **go back and read this chapter several times, again and again, to take all the specifics I've given you and find ways to incorporate them with everything else you'll read in this program.** Admittedly, I've covered a lot of distance in this chapter. But I promise you, if you'll find ways to implement what I've taught you here, your business will dramatically improve.

MARKETING SECRET #56

Direct-mail can give you tremendous leverage. Every direct-marketing piece is a salesman in an envelope! It's out there working for you — without your direct effort!

- Sending out 1,000 direct-mail letters to your best customers is like sending out a sales force of 1,000 of the best salespeople!

SECRET EIGHT:

Using Information Products to Build Your Business

No matter how thorough a business education you receive, no matter where you receive it, it's likely to have some significant gaps when it comes to the realities of modern marketing. There are certain methods and ideas that either don't fit the prevailing theories or that most academics find distasteful, so they don't bother teaching them — a practice that can hamstring their students when they get out into the real world. The purpose of this chapter is to redress at least one aspect of that problem. **I'm going to teach you about a specific marketing method that's too often ignored, even by entrepreneurs who should know better.** You're unlikely to hear most of this information from any other source — in fact, I know of only a few people in the world who are teaching this information, because it's totally non-traditional.

What I'm going to teach you in this chapter is how to use informational products to build your business. In particular, **I'm going to outline, in detail, what informational products can do to help to establish your credibility and expertise.** Some of the ideas here are very subjective — that is, different things will strike you at different times — so I recommend that you study this chapter repeatedly to get the maximum benefit.

An Introduction to Information Products

In his book *Future Shock*, Alvin Toffler wrote, "Our society is moving so quickly today that our children have to learn twice as much in half the time just to keep up." The old saying, "Knowledge is power," is as true now as it was a hundred years ago, and it'll be even more true a century from now. Today, it's possible to transfer information freely and easily in a variety of formats, and the number of formats will only increase as our technology advances. Therefore, any business that offers knowledge as one of its products or perks has an advantage. This works for any business at all — offline, online, whatever industry you're in. You couldn't throw an example at me where I wouldn't be able to come up with an informational product that would be useful in attracting customers to that business.

I'm very excited about informational product marketing, because it gives normal business owners the ability to turn themselves into experts and draw in additional business in a very short time. It's not that difficult to accomplish, because it's very easy to self-publish nowadays; in fact, most people can create information products they could never have come up with just five or ten years ago. Self-publishing, especially on the Internet, is also a great tool for getting through that wall of skepticism we, as marketers, constantly face. **People are skeptical because they're not sure what company to go with; they're worried about getting ripped off, and so what they look for is an expert, a respected person in that niche in which they can put their trust.** By creating information products and putting yourself out there as that expert, you're able to take advantage of their skepticism. Plus, there's the added extra benefit of the cult of "celebrity," which I plan to discuss in more detail later. As a rule, celebrities fascinate us; so **if you're a published author, you've got a little hint of celebrity that attaches to you and gives you an extra edge over all your competition.**

Keep this little tidbit in mind when considering informational marketing: no matter what you know, or how little you know about it, somebody's going to know less. In fact, there's a good chance that there are enough people out there who know less than you do that you can make money by sharing your knowledge with them. Let me say that again. *No matter how little you know about something, there are people out there who know less than you, so you can make money by sharing your knowledge with them.* That's what information publishing is all about. Even if you just have an interesting hobby, in many cases your expertise can be turned into an information product that you can share with fellow enthusiasts — whether it's gardening, golf, bird watching, or skeet-shooting. Many information products start out in the minds of hobbyists who felt they had some valuable information they could share with other people.

It's easy to go on and on about information marketing. In my book (which this is, by the way!) information marketing should be an important aspect of any business — and why is that? Because **there's a lot of money out there that you'll leave sitting on the table if you don't have at least one information product in your moneymaking arsenal.** An information product is one key to dominate your marketing. If you work it correctly, it's an extension of yourself. It's like a solid salesman who goes around screaming to the world, "Hey, this guy knows what he's doing! His stuff works! Listen to him!" **Like a good Direct-Mail Marketing piece, your information product is working for you 24 hours a day, seven days a week. You pay for it once, and it just keeps right on working. Your business never closes.**

Another thing an information product can do for you as a business owner is this: it can credentialize you. **It can help you dominate the marketplace by making your clientele begin to view you as an expert** — the person who comes to their mind when they think of a problem that needs to be solved, or a desire that needs to be fulfilled. If you think about it — and I've made this point before — marketing is all about separating yourself from your competitors, those people who are after the same customers and the same *money* that you're after. You want to make yourself unique, set yourself apart in the eyes of the public. There's no better way to do that than by publishing your own informational products. **It's a way of gaining credibility in the marketplace by making yourself an expert, and it's a way for you to let the best** prospects and customers raise their hands and say, "Yes, I'm interested in what you have to offer."

Remember my best friend who has a pest control business? She has a report she gives away in her Yellow Page ad titled, "10 Things You Must Know Before You Hire A Pest Control Professional." That's just one of her lead-generation informational products. It helps educate the customers about her company, and lets them know what sets her apart in the marketplace. She needs this, because her prices are more expensive than all the other rip-off artists in her business. She has over a hundred competitors just in a small town like Wichita, Kansas, and she charges more money than they do, and so she has to prove to the customers that spending more money with her company is going to make all the difference in the world. To do that takes an effective presentation, and that's basically what her informational product is. **It's a way of making herself shine brighter than all the others, by telling her full sales story, establishing herself as an expert, and becoming somebody with whom people _want_ to do business. When they're in the market for whatever it is that you're selling, they're going to come straight to you.**

Putting Informational Products to Work in Your Business

Before you throw down this book in disgust and say, "I can't *do* informational products in my business," do me a favor: read on for a while, because I'm going to discuss a variety of different types of businesses and give you some ideas about informational products that you can put in place right away. **One of the challenges I see with small businesses is that people don't understand the kinds of informational products they could be providing to their customers.** They haven't seen any in their market, so they don't have a template to follow. In this section, I'm hoping to fix that for you.

The majority of the informational products I'm going to go over are for lead generation purposes. This works just as well for a small business as it does for a large multinational corporation. As I've mentioned previously, my friend Kris Solie-Johnson, of the American Institute of Small Business, works with a lot of hobby stores — knitting stores, bead stores, and like. Now, if you've got a hobby store, it's going to be focused on one niche market — and there are lots of different things you can do to expand your business through informational products.

Let's take a closer look at the knitting store example. Kris recently told me about a meeting she had with the woman who owns her favorite knitting store; that woman had decided to publish a book about knitting scarves and hats. It's full of different patterns that she's modified from other people, and others that she's created on her own. You can do that with any kind of business: beads, model cars, even Boy Scout Pinewood Derby cars. With hobby stores, no matter what the hobby is, you have the opportunity to start with something small. **It doesn't even have to be a huge book — just a useful, informational booklet that makes you into an expert on your subject.**

Let's talk about dry cleaners. If you own a dry-cleaning establishment and can't quite figure out how to get started with an informational product, start with a tips list. Maybe you can include tips on how to get certain stains out, or on how to preserve your clothes. Suppose you include tips on how to treat your furs going into the winter or summer. Where do you store them? How should you store them? How do you get certain types of stains out? How do you preserve a wedding dress? **What are all the different tips lists that you could give to people?** Maybe they're in the form of a little booklet that's only $2.00 per copy. As you start producing more and more of those, you end up with a product line that's profitable. A $2.00 booklet can add to your business — not in a huge way, of course, but if you start doing more and more of these things and get used to information products, you'll start thinking bigger.

Or maybe you own a bookstore. Set up a few Top Ten lists. What are the top ten moneymaking books? Science fiction books? Submarine books? You can publish a variety of different information products about the top books in a particular field, or maybe the best movies ever made from novels. Think about those Top Ten lists as a way to get started in the informational field.

Let's talk about attorneys. **There are many, many topics that we, as consumers, have no desire to learn about — and yet we know we *should* know about them.** For instance: estates, wills, and health directives. There are all these different documents we know we should have. What's a trust? What would it be used for? A lawyer might have a great opportunity to put together a handy information product on this type of thing; maybe it's a "CD of the Month," an information product with audio presentations about the various topics. **For some folks, it's easier to listen than to read the material, so a CD is a good idea.** If an attorney did something like this, he'd separate himself from every other attorney out there just by giving people information in a better format than what's currently available.

Let's move on to clothing stores. Let's say you own a men's-wear store. Maybe you target teens. What are the fashion trends? What related events that are going on in your vicinity? How do you get into fashion merchandising? One of the hottest careers for high school students — especially young women — is getting into the fashion industry. What are some ways that you can get into the fashion industry? They're not going to learn that from the Gap, or Banana Republic, or any of the other big chains. They're going to learn that from you. **If you can continue to feed them information, they're going to keep coming to your store and buying things.**

How about flower shops? You've got "Flowers of the Month." You've got tips on how to cut flowers, and how to create an arrangement. How do you arrange them in a vase? What type of vase should you use? What size of vase? What colors go together? What types of flowers? There are many, many different things that can be done with flowers. How do you care for your flowers? Is a crushed aspirin the best? Does it matter if it's Bufferin? What are the tips that you could offer people?

Accountants have the same issues as attorneys. There are lots of topics that accountants can cover in which they specialize; if the information is currently available at all, it's usually in a hard-to-read format that's difficult to understand. If only you could pop in a CD in your car when you're driving and have someone tell you about tax tips... then you would know to call that accountant to get more information. **You see, all this information you're giving away or selling for next to nothing is really a lead generation tool.** How do you get more of these CDs to people who want to learn more? You could use a Yellow Pages ad, just like my best friend does. **Even when you're sitting next to every other accountant in the Yellow Pages, you can set it up so that your ad is offering something — for free — that actually helps people come back to you.** Here's a good title: "How You Can Cut Your Taxes By 25% And Let The I.R.S. Pay For Your Next Vacation." Everyone will want that report!

Let's talk about professional organizers. These are the people who come into your small business or your home and help you get organized. If you're an organizer, you could put together a variety of different tips booklets that you could hand out to help folks organize smaller spaces — for instance, your junk drawer. Could you come up with a small book that you could sell or give away on how to organize a junk drawer? Or how about a CD titled "7 Secrets For Turning Your Junk Into Cash?"

Insurance agents have many of the same issues as accountants and attorneys, and they have access to plenty of specialized expertise they can use to create an audio product. Of course, they could produce written products, too, but audio isn't currently something that's consistently being delivered to consumers. **If you buck that trend and hand out an audio product, it's going to set you apart from all the other insurance agents out there, guaranteed.**

Getting It Started

Here's a quick rundown of the typical process for creating an information product. First, start out with a Top Ten list: say, the top ten stains and how to get rid of them; the top ten movies out there and what they mean, or how many people are seeing them in your local area; the top ten western novels of all time. Try Hot Trends lists, too. Lists like these are easy to create. Once you have them, compile them into a booklet. **Booklets can, over time, be formed into a larger book:** for example, the knitting store owner started out with one pattern, and then she had two patterns, and then she had ten patterns, and then twenty... and then

FREE GIFT! Go to www.RuthlessMarketing.com/freegift

she put them together in a book that she could sell to her clients. Audio is another great way to sell or give away information products. There's some inexpensive recording software on the Internet where you can record right into your computer, and then cut audio CDs right there, if you're burning them in low quantities. These are all very easy things that you can do, and how you mix and match them **is only limited by the imagination.**

But here's the danger, once again: everybody thinks their own business is unique. I can imagine the skeptic reading this and thinking to themselves, "Oh yeah, right! That won't work for my business." Well, maybe it won't. The examples given in the last few pages are specific examples for specific businesses. **Here's the real secret: what do *your* customers want? How can you help your customers get more of what they want? I think the more you're focused on why your customers buy the kinds of products and services you sell, the more intimate that knowledge is from an emotional place inside of you. The more you know that intuitively, the more you're going to be able to develop perfectly-matched info products for them.**

Here's something that Levi's jeans did a few years ago: they created an information product, a game, because they wanted to target the teen market. They had teenagers go to a website and play that game. But the code for the game was attached to the label on the Levi's jeans, and *that* drew them into the store. So really, if you use these information products as lead generators in whatever business you are, they're going to bring people into your business, into your store — and that, in turn, is going to make your profits skyrocket.

The Perfect Salesman

Never, never forget this simple but awesome fact: an information product is a perfect salesman in disguise. Here's an example. You put out an ad, and your ad has a little teaser about one of these little information products with a great little title, and it gets people excited about it... and you get them to call an 800-number to request that information. When the information comes, it can deliver exactly those things you've promised, but it can also deliver the perfect sales message, the perfect argument as to why that consumer needs to come in and buy your product in order to fulfill their needs. **This is a situation where you can invest a little time into developing one information product that can then make hundreds or even thousands of sales for you — just by using the same information over and over again.** The greatest thing about an information product is, it doesn't forget to say this or that about your product, like a flesh-and-blood salesman might, and it doesn't forget the product benefits — what I call "the reasons to believe in your business." It doesn't have "mind-hiccups" and "senior moments," the way a salesman on the phone does, so it's a much more efficient and effective way to communicate with your client base.

Some of the best informational products are designed to do just one thing: and that is, sell more. They're not really designed to educate people *per se,* **as much as they are to educate people on why they should be giving you money. It's sort of the appearance of "how to" without the "how to."** What you're doing is disguising it. But the specific design, of course, has to do with what people do when they get done with it. If you've done it right, after they're done reading or listening to the product, now they *want* to come to you and they *want* to do business with you, **because your disguised sales message that's buried within the product itself is calling them to action.**

Helping Them Help Themselves

Often, people will seek you out hoping you'll be able to do whatever they need done — but they still want to think about doing it themselves. If you're in a business where you can offer people information that shows them how to do something for themselves, then you can do that — but in a way that's complicated, so a lot of people won't want to tackle it. But hey, there you are, and that's

FREE GIFT! Go to www.RuthlessMarketing.com/freegift

why you're there: you're the expert in that field. You're the one who can do it for them, so they don't have to mess with it. Even if they *can* do it, they might still hire it out. **The prospect reads up on the subject (courtesy of you), so they feel like they did their homework — yet it may be more efficient to let you do it for them.** This works with most people, because you're getting your information into the hands of people who then can choose to do business with you.

Now, some people reading this section may be thinking, "But I don't want to tell them what I do, because then they're looking behind the screen and they'll know my secrets. They'll know what I'm doing, and they may think they can do it themselves." Well, sure. But if you write it so that you outline every single step of what you do in excruciating detail, then what you're doing is training them that this is a complicated process indeed. You're telling them that it takes an expert to do it right, and so they need to hire that expert: you.

Once upon a time, a highly respected advertiser literally took all his secrets, and put it into a single book that's hundreds of pages long. My buddy Eric Bechtold talked to him once and I said, "I can't believe you're giving away all your secrets, because normally you'd charge $15,000 or $20,000 to write a sales letter — and with this book you're telling people exactly how you do it, and you're only charging a couple of hundred bucks." The advertiser said, **"Yes, and that's the best marketing tool I have. Because once somebody gets this thick package in the mail, and they realize they have to read through everything to even come *close* to writing a sales letter like me, they'd much rather fork out $20,000 to have me do it." You see how that works? You have the ability to lay out your entire system and all your secrets, and *still* generate a lot of business.**

The plain truth is that people like to feel as if they've made an educated choice rather than having been sold on something. The idea's really to educate them to make you their choice. It's good for both of you, really. They understand more of the factors they need to consider in making a choice, and luckily, your business is there to provide those things to them. But **they want to feel they came to you — they want to feel they have the power in the relationship.** No one likes to be chased around! Just as dogs can sense fear, some people can sense weakness. No one wants to do business with somebody who's begging them. **Too many businesspeople are selling themselves too cheaply, practically begging for business rather than creating a marketing position where people are beating a path to their door and standing in line to give them money. That's what an information product can do.** It can establish you as an expert, make you the one everybody else is following — the one that all the other competitors look to and are trying to emulate.

Instant Expert, Just Add Words

We're living in the Age of Self-Publishing, and what a great time it is for a marketer to be alive. With the Internet and the various types of software that's available, publishing isn't something at which you have to work hard anymore. In the old days you had to write a book, find a publisher, and then have it published. That was the only way to reach a large audience. **But nowadays, with the freedom of the Internet, you can get a message out there** and set yourself up as an expert, and give your clients and prospects the information they need in order to establish that credibility in their minds. This will situate you to do business with them over and over again — because everybody wants to work with experts. If you do a good job of presenting yourself and a good job of adding value and giving more to your clients, they'll give you more in return, and that's what it's all about.

Self-publishing is flat-out one of the best ways to become an expert. If you think about it, you've probably seen this tactic used numerous times: say there's someone on TV who says, "My name is John Smith, the author of *How To Become The... blah, blah, blah*." A lot of people throw the titles of their books around as a credibility-builder, because it's almost like being a doctor or a scientist. **You instantly get more credibility if you're a published author — and the great thing is, you can publish yourself with ease.** You can sit down, hammer out a book in a couple of days on any given topic, and suddenly be a published author and an expert in that individual field. I think that's really amazing!

One of the things I want to make sure you understand is that it's rewarding to be able to write a book like that — or even a little information pamphlet — because it's going to be doing two things for you. Not only is it going to give you an information product you can use to build rapport with your clientele and prospects, it's going to give you a better understanding of how your business works. This kind of research puts you more in the mindset of your consumer, which is something that's always profitable. And this is a great way to market inexpensively, if you're watching your budget and want to add some flair to your marketing campaign.

One way you can do this effectively is to **create information products for your website, distributing them electronically so you don't have to deal with physically printing brochures or booklets and mailing them out.** One example you'll see on a lot of websites these days (and we've touched on this briefly) is the eZine — a little newsletter you deliver through email. People can subscribe to it on your website. In all the ads and materials you're putting out there to market your company, you drive people to your website and say, "Hey, thanks for visiting my website! Make sure you sign up to get this free informational eZine, which will give you hot tips and tricks on how to save money or solve problems with your business" — or whatever it may be with which you're dealing. If you put enough of these little eZines out there — if you write a few of these every week, or one a week or one a month, even, and you do it for a year or so — then you've got enough material to compile into a book, which can then be sold or given to your customers as a gift or added-value incentive. The key here is that by taking the time to understand your business and put together proven information — information that you know is going to benefit your clients — you're going to be adding value to their experience, and opening up a line of communication that you otherwise would never have had access to.

One of the keys to making money in any business is what's called "branding." You put yourself in front of your consumer so often that when they think about any given product, your name or your product's name is the first thing that pops into their mind. It's also called "top-of-mind awareness." But one of the things you need to understand is that in order to get yourself positioned properly in your consumer's mind, you've got to be in front of them over and over again. By doing an eZine on your website — driving people to your website and getting them to sign up — you can do this. **If you don't feel that a website is a good medium for your business, you can always print up an offline newsletter and send it out in place of an email, and get people interacting with your business that way.** If you give them something that's going to help them, it's not only going to establish credibility in the minds of your consumer, but it's also going to get them interacting with your business on an ongoing basis — which is going to translate into more money in your pockets. That's an easy way to think about information marketing: all you're doing is giving your consumer more of a reason to work with you, and adding value to that process.

Like I said earlier — all the recent technological advances make it easier now to self-publish than ever before. And the neat thing is, **it's actually fun to create informational products! It's enjoyable to share your expertise with people and reach out and try to show them all the ways you can help them. It can become very altruistic.** Then too, when you meet these people face-to-face, you've got a little bit of a celebrity thing going. People value you a great deal; it still shocks me when people come up to me and want me to sign my name in some little booklet that was designed to sell them stuff! It's good for the ego, but it's also good for business.

That's a type of branding in and of itself. My friend Michael Penland recently pointed out to me the example of Lillian Vernon, a leader in the catalog industry. Her catalog became her information product, because it solved problems through the products she offered. Recently a company did an opinion poll nationwide, and according to that poll, more than 39 million Americans now recognize the name *Lillian Vernon*. Think about that. More than 39 million consumers recognize that name, because she's branded herself through her information product — her sales catalog. In that sales catalog she always includes a personal letter and a photo of herself. A small business owner can do that as well, by simply connecting a picture of themselves and information about themselves with every information product they put out into the marketplace.

One of the reasons this works is pretty simple: **there are so few experts in most marketplaces.** Most companies are doing the same thing every other company is doing: they're not separating themselves out from the crowd. **Nobody seems to want to stick their neck out and claim that they're an expert, and I think people are afraid to.** Maybe it's because they've been conditioned all throughout their childhoods not to show off or make themselves out as experts... I don't know. It's hard to say what is it that stops most people from standing up on their soapbox and saying, "Hey, I'm the professional. I'm the one you should call. Forget all my

A two-step marketing principle:

- Make BIG promises in the front-end sales letter...

- Then scramble to fill these BIG promises in the back-end package!

competitors because they don't know jack compared to me!" Maybe it's just insecurity: they haven't been validated. It probably goes back to some Freudian psychology where they think deep down that they're worthless, or were told they were worthless when they were younger. But the fact is — and I can't emphasize this enough — **you only have to know a little bit more than the other people in the room to be the expert.**

So really, most people qualify to stand up and say, "Hey, listen to me. I have something to share." **Once you take that and put it on paper, that's what validates it — in most peoples' minds, anyway! It's like the old joke, "If it's in the newspaper, it must be true." There's a grain of truth in that joke: you gain instant credibility by putting your words in print.** You could be saying the same thing on paper as you have while preaching from your soapbox, but when you put it in print you multiply your credibility by a thousand. So becoming an authority, an expert, a guru, somebody people look up to — it's really like most things in life and in business. It's not that hard to stand out and become great, it's just that so few people are willing to do the things it takes to become the expert, even though it's not that hard. Most people just don't have the confidence to do it.

And here's another thing: **if you tell enough people the same message again**

and again, it becomes reality, in a sense. That's what we, as marketers, have to do, within the bounds of both good taste and legality: we have to think like a consumer thinks. What do they want to hear? What do they want to know? There's always something a business owner knows that his marketplace doesn't know. If you can tell them consistently again and again, "Look, I'm the expert. Here's how this works; here's what will benefit you." Then, in time, that effort (whether it's in an information product or verbally) is going to etch that fact into their minds. Eventually, when they think about that, they think about you.

Want to know something else? I think a lot of people don't realize how many people actually want to hear what someone else has to say, especially if that someone is selling something or is in a service industry. **People want to know as much as they can about those with whom they're working.** Of course, you can take this full circle. **If you tell them every little detail of what you do, all the little stuff that you take for granted and just do unconsciously, this makes it even more complicated in the consumer's mind.** They're thinking, "Wow! That's just one more thing they do that I didn't understand or that I didn't even realize they were doing for me, and that makes me more excited about working with this person." Do that in your information product without over-killing it, and you'll make money. Obviously, you don't want to write a novel as a sales piece, but you want to make sure that everything is clear and concise. Often, things you never thought would be sales points are the ones that are pushing people over the edge and getting them to work with you. **Don't be scared to go out there and toot your own horn. Tell people what you do for them, and they'll be more willing to let you do it.**

Making Yourself Indispensable

One thing you need to do to succeed is to gain customers for life; this gives you a heckuva competitive advantage. It's like my friend with the pest control business: she charges premium rates for services others offer for less, but people keep coming back, and they're getting good value. Why? Because **my friend has made her business indispensable to the client, which may be the most important thing any business can do. Any business can do this by providing customers with the information they need, in a form they want, and making it easily available to them.** Whether the information is the product itself or a supplement to the business, that's a great way to become indispensable, and that should be your ultimate goal.

A lot of businesspeople never consider this option. It's not just that they don't think about information products; they've never thought of themselves as experts, or believed that they could become indispensable to the customer. What they know is that this is the product they sell, this is the business they're in, and this is how they do it — because this is how everyone else has done it for 50 or 100 years. So they're really focused on being more like an employee of their business than anything else. They have their business; they know the product they sell; they may even sell it extremely well, but this is just the routine, the way they do things. **They've never thought about it from another angle. They've never considered the dynamic of stepping back, putting yourself in the expert position, and then being able to use that expertise to make yourself more money in your business** — and then to also teach other people and become an information marketer who is indispensable to their customers.

My colleague Jeff Gardner recently told me about a lady who runs a website design firm. It has 26 employees, and it's growing by leaps and bounds. She often goes out into the local community and gives seminar speeches; she does a great job, and gets a lot of business from it. When Jeff spoke to her, he said, "Well, that's great! But you're limited in terms of how many people you can reach, both in the amount of time you have to do your seminars, and by the number of people in your local area. What you could do is **take that seminar speech and record it, and you'd have a simple audio CD that's no longer limited to your local area. You can offer it, free of charge, on your website and send it out** nationally and internationally. Or, you can have it transcribed and create a print product."

When you're thinking about information products, I don't want you to think, "I've got to be a big-name author like Stephen King, and it's got to be perfect." That's not true! **An information product that makes you an indispensable expert can be as simple as talking into a tape recorder about what you do in your business — what it is that makes you an expert (which you are). Have somebody transcribe it for you and BOOM!** You've got an instant information product without having to be some English professor who knows all the grammar rules inside and out. People don't really care about that. What they care about is that you come across as an expert who knows what you're talking about — a person has an information product that's going to help them in some way.

It's natural to be a little hesitant, a little afraid, when going into something like this — but don't let it stop you from taking that step. **So what if you're afraid of what your competitors are going to say about you? Who gives a damn about them? You *want* your competitors to talk about you! You want them to be a little bit intimidated by you — or at least to respect you. You shouldn't care less about what any of your competitors say, because you want to be the company they follow!**

I can't help but think about the first seminar my wife Eileen and I ever gave, on September 22, 1990. Russ von Hoelscher hosted it for us. We'd been in the business about two and a half years at that time. The seminar was dirt-cheap — we sold it for something like $195. We had a couple of hundred people there, and we were too afraid to get up in front of the group and just say hello. It's funny, now that I think about it. We were so insecure, so afraid of our own shadows, that we stood in the back and wouldn't even get up to the front of the stage just to wave at people. But all throughout the seminar, people kept coming up to us and talking to us. Finally, by the end of that day we were loose, we were relaxed, we were focused on the customers, we had groups of people around us, and we were animated and passionate and excited. One thing leads to another! **Confidence is something that builds on itself. You don't just come out of your mother's womb with total confidence, do you? I think it's something you have to develop. The more you focus on the customer... that's what really gives you confidence. If your heart's in the right place and you're focused on trying to help people, then you're going to want to crank out as many informational products as you can.** You're going to want to have workshops and seminars and consulting sessions and tele-seminars. You're going to want to produce guerilla videos and all kinds of different ways to educate your customers on all the reasons why they should be giving you more and more of their money.

If you don't have the time, patience, or ability to create your own information products, there's no shame in having someone else create them for you. There are plenty of freelancers out there who'll jump at the chance. Randy Charach recently told me that although he likes to do his own writing, he doesn't like to do his own editing anymore. So now he takes all his rough thoughts — whether text or voice recording — and hands them over to a freelancer to transcribe or edit. He's not looking for people to change or correct his grammar, just to take out some of the major

FREE GIFT! Go to www.RuthlessMarketing.com/freegift

problems he makes when putting these things down — the spelling mistakes and such — and to make it easier to read, in a formatting sense. So that's how he does it, and that's how a lot of us do it, because we don't have any problems creating information.

A very popular place I've talked about before is Elance.com. You can go to Elance, hire a ghostwriter, and have somebody write something for you: say, a 30-page eBook about how to sell something. Just remember this: nobody knows your business better than you. If you're going have somebody else put something together for you, let them interview you. If you hire somebody who's going to do all the work putting together a Ten Tips lead generator or an eZine report or whatever, don't be lazy. Don't expect that person to know more than you, because they won't. Provide them with all the information they need: don't make them do all the work, because they won't do as good a job.

Then Again, Good Enough is Good Enough

At M.O.R.E., Inc., we've produced hundreds of informational products. **As long as they're focused on really helping people and giving them the information we know can help them benefit, then who really cares if it's not done perfectly? Nobody, that's who!** We've been doing this since 1988, and it *works*. You know, I only see some of my family members once or twice a year — but every time they see me, they just scratch their heads and say, "How in the world can you charge four or five thousand dollars for people to come listen to you at a seminar?" They think we're ripping people off or something! The blunt truth is, some people charge a whole lot more than four or five thousand dollars: one guy in L.A. charges $25,000. Why charge so much? Because you're offering people information that can do a lot for them, **information that has a super-high perceived value. It doesn't matter what it costs *you*.** In many cases — and I know this is going to sound unbelievable, but it's absolutely true — we've sold products for a couple of thousand dollars that cost us less than $100 to actually produce! When you tell most people that, they'll say, "Oh man, you really *are* doing something illegal." So we don't tell people that. They just don't understand the business.

What matters isn't what it costs you to put the information on the DVD or on the audiocassette tapes or into print. What matters is the perception of its value, and what the information can actually do if it's used properly. Sometimes, just one idea is all it takes to make a few million dollars. If you can clearly express that one idea, so that somebody can really grasp it and use it to make lots of money, who gives a damn if it only cost you a couple of bucks to create and put in that pamphlet or on a CD? If it can make people millions of dollars, then it's worth the thousands of dollars we charge for it.

This brings up another great point, and that's the incredible value of information products in the business sense. You have the ability to create simple products — whether you completely create the product, or just mold it into its finished form — that have an incredible level of mark-up. **You can literally create something that costs $100 to produce and then sell it for a couple thousand dollars, legally — and have people buy it in droves, because they're getting good value from it.** Not only can you sell them the product itself, you can sell them resell rights and make them pay even more money for it. That value is intrinsic; it's built right in.

Now, think about this. First of all, an informational piece doesn't really cost you much to put it together in the first place, because you have the expertise — and if you don't, you can get it cheaply. Experts are willing to submit to interviews with you to get their names out there, and may even provide pre-written articles you can use to boost their branding through viral marketing. It's really a fairly simple thing to do.

Second, you can make a tremendous amount of money on an information product. A jeweler is really happy when he can get double his money on a piece of jewelry. In retail it's called *keystoning* — where you take something and double the price in

FREE GIFT! Go to www.RuthlessMarketing.com/freegift

your mark-up. Our way is *better* than keystoning. We usually multiply by ten — and that's just in selling the information. If you're selling resell rights, you charge even more. **Information is super-valuable whatever form it takes.** Look at it this way: if somebody were to offer you the winning numbers to a lottery, and you knew you'd be the only one with that winning ticket, and it's a million-dollar lottery... are you going to care if they present it to you on a nice plaque or on the back of a napkin? No way! **It's the *information* that's valuable, not the presentation.** That information is worth a million dollars. What are you willing to pay for it? Are you going to look at the value of a napkin that only costs a penny, or is this worth a million dollars to you? The answer is clear.

Consider this very information product you're reading now. It started out as a weekly session in which a total of fourteen people participated over the course of thirteen weeks. Each of us in the session had a minimum of ten years of experience. If you assume each of us made only $100,000 each year (and this is really just to make my math better), you have $100,000 times ten years times the fourteen of us. You get about $14 million of information, which seems extreme! But even half that, or a quarter of that, is a lot of information — and we learned it the hard way. You, the reader, don't have to go through the ten or twenty years of struggle trying to get there. We've run up your experience and told you exactly what you can do to make money; it's up to you to make good use of that information. **How much you paid for this book, and how much I had to pay to have it printed, is irrelevant compared to the information that you're getting.**

Another way to look at it is that if you were to hire any one of us for an hour for consulting, we'd want at least two or three grand, because each of us knows that that's how much we can make in our own businesses when we're working. It's an easy calculation. So sure, the value is there, though some people find that difficult to comprehend. You've got to ensure that they're viewing the situation the right way — that they're not comparing apples to oranges. While it may be true that someone can buy a 250-page book that costs just $20, while you're selling a $1,000 product that costs you $100 to produce, they're not necessarily the same thing. We're in the business of teaching people how to sell dimes for dollars — how to make more money. So when you're selling information on how to make more money, you can charge much more money for that information; the market dictates this. You're not going to buy a book or an informational product on knitting and spend as much money as you are on one that tells you how to make more money in your knitting business, for example. One would be "how to," and one would be "how to make money." It's the same general subject, but the product teaching you how to make more money at it is more valuable. People will desire it more, and they'll pay more for it because they're going to get more money back — as long as the information is good, and they use it right.

Star Power

Earlier in the chapter I wrote about the value of being recognized as an expert in your field, and **there's one type of expert to which people really pay attention: the celebrity expert. People look up to celebrities.** It's more than just putting yourself out there as an expert who knows everything about a particular business. People want to be close to celebrities, and **this gives you power if you can create your own celebrity by proclaiming** yourself an expert and creating an associated information product. After all, it's printed or recorded — there's the proof of your expertise. If the information is valuable, fame may just follow.

Here's why. When you create any type of an information product, people seem to believe that some magical being has to come down and hit you on the head with a wand and say, "You're an expert," or, "You're an author," before you're special. That's not the way it is! If you've written an information product for your business, then BAM! You're the author of such and such. Let's say you have parents in another state and they respect you, and your aunt and uncle in another state respect you too; hey, you're a nationally respected author! You can actually start using that in your marketing. **People don't actually have to read your book or report for you to be able to benefit from the fact that you have information products out there.** Yes, that can be an additional income stream, and a great way to generate prospects for your business. But just by saying, "I'm a nationally recognized author of this book on carpet cleaning..." — or law or bookselling or whatever — can really help you out in your marketing.

Recently, Jeff Gardner was looking for an attorney to look over some business documents, and he went online and found a lady who was the author of a law book. Jeff thought, "I want her!" Obviously, she's a bit more of a celebrity than everybody else in the field. He didn't have to read the book; he just took her word for it. What I've also discovered is, when you start doing that, you're going to be getting some attention from outside media sources. Jeff did the same thing in acquiring a financial advisor: he looked for someone well known locally — in this case, he chose a guy who was on TV, giving financial advice every Wednesday. Jeff set up a meeting with him, and now he's Jeff's financial advisor. Is he better than everybody else? Probably not; but hey, he's on TV, and his business is growing by leaps and bounds. Not because he gets 200% returns, and not because he's the top expert out there; he probably offers the same financial advice everybody else does. Still, he has that little bit of celebrity that interests people.

How do you get that little bit extra? By putting yourself out there as an expert and letting the media know it. Once you do that, people are going to be pushing your competitors aside to get to you. It's just another way of setting yourself apart from your competition, like I've been telling you over and over throughout this book, so that you're the big winner in whatever business you are. **By creating information products and even going to the next level and becoming a celebrity, you're going to be the Number One name in a person's mind whenever they're looking for any type of product or service in whatever business you are.** That will transfer into a lot of dollars in your pocket.

I know I may seem to be harping on this, but as you read this chapter, I hope you can overcome the notion that your information product has to be perfect — that it has to be a book that looks like all the books in a bookstore. In fact, in most cases the worst thing you can do is to create a product that looks like a book in a bookstore. **Putting it in a format that's too slick may be a turnoff for some people. What you really want to do is create an information product that looks like it was made just for the person you want to attract. It's the quality of the ideas you need to express, not the packaging,** that's important. And then there's the fact that your information products will get better over a period of time. Don't get too bogged down by analysis paralysis: realize that perfection comes with experience, just as confidence is developed over a period of time.

My friend Eric Bechtold produces a lot of information products, just like me. He told me about something that I think all my marketer friends have experienced, and it's something I want you to experience. He talks to people on the telephone fairly often because he's selling these high-dollar packages, and many times, in order to get the largest conversion rate, he actually has to do some phone selling. **People call him and say, "Oh my God! I can't believe I'm talking to you!" That's the kind of thing we want all of our prospects to say.**

If you think about it, most marketers are a little scared, or even ashamed, about having something to sell. But when you get somebody on the line who's like, "Oh my gosh! I'm so excited to talk to you, and I can't believe you're taking the time to actually tell me more about this!" — well, that's just an open invitation. They're saying, "Hey, sell me what it is you have. I'm already excited about it." **Because you automatically have that star value in their eyes, you can almost walk on water with your prospects if you do it right.** You don't feel intimidated at all when you're talking to somebody who views you as a celebrity. You're up on a pedestal already, so all you have to do is just come down to Earth with them, talk them through whatever it is you want them to do, and it's the easiest sale you'll ever make. **You've basically already won them over, and they're excited about what it is you have to say before you even open your mouth.**

With any other way, I think you're spending too much of your own time selling the person on the fact that they want to be sold. But **if they come to you and they're already excited and ready to buy, all you're doing then is putting your arm around their shoulders and answering their last-minute questions — and closing sales right and left.** I know this sounds amazing if you've never done it before, but Jeff brags about closing ten to twelve sales for more than $5,000 in one day, just sitting on the phone taking phone calls — only talking to the people who are calling him. Few people in any industry can make that claim.

This works because with information products, you establish yourself as an expert. Pretty soon you're no longer a salesman: you're a celebrity who just happens to be selling something on the side. Society really places celebrities on a pedestal, whether they deserve it or not — actors, athletes, even authors. If you can add "author" to your list of credentials — your title — you're right up there with, and maybe even *above*, more commonly-known people like doctors or teachers. All of a sudden you're a celebrity, and why not capitalize on it? Most importantly, do your best to live up to it so it isn't just a nominal title — so there's a good reason for it,

How do you become a powerful result-getting copywriter (or anything else you most want to be)? The answer lies in this quote from Stephen King:

- "When I talk about my craft, I emphasize one point over and over again: You don't have to be great to do a thing, you just have to not get tired of trying to be good at it."

because you're sharing great information, you're sharing it generously, and you're sharing it in an ethical and proper manner.

Make That One Simple Change

As I wrap up this chapter, I want to re-emphasize the value of adding at least one information product to your business arsenal. As I mentioned earlier, many business people don't think about this dynamic. They know what they do; they know what they sell. They come into their workplace, their office, their storefront every day, and they know customers will come in and they're going to sell products — and that's all they do. They've never thought about the dynamic of adding an information product to their income stream, but it can work wonders. **In some cases, you can even make more money selling information than you can by selling your everyday products and services.**

I've discussed the formats you can use to accomplish this: on audio you can deliver on cassette or CD, even MP3 and digital audio. You can also deliver your product in printed or electronic book forms, or through live and telephone seminars. **There are all kinds of ways to deliver information to people, and all kinds of angles you can take to do that** — and that's what I'm going to talk about in this section.

One way is to sell information to other people in your industry — other competitors, really. It's a common practice among successful information marketers. If there are other people in your business, they can probably learn something from you; you've probably got some secrets you could teach them, or some specialized information you could share with them. Maybe you've discovered a process that makes it easier to do a certain task, whatever that might be. Your information product could explain that process to them — how you do it, how you've learned to master this problem with which everybody else in your industry deals.

A side note here while I'm talking about dealing with your competitors. If you're a local business, keep in mind that you could sell this kind of information to people outside your immediate selling area without ever worrying about competition — as long as you keep it out of the hands of people in your local market. **You can sell information all day to people who sell the same kinds of products and services, all across the country and even around the world in some cases, and you'll never have to worry about them, because they're not your direct competitors.** They'll be happy to buy information from you if you've got a system to help them succeed in their communities. **As long as your local competitors don't get ahold of it, you're okay.**

If you don't want to sell your expertise to people in your own business, you can also profit from selling information to your customers. I've already talked a lot about this, but here are a few more good examples: if you're a photographer, you could sell a book or a report on how to take professional-looking photographs at home without a studio-quality camera. The product is simple: all it does is show people how to take decent photos at home. Naturally, people will trust a professional more than their Uncle Bob. Along with that information, you could talk about why they should still choose a professional photographer for their more important photographic needs, showing them the things you do specifically and the benefits of employing you.

If you have a lawn and garden business, you could create an information product called, "How to Have the Best Yard in Your Neighborhood Within 30 Days Without Busting Your Budget." This could cover all kinds of tips for creating a nice-looking yard without spending a lot of money. Then, of course, you offer your own service: you'll come out and you'll look at their yard, and for a fee you'll customize something for them specifically.

Like I said earlier, a lot of people just want to feel like they've made a good decision. For them, **getting the information you make available makes them feel they're in control.** They've looked at what you have, they've realized that maybe they could do it themselves, but they still want to hire a professional: they still want to have someone else take care of it all for them. In giving them that kind of information, you're making them feel like they're making an educated decision. **This helps them choose to make a purchase rather than being sold, so that can put them in the position of power in the business relationship.**

Some businesses actually use information products as a front-end — as something they use to attract new customers, to attract new businesses. Here's an example of how a chiropractor might run an ad in the local paper that offers free information: "Attention back-pain sufferers! Here are five things your doctor won't tell you about your back pain." When a person requests the free information, you send it out and talk about your chiropractic approach to back pain and what makes that better, and all without the use of medicine. **You can use your information product as a way to get new customers to contact you and then talk about the benefits of doing business with you.** The free bonus also approach works wonders: **when someone orders something from you, you can give them that free bonus to helps separate you from your competition.**

So there it is. You can either choose to create information products for your competition, or you can sell or give away information to your customers and let them choose to do business

FREE GIFT! Go to www.RuthlessMarketing.com/freegift

with you. But the main thing is that you add information products to your marketing mix. Use them to create an additional income stream. Some highly successful information marketers have actually dropped their main businesses and gone to a 100% information marketing-based business, because of the success of this approach — so it's definitely something that can take you above and beyond what you've experienced to this point.

Will you make a few mistakes along the way? Of course you will, but they'll be worthwhile mistakes — because that's how you learn. **As a Nobel Prize winner once said, "An expert is someone who knows the worst mistakes that can be made in his field, and who also knows how to avoid them." Sometimes the best expert is someone who's failed, because he not only knows what to do, he also knows what *not* to do. So everybody out there qualifies as an expert.**

Some Final Words

Remember this: *you're an expert the day that you say you are*. People want to follow somebody who knows more than they do. They don't like to be chased around, either: they like to feel that they're coming to you. I wish I could just grab some business owners and shake them a little bit, because they simply ignore information products. There are so many benefits to publishing these products, and I hope you'll think deeply about some of the things I've shared with you in this chapter. When you get a prospect or the telephone or meet them face-to-face, they'll be grateful for the information they purchased or received from you absolutely free. They *know* you're the expert. You do have a little bit of celebrity status, at least to some degree. They don't have to be sold anymore; they're *already* sold. All you've got to do is finish the paperwork and agree on some terms of the sale. They're ready to buy, and that's the really great benefit.

Look around. There are people doing this right now in your local area, and there are plenty of people doing it in other industries. All this is quite common. So develop your awareness, **get involved with this powerful marketing method, and you'll gain a tremendously unfair advantage over all of your competitors.**

The very act of buying something satisfies many people's desires to gain the benefits of your product/service.

- It makes them feel good about themselves.

- It makes them "feel" they are doing something positive.

- The very act of buying satisfies them!

FREE GIFT! Go to www.RuthlessMarketing.com/freegift

SECRET NINE:

Work *On* Your Business, Not *In* It

In this chapter, I'm going to teach you how to work *on* your business rather than *in* it. That may seem like a minor semantic distinction, but it's actually what separates the big dogs from the whimpering puppies. Too many business owners out there — the puppies — spend all their time and energy working *in* their businesses. They come home tired and stressed-out every day; they have stomachaches; they're always short of money, they're always tired, their businesses don't work, and they end up going broke. **The smart people out there are the ones doing everything possible to focus all their time and energy on the things that bring their businesses the largest amounts of sales and profits, while delegating everything else.** That's what working *on* your business, rather than *in* it, means.

While it may not seem to be the case at first, working *on* your business rather than *in* it is where this whole outlook gets truly ruthless. Why? Because that tired guy I was talking about in the opening paragraph, the one who's always constantly struggling to keep up, and the bank isn't full, and he has no time, and he's exhausted... well, he's already got two strikes against him. How can he keep an eye on his competition? How can he have the time to devise the next neat trick to out-step and out-sell them?

The key is systemizing your business: building it into something that runs itself. **This frees your time up not only so you can continue to build your business, but so you can enjoy life too!** I love the ruthless aspect of waving at that poor schlep who's still working his business — working *in* it and not *on* it —

---

as you go by him in your yacht. That's ruthless, because you've got the free time and you've got the yacht — and he's got twelve more hours of work today, and an empty bank account. Working *on* your business instead of *in* your business involves the creation of a business that serves, rather than *consumes,* your life. **When you work *on* your business, you're creating systems and setting things up so that other people can do what needs to be done for you,** without going through major training and facing a steep learning curve — because everything has been documented properly.

You need to take everything that you do more than once, document it completely, and put into a manual. That way, you don't have to reinvent the wheel every time somebody new comes into a task. Even if you're an individual working alone, you still want to do this, so you don't have to go through the whole thought process and difficulties of re-creating everything from scratch. Take emails, for example. You can set up templates for emails, letters, even scripts. **Everything you do can be broken down and made easy for you or someone else to do. Then you can focus on the important things in your business and in your life.**

By doing this, you have several advantages. Not only can you put your focus on more important things, but if you ever want to sell your business, you now have a nice neat package that has more goodwill (in both the social and financial senses of the word) than it would have if you hadn't documented everything. Also, if you decide to expand, you can pay less for new employees, because you can get people with fewer skills. They may still be good, qualified people, but because everything is all laid out for them, you don't need to find people who are completely innovative. I like to look at McDonald's as an example. They have everything down to a "T"; that's why they're so uniform all over the world. You go and get a Big Mac, and in Japan it's the same as it is in Canada or anywhere throughout the U.S., because they have systems for everything they do. That lets them bring people in at a relatively low wage. They do put them through training, but they're training them based on pre-existing procedures and manuals. When you do this yourself, you'll tap into a great sense of freedom.

You see, your employees don't have to be entrepreneurs: that's your job. When you're working *on* your business rather than *in* it, **they're the craftsmen, the engineers, who help move your business forward under your guidance.** You've got totally different perspectives, totally different responsibilities, totally different objectives, totally different accomplishments in your lives. There's a difference between being a craftsman and being the business owner. You've got to run your business, and as a business owner you *must* have the ability to make a lot of money.

Over the years, **I've learned that working less in my business is the smartest thing I can do — and I happen to know that many of my fellow marketers feel the same way.** My friend and mentor, Russ von Hoelscher, usually works from about 10 AM to 4:30 PM at his office. People who don't know him too well say, "Gee, Russ, you've got the life of Riley! You work only five or six hours a day, five days a week." But you see, it's not true — because he works at least three hours a day at home. He's found that it's a good idea to get up early in the morning and get to work on the advertisements, letters, and issues that concern his business. Once he gets to the office, his employees bring him all the hassles. They're mostly little hassles, but there are always problems with which he has to deal himself — some of which do, admittedly, help to build his business. But **most of the real satisfying work to build his business, to make his business profitable, comes when he works at home. When he goes to the office, it's just to manage the business.**

A lot of businesspeople today manage their businesses *all the time*. They're no better than employees. They may be managers, but they're not really entrepreneurs. To be an entrepreneur you've got to get away from your business, or set aside time at your business when no one can disturb you while you work on those issues that will build your business.

One of the things that really motivates most business owners, at least initially, is the fact that they're tired of working for someone else. They see an entrepreneur out there who's living what they think is the life of Riley — but they don't understand exactly how they got from Point A to Point B. **Many people start a business with great intentions, but then they get mired down with the little stuff. They quickly find they're swimming in all this minutia that has to do with running their business.** They find it hard to disengage, often because they've been taught, "If you want something done right, you have to do it yourself." But that's not what an entrepreneur does — not for everything, anyway.

You have to realize that there's a whole different set of rules that you need to focus on as an entrepreneur, and having to deal with mundane tasks gobbles up the time you need to be focusing on your business. So how do you get out of that rut? How do you get out of being so immersed in your business and so caught up in small details and little hassles that you really don't have time to focus on your business? You'll find a lot of good tips on how to do that in the rest of this chapter.

That Good, Honest Cliché

It may sound like something that you'd see in a Dilbert cartoon, but the fact is that **working *on* your business and not** *in* **it is all about working smarter, not working harder.** Hey, it's a cliché because it's true! **One of my favorite quotes is from the great Abraham Lincoln, who once said, "If I had three hours to chop down a tree, I'd spend the first two sharpening my axe." That's what working smart is all about!** Think about it. If you had three hours to chop down a huge tree, and you sat there very calmly and quietly sharpening your axe for two of those hours, you'd get the tree chopped down with a lot less effort. Ultimately, that's what we're talking about.

Here's a list of nine basic things you can do to work smarter, *on* and not *in* your business.

1. **Focus on things that increase your sales and profits,** such as developing and promoting new products and services.

2. **Spend time planning, scheming, and plotting,** coming up with new kinds of strategies to do things better, and ways to serve your customers better.

3. **Work on a new promotion: either to attract new customers, or to re-attract old customers.**

4. **Think about your competition** — even do things to spy on them. Think about all the things your competitors are doing right, all the things they're doing wrong, and how you can do it better.

5. **Spend some time trying to deepen your understanding of your customers, and thinking about ways to strengthen and solidify your relationships with them.** How can you do more business with your customer? Write that question down, spend a half-hour every day answering that question, and I promise great things will happen.

6. **Spend some time planning your day, week and month in advance.** Don't just wake up in the morning without a

solid plan. You need to spend some time trying to determine the maximum use of your time, for maximum productivity. And I can tell you this: **when it comes to time management, the more stuff you have planned to do every day that will serve the company and make you money, the more productive you're going to be.**

7. **Spend time dreaming, goal setting, studying marketing materials, and just thinking.** Think about where you want to go, what you want to accomplish, and how you're going to accomplish those things.

8. **Develop information products designed to establish your credibility** and position yourself as an expert in your market. Information products are a great way to attract the best prospects in your marketplace.

9. Combine different aspects of what I've been sharing with you. **Ask yourself the tough questions that none of your other competitors are asking themselves;** sit down and really try to figure out the answers to questions like,

   ✓ "How do we attract and re-attract the very best customers in our marketplace?

   ✓ "What do we have to do to accomplish this?"

   ✓ **"What do the best customers in our marketplace want that nobody else is giving them?"**

   ✓ "Where are the untapped opportunities right here in front of us, right now, that nobody else can see?"

   ✓ "What could we be doing differently that could make a bigger impact on our best customers and help them do even more business with us?"

   ✓ **Here's a great one: "How can I steal the best**

FREE GIFT! Go to www.RuthlessMarketing.com/freegift

customers away from my biggest competitors?" If you could find a way to divert those people over to your customer base somehow, you can claim money that's right there for the taking.

✓ **Another good question:** "What are the three things we can do right now that will dramatically increase our sales and profits?"

✓ How can you cross-sell to more of your best customers?

✓ How can you get them to buy more of your stuff, for a larger amount of money each time?

✓ **And, last but not least, another great question that will lead to lots of interesting answers and more questions: "What are the innovative companies, both in and out of my market area doing that I can imitate?"**

These might be companies you wouldn't even think of as competition, because they don't sell the same exact types of products or services — but they're doing innovative things that you can adapt for your own business.

If you just spend some time every single day sharpening the axe, thinking very carefully about the answers to these questions, some days you're going to get some great answers. Some days you're not going to get any answers. But keep a notebook, think and dream and scheme, and keep asking the questions, and you'll be surprised at the answers you'll come up with.

Now, you might think that nothing in those nine topics sounds particularly ruthless — but applying them properly is what makes you a ruthless marketer. It's all about focusing on what's really important. I hope you, the reader, are willing to incorporate all these points in your thinking.

One of the most important points I've mentioned here involves how you can sell more to your existing customers, especially your best customers. Most businesspeople focus on one thought: "How do I get more customers?" While that's always important, it's more important to say to yourself, "OK, I've already got "X" number of customers. How can I sell more things to these customers?"

Why is this more important than acquiring new customers? Because I've found the 80-20 rule works. That is, at least 80% of all the profits you make will come from 20% of your customers. It's okay to go after new customers; we have to do this. But **98% of businesses aren't selling enough to their present customers.** If you can create new programs, new products, new services, and new ideas to enhance the business from the customers you already have, you're way ahead of the pack.

This includes what I've referred to as "stealing other people's customers." That's ruthless, sure, but how else do you build up your customer base? Now, **there are companies out there that are doing such a great job of serving their customers that there's not a damn thing that you can possibly do to steal them away.** My best example of that is my printer. I've got such a great relationship with him — and we do millions of dollars worth of printing every year through his company — that there's no way any printer could ever court me away from him. Ever. He's just doing too good a job; he's serving me too well.

But that's an extreme example. **A lot of businesspeople are getting less than desirable service, and they're less than happy with their present suppliers.** They just get into the habit of doing business with the same companies over and over again, because they don't want to change. **Those disgruntled customers are the ones you can steal.** As I taught you back in Chapter One, part of developing your overall marketing strategy is to create a Unique Selling Position in the marketplace that answers the problems with which your potential customers are faced, whatever they might be. If you know what those problems are, you can develop advertising that's aimed at those people, and you can let them know that your company is built to answer and address those issues — whereas their existing suppliers aren't. **The more you know about your very best customers, then the more you'll know how to attract other customers that are just like them, and many will come from your competitors.** A buyer is a buyer is a buyer, so the more you know about *your* best customers, the better you'll know your competitors' best customers too, and the more you'll know about their dissatisfactions. You should also get to know y*our competitors.* **Go out and buy everybody's stuff you could find, not just to see what your competitors are offering, but also so you can understand their sales processes.**

Here's another way to make your customers happy, and make more money from them in the long run: just give your best customers a better deal. My friend Russ von Hoelscher used to do business with Staples for office supplies, and also whenever he had to print up 500 copies of this or 1,000 of that. That amounts to a substantial amount per month. Then Office Depot opened just four blocks from him, and he went down there and said, "You know, I do a lot of business with Staples and they give me 10% off their regular prices on all printing and some of the office supplies." The manager was called over and he asked, "How much do you do?"

Russ said, "Oh, about three thousand a month. I take my major business to a big printer, but I do a lot of small-scale printing and I buy plenty of office supplies." Well, the manager knew a golden goose when he saw one, so he said, "Look, we'll give you 20% off if you do that type of volume every month." So now Russ is one of his best customers. You can do things like that for your best customers — you can treat them special. When you do that, you can steal 'em from the competition.

Always Remember, and Never Forget...

One of the most important things you should remember with this kind of marketing is that **you absolutely have to take the time to study and think in order to come up with the right strategies. Don't get so wrapped up in those everyday business details; slow down!** Ask yourself the questions I said you should ask yourself in Point Number Nine on my list. When you ask yourself those questions, answers will eventually come. One good question I'd add to the list is this: "What do my customers really want?" I don't care if you're selling shoes or printing or you run a restaurant, what do your customers *really* want? Because it's always above and beyond the obvious. When you start answering that question satisfactorily, you can serve your customers much, much better.

Ask yourself the questions, and the answers will come — and over time they'll be better. That's the big secret. I think **the reason a lot of people *don't* ask the questions is because they're afraid. Well, guess what? You'll get some wrong answers. There's no doubt about it. But through the process of asking and answering questions, you'll eventually come up with better answers — which will lead to better questions, which will lead to better answers.** I think a few other questions that are really nice to ask yourself as you're working *on* your business and not *in* it include, "Where are my biggest strengths? What do I have to offer that other companies can't or won't? How can I do better at the things I'm already good at and delegate the rest? What am I spending my precious time and energy on right now that someone else could be doing as well or even better than I'm doing? How can I produce bigger sales and profits with less time and work?" That last one's a good question, because too many people are working their asses off and they're not getting nearly what they should be getting. Or ask yourself, "Who in the marketplace is making the largest amount of money?" And, "What are they doing that I could be doing?" Or, "What are they doing that I could be doing *even better*?"

All this boils down to making a short list (no more than ten) of the activities you can perform consistently to bring in more sales and profits every day — and then delegating everything else to the most competent people you can find, so you're not trying to wear all the hats. **What you're doing is trying to put your time and energy into the smallest number of things that bring you the biggest results.** Assuming you can find the most capable, competent people, you're letting them do what they do best while you're focused on what you do best. It's a much smarter way of doing business than most people will ever devise. I often ask myself, **"Why don't more people do this kind of thing?" All I can think of are these six things:**

- **They're just lazy.**

- **They're delusional.**

- **They just don't know what to do.** If you read this chapter and take it to heart, you'll be ahead of them because you'll know exactly what to do.

- **They're just following the follower.** They're just doing what every other business in their markets is doing — it's the blind leading the blind!

- **It doesn't fit our great American Judeo-Christian work ethic.** People think that if they're not working hard physically, then it's not work. It really *is* work, but it's the cerebral kind; you might get a headache, but you're never

All of us are in the exact same business:

- The business of giving our customers more of what they want.

- The business of customer acquisition and development.

Every person who is truly an entrepreneur knows this. That's why these people can move from business to business — and make money in all of them.

going to break a sweat doing any of this stuff. A lot of people feel like they have to work hard and try to do everything at once — and if they're not really tired, then they don't feel like they've worked that hard.

- **People are miseducated.** They don't even know what they need to know, and in fact they don't even know what they *don't* know. For example, many people think of location as the most important thing for a business, but it's not. Location is important for some types of businesses, but that alone will only get you so far. **Most people don't realize that if you use some of these strategies and techniques about which I'm talking, you can double and triple your business regardless of location.**

That's the gist of the "work smarter, not harder" argument. The people who are making the most money are doing these things, and I'd like to include anyone reading this book in that category. I'm practicing what I preach, and so are all the other top marketers out there.

What You Absolutely Must Start Doing, Today

In this section, I'm going to share a few tips about what you absolutely *must* be doing if you expect to work *on* your business and not *in* it. These tips can make all the difference between living the good life and actually living *for* your business, which is exactly what you don't want. Nobody I know of wants to live *for* a business. It's a job at that point, and you think to yourself, "I've got to keep doing this to survive." Instead, you have to put your business on autopilot, and systems and planning are key to doing that. Simply put, the truly ruthless marketer hires the best people to do everything, or out-sources wherever possible what he can off-load from his own plate.

The biggest problem I see, when someone is starting out in a business, is that they end up wearing all the hats — and that puts them between a rock and a hard place. They think, "I don't have any money to hire people; gosh!" and, "When do I know to let go of that?" **Obviously, it very tough to let go of tasks when it's your business. I understand that; I've been there. It's your baby. It's tough to let somebody else come in and give the baby a bath. It's tough to let somebody else take your baby for a walk in the park. But you know what? Maybe it's more productive if you do.**

You can't do it all — period. I don't care how much you're good at. You can't possibly provide, for example, the same quality of Web design for your business as someone who only does Web design all day long, day in and day out. Even if you're a Web designer, even if you're a great graphic artist, if you're also paying the bills and running the errands and doing everything and whipping out whatever you can, your work is more hurried. It's not going to be as good as your best. You can't provide the same quality of customer support as someone who does only customer support all day. You can't even sell better than someone who sells all day — and that's a tough one to take, because most of us feel we're the best person to sell our own business. But if you're the salesman for your business, you're selling yourself short. **You need to be building the business, building new products, and you can't build your business consistently if business building is just something you do in between all the other chores.**

If you haven't already, *immediately* hire someone or find outsourced labor to replace the repetitive tasks anyone can be trained to do. As I pointed out earlier, you should **document your repetitive tasks so someone else can step right in and do it from there. Off-load your workload as soon and as often as possible — and continually re-evaluate everything.** Once a month, here's what you should do: list every task you do every day for a week. Create an hour-by-hour log. Put an asterisk beside everything you did that will build the business and increase revenue, not just save you a few bucks because you did it yourself. Put a plus sign beside every task you did that *someone else* could be doing right now just as effectively. I bet you'll find that you've marked a lot of the same tasks with both symbols. Once you've done that, figure out if it's more cost-effective to have someone else do those tasks.

Here's what you need to remember to figure that out. Even when the money doesn't seem to be coming in to cover it, realize that **your time is the most valuable asset you have in your business.** Add up your business's total revenue. Divide it by the hours you work. You're the driving force behind this business. This is how much each and every hour of your day is worth. Now, maybe you'll find out that it's easier to put some more plus signs on that time ledger. Then make a list of all the things you need to be doing that you're best at that will generate more sales, revenue and growth for your business — but that you never seem to have all the time you really need to do. Calculate how much money you're losing by not doing this, then move out those repetitive tasks that could be done by someone else and make more room for the profitable tasks that you don't do enough. Remember, **you can always generate more money, but you can never generate more time.**

All it takes is a little documentation. Take every repetitive task you do — for example, database entry, building that mailing list, keeping track of who's purchased what — and describe it, step by step, in a few pages of documentation. Put it in a notebook for new hires to read. Outsource graphic arts and Web design work, even if you can do it yourself. Get an accountant to do your payroll and pay most of your bills for you, assuming you bring in enough money to do that. I'll tell you a little trick about outsourcing I've found, too. I sometimes hear people say that you should outsource everything, because employees are a hassle. Well, sadly, nobody will deny that. But I've found that there are certain situations (and it can sometimes be tough to decide which those are) where it's good to have someone in the office with you working, not outsourced. It's good to know they're going to be there tomorrow.

Caveat emptor: outsourcing can lead to some disastrous results, so you want to be careful with it. And here's something extraordinarily important that someone told me a long time ago that's helped me a great deal. I've never forgotten it, and I'd like to pass it on to you. It's just this: **never, ever delegate your marketing to anybody else. You can delegate everything else.** Accountants are a dime a dozen; good employees are harder to find, but you can find them. **And by "marketing," I don't mean selling. Selling is only part of marketing, and you can find salesmen to do that.** In many ways, selling is where they're repeating your marketing on a script page, doing the repetitive part of selling and following the steps you've created to close a sale. That's the manual labor part of it, where you can train somebody to sell either by phone or out there eyeball-to-eyeball, belly-to-belly with the customers. **What you have to do is develop the strategies and methods to attract and re-attract the best customers, to create the advertisements you need to use, the marketing messages, the *ideas* you use to create new products and services.**

Marketing is all of the things you do to go out there head-to-head with your biggest competition and win. Those are the things you *don't* want to delegate, because they're too valuable. At the same time, those are often the very things you'll find that you wish you had more time to do. Those are the things that get pushed aside all too often. Those are the things that get ignored because you get busy in your business, rather than standing back and running your business. There's a big difference between

MARKETING SECRET #68

A great salesperson cannot make anyone buy something they don't want... That's why we must get prospects to "raise their hand" and show us that they are interested.

- Let the prospects qualify themselves by jumping through the hoops we hold in front of them!

- This is the secret to making easy sales!

running a business and having it run you. **If you free up all your time to do nothing but marketing your business and creating new products, your business will do nothing but grow.**

I know how hard it is to start delegating all those things. If you're focused on really building your business, you'll find that while it may seem expensive the first time you take an employee in or when you outsource a copywriting job, it's more costly *not* to do them. **If you're stuck writing your own checks or putting out fires instead of marketing, then you're doing the wrong thing.** You ought to evaluate what that's costing you compared to what it would cost to get someone to do it.

Here's an example. I met this copywriter who did some work for our company about ten years ago, and at first I didn't like him at all. He's a famous guy out of Orlando. I won't mention his name, but he's got a limousine that takes him everywhere. He's a little tiny guy and I started out thinking, "What an egotistical monster. I don't want to do business with anybody who's got a bigger ego than me!" But then I found out that **all the time he was getting chauffeured around in his limousine, he was working his ass off. He was writing copy, coming up with all kinds of ideas. He was on the phone with clients, and he was making maximum use of his time.** That's when I decided that

FREE GIFT! Go to www.RuthlessMarketing.com/freegift

I'd prejudged him wrongly; because that's exactly what I'm talking about doing here: freeing up your time so that it's best spent doing the handful of things that produce the biggest profits. He didn't even want to bother driving himself around; it was more profitable to have someone else do it. And there's another point in this guy's favor: doing this was helping further the image that he wanted to create. He makes himself seem rich and successful, and all of a sudden his value goes up!

I know how hard it is to take off some of those hats you have to wear when you first start out in this business, especially since it can cost you initially. But if you just reassign some tasks to other people and apply the extra time to your marketing, you'll soon see much more coming in than what you're spending to off-load those tasks. Your revenue will grow to cover it. I'd bet money on it.

That said, **don't confuse delegation with abdicating.** That's been the source of some of my worse mistakes. There were cases when I thought I was delegating something, but what I was *really* doing was abdicating — just giving up a task and forgetting it. **Abdication is where you just throw things at people and say, "You take care of all that for me," but then you don't check up on any of it, and you have no way of knowing what's going on. There are no checks and balances built in, and the people you trust could be stealing you blind or doing a terrible job, and you'd never know it until the very end.**

There's a BIG difference between abdication and delegation. I see so many business people making the mistakes that I've made in the past, where I'd try to be involved in every aspect of my business. I spent several years doing this, and at night I'd come home beat-up, exhausted, and my stomach would hurt and I wasn't feeling good. It was all because I was trying to wear all the hats, and I was trying to be involved and micro-manage everything — trying to be a manager more than a business owner. That's a terrible mistake I often see other business people making. Sure, you have to oversee things, and there are some things you may decide you'd rather do yourself. **But you also have to build in the necessary checks and balances, and document everything that's repetitive so that *anyone* can do it. That's the basis of one of the most successful business models ever: the McDonald's model,** the one I talked about earlier. They teach you how to make a burger, and anyone can learn. They even have a Hamburger University where they teach you, "This is how *we* make burgers the McDonald's way." Every McDonald's you walk into, it's the same burger, and that's why. That's a selling point, and it's also a business tool.

My friend and colleague Randy Charach spent six years as Ronald McDonald in a previous life, so he's actually been out to Hamburger U. in Oakbrook, Illinois several times. At the time, there were about a hundred Ronalds, and he was one in Canada, where he lives. Even their shows were all scripted the same, and they had very little artistic freedom — which is why Randy stopped doing it. But it's effective for them and it was fine for him for six years, until he got bored and wanted to do his own thing.

Sit down and tell yourself, "I'm going to spend the extra time and effort now to document everything." While it may take you a while to document everything you do, in the long run it's just going to save so many hours and so many headaches and create so many benefits that you'll soon be wondering why you never did it before. Even if you're the kind of person who never wants to let anything out of their control, you've simply got to do this. Once something is documented, you're never beholden to any individual; you never have to rely on somebody to do things right. If you try that, you're screwed if that person gets sick or decides to quit. That could generate a lot of havoc and personal distress, and create problems in your business. Get around it by documenting.

That's a significant part of a mindset that you should put yourself into if you want to succeed. **The mindset you should use is that you're setting up this business so you can franchise or sell it. Not that you necessarily will, but if you have the mindset that everything you do has a greater purpose — and that's to**

create this turn-key business path you can then duplicate, sell to somebody, or take a year off and have it run itself — you'll be looking at it all the right way. Maybe you'll never sell or franchise your business, but if you've got everything all documented, the value goes way up. It's also a precaution in case you or your key personnel ever get sick. Document even the most mundane, simple things that you take for granted — like sending a fax, for example. You don't know the experience of the other people who are going to come in and do this for you if you're out of action.

Here's an example, again from Randy Charach, who once owned a toy business. One year he was so ill during the Christmas season that he had to be in the hospital during his busiest week of the year. Back then he didn't have everything documented, so he had to make do with good employees and a lot of telephone calls. You can bet he knows better now, even though he says it was a lesson that took him several years to really understand. Now, thorough documentation is his insurance policy in case something goes wrong — and it should be yours, too.

Becoming Someone Else

You need to realize that you're a different person when you're working on your business than you are in all other parts of your life. No matter what you're selling and no matter why you're selling it, when you're developing and growing your business, **the business is your product.** Let's look at McDonald's again. The great Ray Kroc built McDonald's from a small family business to the powerhouse it is today. And you know what? His product wasn't hamburgers, and never was! Ray Kroc's product was businesses.

You don't want to get stuck believing that you're selling a product. Let's say you own a dance studio; well, don't think that you're selling dancing. **Your business is a mechanism, a way of bringing in money.** Once you start doing that, you've gone from being a hobbyist or a bibliophile or an engineer to something new — a marketer, an entrepreneur, a businessperson. As such, one of the things about which you won't ever be confused — unless you start working *in* your business — is that you're teaching dancing, because that's not what people are buying. People are *really* buying the fact that they'll feel good, feel healthy, and meet people of the opposite sex more easily. Once you understand all that and focus on the needs of the customer, then you find out where people are really going.

Plain and simple, you're a different person as a business owner. To maximize your profits and build your business properly, you have to leave behind all this craftsman stuff, all this engineer stuff that you might have taken great pleasure in in your former life. **When you're a business owner, your product is your business, and you need to optimize that. Like I said before, one way to do that is to work as if you're planning to sell your business, because that forces you into upping your revenues, systemizing everything and making it attractive to other people.**

In addition to being a different person with different concerns when you're really working on your business properly, your rewards are a whole lot different than when you're laboring *in* your business. You're the one who's really playing the game. Let's say you hire a dance instructor.

They're not playing the game; they're getting paid to do it. Sure, they're having a good time and probably for them, at that level, that's really good. But you're the one who's got the juice. You're the one who's living or dying by your marketing efforts. You're the one who's growing your business. You're the one who's boating around in a yacht and riding around in the backseat of a limousine, right? You're the dealmaker. You're the creative entity. Money is what brings all the rewards in, and money is how you keep score!

You know exactly when you need to be doing the most productive things for your business. There's an old book by the famous writer Arthur Haley, who was once an on-the-street salesperson. For him, the most productive time of day was 5:30a.m. to 10:00a.m. He was in the insurance business. During his productive time he'd have meeting after meeting and sign people up left and right. It was afterward that the business took place; the "busy-ness" of making sure the accounting was done, making sure the policies were actually signed out, and getting any questions answered or follow-ups done. That was done in the afternoon, in low-priority time — time when he couldn't be selling anyway, because everyone was at work.

You should do the same, whatever your productive time might be. You know better than anyone the time of day that you do your best work, whether you work best in the morning or at night. Then prioritize the most important aspects of your business. If you get these things done, no matter what else you do (or don't) get done, then the day has been a success. You've made progress in your business in the big picture. How you want to do that is up to you. I belong to what I call the "5 A.M. Club," along with my friend and fellow marketer Ted Ciuba. If I can get up any time at or before 5 A.M. then I've made it. I have other friends who work best in the late afternoon or evening. I know that for somebody like my friend Alan Bechtold, it's impossible to join the 5 A.M. Club, because he's a night owl. He does a lot of his deep thinking at 1 A.M. Like any good entrepreneur, his business doesn't run him, so he can go in when he wants to, and spend at least two hours of writing when he's at his freshest — before he's been distracted, before he knows what distractions are going to pull him away from it. **Most of us get an hour or two of writing in each day, whether it's on product development, ads, or whatever. Some of you guys, as you're starting a business, may only be able to do that for 30 minutes. That's fine. If you can do that consistently and then extend it to a few hours a day, you're going to be so far ahead of your competitors they're going to be freaking out, wondering what the heck you did to bypass them.**

You may actually spend a lot of your time studying, which I highly recommend. There are many courses and information resources and books related to your business. If you owned a pet shop and **got up every morning and spent two hours a day — or even an hour a day** — just reading about the various products and animals and care that you sell in your store, you're going to have the equivalent of a master's degree in five years of reading. Meanwhile, you're going to be learning all about marketing, too. The bottom line is, in the end **you will be a master at what you do.**

Just do the important stuff during your most effective period, and spend your other time taking care of that "busy-ness," fixing up the details that keep the business running, answering emails, doing rote tasks that don't require much thought. If your business is systemized, then you've got it made, and you don't have to do everything yourself. As for me, if I can't run all the business aspects of my business in a few hours a day, then *I* am doing something wrong — and that's just too bad, because that's all I'm going to give it! The rest of my time needs to be spent creating.

What should your priorities be? Anything that sells or builds your business. Studying everything you can about your business. Of course, it's critical that you spend a lot of time in product creation. Production is really what I call it, because it's not only product creation, it's product copy, writing ads, marketing your ads, overseeing your website, making things work better. Product creations and the associated marketing are the big priorities, things you definitely want to carve out time for and do every single day. This is what *nothing else* can interfere with. Everything else, even your other priorities, can slide — but you have to create and market. Here's a suggestion somebody gave years ago that's helped me a lot. **Every single day, do at least one thing that's going to dramatically increase your sales and profits, that stands the greatest chance of bringing you some serious business. That's proactive: it's being offensive, rather then defensive.** You're setting out to do this and to make this happen. If you don't let a day go by without doing something concrete to grow your business, then your business will thrive.

How extensively you want to structure your day is something you'll have to work out by trial and error, and how you do so may evolve over time. Here's an example. My fellow entrepreneur Chris Hollinger used to be a teacher, and he had a lesson plan prepared for every day. Every single day, he knew what topic he was covering and how he was going to cover it. When he became an entrepreneur, he kept that part of his daily routine in place. It worked out well, and kept him on task. But then he started looking at his lesson plans for the business he was putting together, and he realized, "Okay, I'm spending too much of my time on things that I shouldn't spend so much time on." That included things like answering emails and taking care of mundane tasks. So he forced himself to say, "I'm going to make a commitment to free up the time so I can focus on these things that make me the most money. That's what I need to do now as an entrepreneur." As a teacher, it was his classroom; he had to take care of all those details. Now, as an entrepreneur, Chris has a lesson plan for himself that keeps him focused on the times he needs to be selling, and the times he needs to be preparing to sell. He's gotten into the habit of giving everything else up, systemizing it, and having other people do it all. **To do this well requires an awareness of all the things that produce the biggest profits for you in your business, and the willingness to find ways to delegate everything else as much as you can.**

Who Says There Are No Shortcuts to Success?

Within every industry, there are things that you can do in far less time and still receive the same benefit, if only you're spending less time on them. You should look for those shortcuts everywhere. At M.O.R.E., Inc, we've found lots of ways to take shortcuts, and we take as many as we can. Most people don't. I think the reason is this: taking shortcuts sounds like a lazy way to do things. Many people feel they have to work their butts off. What they don't get is the fact that if they can save some time, they can make more money, too! I love what one of my mentors told me early on: he said that **when he goes to the bank to deposit all the money that came in that day, the teller at the window never asks him, "Did you work hard to make this money?" They don't care, and you shouldn't either.** So take your shortcuts. As you get better at the fewer things that produce the largest amount of sales and profits, you'll come up with all kinds of shortcuts. You'll end up spending less time making more money, and probably thinking more. This is a very, very powerful principle.

The Good and the Bad of Having Employees

Employees can be huge assets to your business — but the fact is, they're also big liabilities! You have to be very careful to hire your employees for the right reason — not because they're attractive, or because you feel sorry for them. The responsibility for hiring the right people is *yours*. **It's up to you to make sure you get the right person for the right job, so you have to interview these people and be sure they have the basic skills.** But more importantly, you want a person who's friendly, upbeat, helpful; a people-person, a person with a positive attitude. You might tell someone their job description is A, B, C, but you always want to say, "Look, sometimes we're going to require you to do other things as well." You don't want someone to tell you a month later, "That's not part of my job!" If you have a small business with just a few employees, you need to make their job description very broad, and you need to fill the slot with a person with the right attitude, who's got the basic skills, who's eager to get to work and has a great "people" attitude. It's so much easier to deal with this type of person. Even with good employees, of course, you're going to have some problems; there's no way around that, but you can minimize them if you're careful.

In short, you need folks who'll help you build your business. **A good employee won't cost you money — they'll actually make you money, both indirectly and directly, by freeing up your time and leading you to places you wouldn't have gone without them.**

Giving Good Customer Support

The very best employees to hire are the ones who contribute directly to your revenue stream: for example, Customer Support personnel. Here's a good ruthless marketing principle for you: Customer Support is a chance to sell more. With Customer Support you answer a question and help the customer; you've now befriended them, so they're more apt to buy more. **Every customer contact is a chance to make a sale.** If you hire the right Customer Support people, and they're trained the right way, they'll bring in much more money than you're paying them.

A good Customer Support worker also knows how to take an irate customer and calm them down. Perhaps an order was shipped but it didn't get there, and the customer's screaming — well, a good Customer Support worker knows how to settle them, to make them realize you're going to do the right thing for them. They can also up-sell, which is another priceless quality. Keep in mind, though, that **Customer Service is a great example of something you can systematize. You can set up scripts for your Customer Service personnel to use, whether they're just directing people to the proper department or actually troubleshooting issues.**

Reaping the Whirlwind... Or Not, as the Case May Be

Most of what I've talked about in this chapter boils down to making up your mind that you're going to develop the systems and time-saving methods that let you slough off all those boring everyday tasks, so you can do the things that will make you the most money. If you're caught in the hurricane of your business and you're taking care of all the minutiae and putting out fires every day, and it's just killing you, then you have to decide to set goals that bring you back to reality. You might decide, "Hey, I only want to spend four hours in my business and that's all the time I'm going to give it," then spend the rest of your time creating your products, marketing, and enjoying your life. Just make up your mind to develop the systems and all the delegation that needs to go with them in order to focus strongly for four hours on the things you *really* need to focus on. As for the rest, you can be thinking and planning while you're sailing around on your yacht. You're working *on* our business even as you sail — which justifies all the fun you're having!

That's what most of us would want. **There are so many businesspeople who get started with the idea that they're going to make a lot of money, and they're going to have this great new jet-setter way of life... and what they find is, they've just got**

another job. Only it's the worst kind of job, because your boss is a bastard and you can't get out now. With most folks, if things go sour on them and they can't stand their job, they can just quit and go to work elsewhere. But if you've built up a company where you owe all kinds of money to all kinds of suppliers, and you've got all kinds of customers you've made promises to over the years, and you've got all kinds of Joint Venture relationships with different people — well, it becomes very, very difficult to just say, "Okay, I'm through!" **You're sort of in prison now — and that's why there are so many businesspeople out there who are anything but free.** They start their businesses with all kinds of hopes and dreams, and they buy into all the hype about how being self-employed is going to lead to all this glamorous stuff. But just a few years they're asking themselves, "Oh my God! What have I done?" They become slaves to their business, and very seldom think about their business on a yacht, because they don't own a yacht!

Now, I'll readily admit that working *on* and not *in* your business is only one strategy for business success, but I think it's the ultimate strategy, because it's more proactive than others. Most businesspeople spend all their precious time doing what I call "putting out brushfires." They go into their company and get sucked into the vortex of it. I used to be one of them, and for several years, that was my life. I was right out there with them, putting out those fires and losing my focus. **Most business owners are just like managers. They're high-paid babysitters and really don't own a business: they own a job.** That's a terrible thing, because we start our businesses with the idea that we're going to move away from that whole J-O-B thing... and then we find that we're back in it. You know, if you're in trouble legally, the worst thing you can do is become your own lawyer and try to defend yourself in a jury trial. In the same way, the worst thing most people can do is be their own boss, because it's just terrible.

As a business owner, you tend to stick to what you know. If you're an engineer, you'll probably start an engineering business. If you're a carpet cleaner, you start a carpet cleaning business. Most people think the work that the business does *is* the business — and that's so wrong it's not even funny! *You're in the business of performing the work that you do.* There's a subtle difference, and it's hard to explain sometimes. **The business you're in and the things your business does, in terms of products and services you provide to customers, are two entirely different things.**

Here's a quick example: suppose there's a handyman who all of a sudden gets more work than he can handle, so he gets other handymen to go out and do the work. Then, all of a sudden, he finds he no longer has time to be a handyman, so instead he's booking out all these other handymen. And now he's suddenly in a whole different business: he's now managing people. It requires a whole different skill-set than he's used to using. That's not to say that this won't work out, but you're now talking apples and oranges. What worked for you as a handyman or an inventor or as a salesman may not work when you make the transition to marketer. It's what writer Michael Gerber calls the eMyth, in his book of the same name. It's the entrepreneurial myth — the person who's out doing the work all of a sudden shifts into a whole different role and thinks that will work, too — whereas in most cases, it won't.

The point I'm trying to make is that just because you're a good dance

instructor doesn't mean you'll make a good dance **entrepreneur, unless you throw off that eMyth and learn the skill-set you need to build a business.** Always remember: *the function of an entrepreneur is to create money.* If you remember nothing else from this book, remember that statement. Look at the average entrepreneur, and you'll find they have a checkered history: they've been in five, ten, twenty different businesses, because what they're doing is *not* the craftsmanship job. In fact, I believe that Michael Gerber, in his book *The eMyth Revisited*, even makes the argument that **you're better off if you *don't* know how to do the tasks and *don't* know how to be the craftsman and *don't* know how to cook hamburgers or be a dance instructor. And why is that? Because then you can go out and focus on building your business, which is a whole separate function from the actual work the business does.** Your expertise is going to sell more than the competition could ever hope to. Do this, offload all those repetitive, dull tasks and get yourself focused, and you're going to build a wall around your business that nothing can penetrate.

A Parting Shot

As I end this chapter, I want to encourage you, as always, to read it over more than once. Take some notes and do some heavy thinking about all of this. I want to leave this chapter with one idea. The answer to these six words will determine the amount of money that you're going to make. And here they are: What are you willing to do? **If you'll only spend one hour, every day, totally focused on all of the things I've talked about in this chapter, you will be** *amazed* **at the results.**

MARKETING SECRET #72

The safest marketing system that guarantees consistent sales and profits:

1. First generate the highest quality leads you can get from space ads — or small direct-mail packages.

2. Get the customer to request more information.

3. Then followup and hit them with all kinds of personalized sales material that takes the place of a live sales rep.

FREE GIFT! Go to www.RuthlessMarketing.com/freegift

SECRET TEN:

Relationship Building

In this chapter, I'm going to discuss the various aspects of relationship building — including all the things you can do to create better relationships with the people with whom you work, including your employees, suppliers, and Joint Venture partners. More important than all those put together, however, are the kinds of relationships you establish with your customers. **Everyone says business is a numbers game; you hear that over and over again. But the truth is, it's really a *relationships* game.** The better your relationships are, the better your numbers are going to be. In this chapter, I'm going to tell you how this all works together.

The Skinny on Relationship Building

It's a fact of the business world that **it's much harder to get a client the first time than it is to sell to the same client over and over again.** A lot of people try to build their businesses on new customers, customers who don't know and trust them, and so they have hurdles they have to overcome every time they make a sale. I believe this is the wrong way to go about it. If, instead, you **take the time to compile a list of clients and build solid, trustworthy relationships with them, it becomes much easier to sell to them and maintain a working business relationship.** So my suggestion is this: **focus your business more on holding onto your current client base and maintaining your relationships with them, as opposed to going out there and always trying to forge relationships with new customers.** You'll get a lot further down the road that way; you'll be a lot happier, and make a lot more money with a lot fewer headaches.

That's not to say you don't need to acquire new customers;

we all do, especially when we're first starting out. **You have to know how to take a looker, an inquirer, and turn them into a buyer. Once you've done that, though, the next job is to turn that buyer into a customer who buys again and again. Ultimately, you need to take that customer and turn him into a long-term, five-star client who trusts you and does business with you year after year.** You'll often hear very smart business people talking about the value of those long-term customers — and for good reason. If you keep records on what comes in from whom, you'll be amazed how much business you get from the same small percentage of your customers. I've mentioned this before; remember the 80-20 rule? You get 80 % (or more) of your business from the same 20% of your customers.

Because the value of these people becomes immense as the months and years go by, you need to learn to cultivate them, to treat them special. Now, we don't treat all customers the same. That's a popular idea in business — that everyone gets treated the same — but it's unfortunately not the case. Your best customers get treated better, period. That may sound a little ruthless, but it's how you play the game. If you're a football coach with a superstar on your hands, you treat that superstar a little different than someone who rides the bench and very seldom gets into the game, don't you? The same thing applies to your superstar customers: you have to treat them better, and you have to *do* more for them. When you do that, your business will soar.

That's because **in business, there's nothing more important than relationships.** Let me say that again: *there is absolutely nothing more important to your business, to your success, to the money that you want to make, than the relationships you build.* Relationship building is what business is all about, and it ranges from those first steps you take when you're trying to get a customer, all the way to the lifelong relationship with that best customer, your own personal superstar. Everything you do is a building block in that tower of relationships you have to build with employees, other businesses, suppliers, and others in your industry, such as Joint Venture partners.

Ask any group of businesspeople, "What business are you in?" and they'll rattle off a dozen different answers. Some may say "real estate;" some may say "marketing," some may say "bookbinding." But the truth is, we're all in the "people" business. That means we have to build relationships on a daily basis. Early on in this industry, I learned that people really just don't care how much you know — as long as they know you *care*. That's what relationship building is about. It's about helping people appreciate their own value in your eyes, so they know you care about them and you have their best interests at heart. Your income as a marketer or as a business owner is directly connected to how strong your relationship is with your client. The stronger that relationship is, the stronger your business becomes — and as a result of that, the stronger your bank account becomes! It's not just a one-way street, either. A relationship isn't just about a conversation going in one direction, or information being exchanged in one direction; it's a two-way street, which means there's a giving and a taking on the part of both parties. That's how those relationships are cultivated, and that's how your business is made to grow — by continuing to build those relationships, continuing to nurture those relationships, and by continually helping people appreciate their value as a part of your business. You've got to strive to make all of your customers feel like they're your true friends. You've got to show them not only that you care about them, but that you respect them, too.

Consider all the qualities it takes to have a great relationship with the people who mean the most to you *right now*. **Think about your most important relationships** — the people you care about and value most. **There are certain dynamics that go into those relationships.** You feel you understand these people, and they feel they understand you. You feel a deep connection with them. You're looking out for them at some level, and they're looking out for you. You feel you can trust them, that there's a certain amount of mutual respect between you. They know they're important to you, and you have the same feeling about them. They like you, and you like them. You enjoy seeing them and spending time with them, and vice versa. **In order to do well in business, you've got to inject some of those features into all your business relationships.**

I find it interesting that many business owners never learn that business is all about relationships. They feel like they're islands; they don't build relationships with other people in their industry. They're afraid of the competition. They see those people as the enemy. Since those people are competing for the dollars that should be theirs, that's a defensible perspective — but it ignores the fact that **there's also a lot of money to be made by teaming up with your competitors, or with people in your industry who sell other types of products that your customers might want.** If you have the same customers, but you're not selling the exact same product, you can build relationships with your erstwhile competitors that are mutually beneficial — relationships where you can both profit. That's what makes for a great business relationship, a great Joint Venture.

Always pay attention to building business relationships of every kind, because they'll pay off for you. The more solid relationships you can establish and cultivate, the more successful you can be, and the more opportunities for profit you'll open up. Sometimes it pays off in ways you didn't initially consider; take suppliers, for example. We work with a printer who's really like a good friend of ours. He's done business with us so much; we've built and established that relationship so strongly that he's willing to do just about anything for us.

However, most of the money you make in your business is correlated to the relationships you have with your customers — the people on your lists to whom you market, and serve over and over. Whether the list is an email list, a Direct-Marketing list, a group of people with whom you do business on a regular basis, a group of potential new customers, or customers that you currently have, the relationships you establish and grow and build over time have a direct relationship to the money that you will make.

What you need to do is think carefully about all the most important relationships you have right now, and the qualities behind those relationships, and then how you can duplicate those qualities for your customers. Strive harder to understand their pain, their problems, and the things that cause them to buy at a deep, emotional level. Then, just like all good friends, strive to make a deeper emotional connection with them to understand them better, to appreciate them better. Do things that make them feel special. Let them know they're important to you.

And you can't make it phony! It has to be real. You have to share yourself a little. You have to be totally upfront and honest with people. When I think of the best relationships I have, both personally and in business, it's with people like that — people I know aren't going to BS me! They're going to tell me the truth. They're going to be honest with me, and I'm going to be honest with them. I appreciate them and I value them, because I know they're not going to lie to me — even if the truth's not something I want to hear. That's what friendship means to me, and that's what you have to strive for in all your relationships with the people with whom you do business. It's very, very important, because when **the right people are working together, you create a synergistic**

effort that adds to all aspects of your business.

The Joy of Joint Ventures

When most people are faced with a new business concept and can't figure out how to implement it, they won't take action at all. You can't think that way if you want to succeed, and that's why you need to understand the sheer value of Joint Ventures. In this section of the chapter, I'm going to give you a foundation on which to build them.

The greatest asset any business owner has is their list of customers. In any conversation you ever have with another marketer, they're going to tell you the money is in the list. That's true, but what's even more true is that the big money isn't just in *your* list — it's in *other people's* lists. Joint Venture marketing and building a relationship with people is the key that unlocks that particular vault, that lets you maximize your list revenue. Now, **the term "Joint Venture marketing" is kind of a buzzword these days. It's real sexy. People think it's a cure-all, a panacea. But it's more appropriately called "host/beneficiary endorsement" marketing. What that means is that there's a host — the individual who has a list, who has a relationship with people in their client base — and then there's the beneficiary, the person who benefits from that person's relationship. That's the person who has a product or a service he can help that host convey to his list of customers. In the end, everyone benefits: not just the host, not just the beneficiary, but also the customer.**

For example, let's say you own a jewelry store. You can approach other business owners and explain to them you've got a tested and proven program, a system that will let them increase the goodwill they have with their customers, and also create new customers — and, in the process of doing that, increase their profits. It's 100% risk-free, there's no investment on their part, and you guarantee the results. Now, who would turn down that kind of offer? No sane business owner, obviously. Here's how this works.

Once you've gotten the business owner interested, that business owner sends an endorsement letter to his list of clients, or gives it to them when they come to his store or his business. In that letter, he tells them how much he appreciates their patronage. But he wants to do more than just say that; he wants to prove it. Therefore, he's arranged with you — as the owner of that jewelry store — to give everyone who comes into that store and brings their letter with them a 25% discount. In this scenario you're the beneficiary. But you should also begin to think of yourself as a host — as a person who has a list that you can use to endorse your partner's product to your clients.

There was once a legendary marketer named Joe Karbo. At one time, **Joe had a list of people who'd bought an information product about horse race gambling. He could have rented that list to other marketers, and he could probably have made $50,000 a year doing that; there were about 50,000 names on that list. But Joe never did that. What he did instead was create Joint Ventures. In those Joint Ventures, he would split the profits with other marketers who had a mailing piece they could send to his list. Once all the costs were subtracted, they did a 50-50 split. The result of that was that Joe Karbo was able to bring in an extra $400,000 a year from that small list of 55,000 names.** Sure, he could have settled for $50,000 renting them. But being creative and cognizant of the power of Joint Venture Marketing, he was able to leverage that and produce a lot more money for both himself and for his business.

I look at doing Joint Ventures in two ways: as a way to acquire new customers, and as a way to maximize the amount of money you can make from your current customers. This involves a very simple equation, provided by my friend Eric Bechtold: List + Product = Profit. There are two sides of the plus sign: the list side, and the product side. The list side — actually going out and forging those relationships — is the hardest part if you're brand-new, or if you're looking to build your business. You need to get some Joint Ventures in place so you can kick-start your business.

Here's what I mean by that. A list is simply a client base. One of the things you've got to know is that you're not going to be able to sell to clients if you don't have the right message-to-audience match. For example, the phone book is a list, but if the people on that list aren't likely to buy your product, it's not a list to which you want to try to sell. What you need is a qualified list. **Think of the right list, a qualified list, as stored moneymaking energy.** It may be that the list you need belongs to another company, so you'll have to approach them with a Joint Venture idea about a product that's complementary to what they have to offer. To do that, you've got to have a product that your Joint Venture partner wants. You can both make big bucks by selling to their list — and you can use that Joint Venture scenario as a way of gathering new clients. **From a ruthless standpoint, you're hijacking other people's clients, if you will. But they're in on it. They want to be doing this with you, because every time they do a good Joint Venture and sell your products to their list, they make more money and they're happy. It's a win-win situation for both sides.**

Here's how you set up this situation. When you go out on the prowl for a Joint Venture you can springboard off, look for complementary lists, complementary products, or complementary companies that have a good, qualified audience base. Then contact the owner of that list and say, "I have this particular product, and it's complementary to your audience base. I'd like to send you a sample of this product, so you can review it and see how good it is, and determine that it's a good match for your client base. Then I'd like to sell it through to your client base and give you 50% of the profits." It doesn't have to be 50%, of course; it can be whatever you decide. I do this all the time, and so do most other successful marketers; it's very effective.

Of course, your Joint Venture partner isn't just going to hand over his client list, and you don't want him to. If you're using Direct-Mail, the best thing to do is to have them send their list to a bonded mail house that you both agree upon, while you send the mail house your offer. The mail piece is sent out, and any people who buy that product now become members of your new list, and offer new relationships on which you can build.

The other side of the business equation I presented to you a few pages ago is the product side. I just talked about how, once you have a product, you need to go out there and pitch it to other people's lists in order to acquire their customers. But when you're on the other side of the equation and you've actually acquired a good list, then you can go out and find complementary products you can sell to your list, and pick up Joint Venture partners (and profits) that way. If your list becomes big enough, people are going to start coming to you, and when that happens you can shop around and start promoting the products and services that will maximize your profitability from the client relationships you've already built. I like to think of it like this: developing product is hard, but *finding* product is easy. As always, your goal is relationship building, and that's how you'll build your business.

Get With the Program

Eric's "List − Product = Profit" principle is great for Direct-Response Marketing, but if you're a Main Street business owner, you're going to be dealing with a lot of merchants up and down your street who don't have a list — and have no idea that they should have one. But you still can use the Joint Venture principle to forge relationships with other local merchants and gain new customers. Let's say you have a restaurant: you can offer "2-for-1" dinners to other merchants in your area. You can go to a real estate company and say, "Why don't you give away free dinners to my restaurant for people who come in for your Open Houses?" That'll get people in the door, whom you can then groom as long-term customers. If you've got a flower shop, you can offer discounts to restaurants. If you're a carpet cleaner you can go to the realtors in your area and offer a discount to all their customers. So even if your merchant neighbors don't have lists, you can still used Eric's principal; you just have to use a different tactic. It's still relationship marketing. **It all comes down to relationships; when you get together with another business to offer something special for their customers and yours, you're benefiting everyone. You're extracting gold from the untapped assets of their list, and making everybody richer.**

Now, Joint Venturing can get complicated, depending on how you structure your deals, but I want to show you how simple and easy it really is. Eileen and I were involved in Joint Venturing before we even realized it was called that. Somebody came along years later and they coined this phrase, and now it's so popular people just say, "Hey, you want to do a J.V.?" But when we first started working with Russ von Hoelscher, we were Joint Venturing and didn't even know it. Back then we just called it a mutual sales agreement, and that's basically all it is: two people who come together to do business. It's like this: you've got something I want, I've got something that you want; let's scratch each other's back. It's simple, it's clean, and it's honest.

That's the one thing that I really love about how business and relationships work. Whoever said that business and friendships don't mix was right — but they were wrong, too, because friendship and business really *can* mix well, if you're careful. As

FREE GIFT! Go to www.RuthlessMarketing.com/freegift

long as the friendship is built around the business, rather than the business being built around the friendship, then it can work. **If you take a pre-existing friendship and try to do business with that person, Lord help you. It's going to be an uphill battle, because the relationship was already established before the business came along, and that can spell disaster. But if you want to do business with somebody who has other resources that can be of value to you, and you develop a friendship that's based around the business that you do together — with the business being the primary factor of the friendship — I think it's a match made in Heaven.**

Here's the key point, though: you've got to keep it simple. If you do an Internet search on Joint Ventures, you'll probably be shocked at all the legal stuff you find about how to set up Joint Ventures, and how you should "Use these forms to enter into a binding Joint Venture agreement," and all that garbage. It'll make your head spin! That's why I say that you should keep it simple; you don't need all those headaches. Make it about two business people coming together and deciding they have something that's mutually beneficial, and there's a way to profit from that. As soon as you start pulling in the lawyers and try to make it all legal, it complicates things. People get scared off.

Just keep it simple; keep it real. If you've got someone else with whom you can do business, someone you feel has a customer base that might be interested in your product, just approach them and work out a deal as friends in the business. **I think the more you can keep it simple, the more likely you are to succeed in finding Joint Venture partners.** All that stuff you'll find on the Internet? It's too complicated, because it's all based upon a one-shot Joint Venture deal. But that's not really what Joint Ventures are all about; they're about developing a long-term relationship with another business owner, and then continuing to benefit each other by building that relationship and branching out with more Joint Ventures for years to come.

Joint Venture Components

Marketing is simply a 3-Step process:

1. Attracting qualified leads

2. Converting the highest percentage possible into sales

3. And then re-selling the largest number of these customers

That's it! There are only 3 steps!

- However, each one is distinct. And it must be done right.

I believe that there are two basic elements to every Joint Venture: you have the mechanics, and you have the relationship. Of course, **the relationship comes first. The mechanics will essentially take care of themselves,** by virtue of the fact that every Joint Venture involves a product or service, and there are certain aspects of that product or service that have to be presented to the customer. You have to put those things on the table, so the customer understands what the product is all about. At that point, you know what you want to market to the customer; you know what your outcome is going to be. You know how much money you'd like to make. All you have to do is put the mechanics in motion to make that happen. Sure, outline them, think them through, brainstorm, figure out what you have to do. But the relationship is the starting point. That's the first and foremost thing you have to think about when you're planning to put together any kind of Joint Venture — or any other kind of business situation involving you and someone else. The benefit is that **both partners end up making a lot more money than they would have ever made on their own.**

I know for a fact that this is true. I've made millions of dollars just by hooking up with people who had resources that I lacked, when I had resources that *they* lacked. Considering all the benefits that

FREE GIFT! Go to www.RuthlessMarketing.com/freegift

Joint Venturing offers, **I asked myself one day, "Why don't more people Joint Venture?" Here are just a few reasons I came up with:**

- **Greed.** I think a lot of people are greedy, and just want to keep it all to themselves. They feel that the pie isn't big enough.

- **Shortsightedness.** People just can't see the forest through the trees — in other words, they can't see the long-term aspects of these relationships.

- **Small-mindedness.** They just don't see the big picture.

- **Touchiness.** Some people are very difficult to work with; they're basically prima donnas. You can work with them, but then you feel like you've had the crap beat out of you when you're done, and so there's not a good taste in your mouth anymore. When you're working with people you really enjoy and people you care about, you walk away feeling energized. But some people are just too much of a pain in the ass to bother with.

- **Simplicity.** Because it's so easy to embark on a Joint Venture, some people deceive themselves into thinking, "Oh, it can't work. It just can't be that simple to make an agreement with someone."

Of course, all these factors are related, and maybe they're all just aspects of the same overarching inability to cooperate for the greater good. This is sad, because Joint Ventures can be extraordinarily effective. My friend and colleague Mike Lamb was telling me recently about a talk he had with a friend who was in the Army. The topic of Joint Ventures came up, they started talking about the simplicity of things, and Mike's friend pointed out, "Two heads are always better than one. If you have two individual soldiers, they each have to make up their cot or put up a tent or whatever the case may be; but two guys working together can do it faster than one guy putting up his own tent."

That's the simplicity of a Joint Venture. You have the ability to reach two different audiences at once. You have two people (or more) working on the project together. You can brainstorm together. Each of you can find mistakes no one else sees, and each of you can find the positive aspects that the other missed. **Working on something by yourself can blind you to some of the aspects of your ideas, good or bad. Then somebody comes along and looks at it from a different perspective, and suddenly you realize how valuable what you're doing really is. You can take one idea that's had moderate success for you individually, and with another person's help, you can turn it into a huge moneymaking project.**

Of course, you still need to pick and choose your projects; don't take just anyone up on an offer. Sometimes there are good reasons *not* to Joint Venture with certain merchants. Let's say, for example, that you had a wine and liquor store, and you were approached by a restaurant with a deal where they would send you business and you would send them business. It seems to be a marriage made in Heaven, right? Not if you knew that this restaurant had bad food and bad service. You wouldn't want to Joint Venture with them then.

And then there's greed, which I mentioned earlier. That's one of the bigger problems with Joint Venturing: **some people want to take the entire pie home with them instead of sharing it with anyone else.** Michael Penland once told me that when he first began doing Joint Ventures, he gave away 70%, 80%, sometimes 100% or the profits, because the real value in Joint Ventures isn't in getting that initial sale; it's in the long-term acquisition of that new customer base, at zero cost and zero risk to you. Sometimes the people who press for a huge percent of the profits are too narrow-minded and shortsighted to realize that; they just want to see the money. Propose a Joint Venture at a decent percentage rate with them and they'll say, "You mean I'm going to give away this much to acquire that customer? No way!" And so they end up with nothing.

You need to remember, too, that Joint Ventures are out there for the taking. **It's easy to get so caught up in your own business, so focused on what you're doing to make money within your own little realm, that you forget that there are all these other complementary products out there.** Here's what I urge you to do: every once in a while, take a break from what you're doing and think about what you need to do to get some Joint Ventures going. **Find somebody out there who has a product or service that complements your client base, and at least let them start making you some additional turn-key, hands-off money.** That's the key. You and your partners can make a huge amount of money for each other in a Joint Venture, money that you'd otherwise never see. It's all about synergy — the sum total being greater than the individual parts.

Not-So-Common Sense

Creating good relationships of any kind is all about working fairly with people. Some of this just sounds so easy, so elementary; it sounds so much like common sense. But if it really *were* common, more people would be doing it. I've talked a little bit about the reasons why more people don't do Joint Ventures — greed and small-mindedness and such — but sometimes it's just because of ignorance. **Many local businesses, for example, just put a sign out announcing that they're open, and the only relationship they have with other businesses in their area is to say, "Hello, Jill," or "Hello, Fred." They salute them if they see them on the street, but they have no relationship with all these people up and down the street who could help build their business. They don't realize that those people are serving the same kind of customers they're serving.**

As long as another business isn't a direct competitor — that is, as long as they're not selling the same exact types of products or services — you should make what I call a "hit list:" a list of individuals and companies who are not direct competitors, but are selling to the same type of people to which you're selling. You learn all you can about their businesses and determine that you're going to work with them. Try to think this thing through. Come up with two or three things you can do for these people, ways that you can help them. **Then, simply write a letter to them that tells them, "Hey, I've got customers who are buying from me and I know you've got customers who are buying from you. Let's come together. Let's share some of our best customers with each other."**

There's nothing that works better than a third-party endorsement. Everybody knows that if I've got a business, I'm going to say all kinds of great things about my business, and I'm going to try to convince you that you should be buying from me. That holds little credibility in the minds and hearts of a skeptical consumer or prospect. A better approach is when I say something nice about somebody else. It's a third-party endorsement. That's one of the benefits of Joint Venturing — **I can say nice things to my customers about you and help bring business to you that you would have never received otherwise, because my customers trust me. They like me; there's a relationship there, a bond that's**

been developed. So when I go to my customers and I say nice things about your business, there's a power that comes from this. It's a testimonial from someone they trust. Let's say the owner of the jewelry store is giving a testimonial for the owner of the flower shop. The customer base in the jewelry store trusts the jewelry store; and they say, "Look, here's a letter that's telling me I should go over to the flower shop for a good deal." It's much, much better! They expect you to say great things about your own business, but when somebody else in authority — in another business — says something good about you, that's a powerful testimonial that can lead to many sales.

If you think about it, a lot of consumers aren't going to catch on to the fact that there's a Joint Venture there. They're not going to see that you and this other person with whom you're Joint Venturing are in a relationship where you're both benefiting. So, to them, it just seems like, "Hey, this is someone who's telling me I need this other service. I should do business with this other company." **It almost comes across as a goodwill gesture, rather than a sales pitch.** Having that third-party endorsement from your partner gives you an angle you don't have when you're just going out to your own customers and trying to get them to buy with you. It works the other way around, too; if you've got a well-developed list, you can endorse third party entities and have your clients listen to you.

Remember what I said before about having stored energy in a list? Let me go over that again. What happens when you've got your own internal client base and spend all this time and effort in building these relationships and staying in touch, is that you build a rapport and this friendship with your client base. Even if you're not talking to them all the time on the phone, you're sending them Direct-Response mailings and they're interacting with you through the mail. I know a lot of people who have really great, almost family-type relationships with customers they don't ever talk to: they just send correspondence back and forth. There are lots of ways to do this, especially with your core, primo customers. **If you've got that good relationship in place, then when you** endorse something to those people, the outside party is going to be ten times more likely to be able to make a sale to that group, because they're leveraging the energy you've already stored within your customer base by cultivating those relationships. It's kind of like you've got this big spring coiled up and wound really tight, and you put all this energy into it, and now they're going to come along and you're basically lending your credibility so they can just unleash that energy.

It may be that you don't have anything more to sell to the people on this list of yours. But by going out there and leveraging somebody else's product and bringing it in and endorsing it, it's almost like you took the time to develop a new product for the same audience base, and now you're able to release that energy, and both parties are going to make a whole heck of a lot more money than if you just said, "Okay, here, you can mail to my list," or, "Okay, here are my clients. Here's how you access them." Your endorsement actually lets you release that stored energy in a very effective manner for both of you.

Cultivating Effective Relationships

Relationships are insanely important to business, whether you're talking about Joint Venture partnerships or anything else. Let me reiterate something I've already said more than once here: **your income is directly connected to the number of relationships you have, and what you do to cultivate those individual relationships.** How you cultivate those relationships is incredibly important. That's the message you should take to heart; that's how you should look at it every single day.

I personally know some people who are a hell of a lot smarter and more talented than I'll ever be. Yet these people are always struggling, and they're envious of my success. True, they're brilliant in some ways, yet when it comes to emotional intelligence, they're kind of retarded. They just don't know how to get along with people. They don't know how to do what some people might

FREE GIFT! Go to www.RuthlessMarketing.com/freegift

call "schmoozing." Maybe it's inborn, or maybe it's just that they've never had the opportunity to learn how to do that kind of thing. Maybe they just didn't have any good role models when they were a kid; hell, I don't know! But I do know this: some of these people are very resentful, cynical and bitter because they know how smart they are, and then they see other people come along and make a lot of money who aren't nearly as smart... but who have their people skills highly developed and well-honed.

You might be asking yourself, "Well, what do I do? What can I do? How do I build these relationships you say are so important?" The answer is, What is it that you *can't* do? Every time I speak with somebody, every time I write somebody — individually or as a group — **I leave them with something that's going to bring them back to me:** a piece of information, knowledge they didn't have before, or an echo of a conversation we had so they knew that I was actually listening to what they were talking about, or to what they needed.

A lot of us do this innately, just because we've done it so long that it's part of our makeup. But if you haven't done this before, you have to create benchmarks. You have to do things people will remember. My friend Mike Lamb recently published a book called *One New Relationship A Day*. That philosophy is something he practices every day now, and he's been doing it for several years. In fact, he's documented most of the days for which he's built at least one new relationship. That relationship can come from any source: it could be a referral, or a person you meet on the street, or someone you meet at a meeting. It turns out that **you never know when the next person you meet will have some beneficial influence, put money in your pocket, bring you a useful scenario or a situation, or introduce you to somebody who could have a profound effect on what you do in business — or just in your life.** If you practice the one-new-relationship-a-day concept, you'll have 365 new relationships a year!

Of course, some of the people you meet are going to be very

incidental; they're not going to be that huge immediately. You might meet a janitor somewhere, and you wouldn't think that relationship could go anywhere; but that janitor might have befriended somebody who may have a profound impact on your business one of these days. So you keep track of the people you meet. You send "Thank You" cards. You send pieces of email to those people, if they have an email address. You leave a unique business card behind. **You do things that, in their minds, help you stand out. You do the things to help them remember you.**

The idea of 365 new relationships a year sounds momentous; it sounds like a lot of work, but it really isn't. You just keep track of the people you meet, and from time to time you drop them a note — and you have to be genuine; this can't be a BS track. You literally have to want to help these people do or obtain whatever it is they want. You don't have to do all the work for them; you don't have to do the things they want you to do, even. You just have to pay attention to them, in many cases.

So let's say you want to make $50,000 a year in net income. That means you need to have a model in place, whether it's yours or somebody else's, and you have to be able to build and cultivate relationships with those people. Let's say 50 of those people you meet have the potential to make you $1,000 each in net income. It doesn't matter right now how you do it, and I don't even

FREE GIFT! Go to www.RuthlessMarketing.com/freegift

worry about that anymore. **You make a concerted, consistent effort to share yourself, your information, your knowledge with other people, about other people, things you know that they don't, things you've learned. You make a concerted effort to meet new people. You take advantage of situations in which you're placed for one reason or another, or because of one person or another. You allow yourself to meet or be introduced to new people. You do those small things about which I've talked, like leaving a unique business card behind. You do things that help them remember you, so they were so impressed and so interested that you were so interested in them, that you thought enough of them to send them a note or catch up with them later.**

Like him or not, former-President Bill Clinton is a master of this technique. Many successful businesspeople are too. Sure, we're all busy. We all have too many things going on, but if you think about it, successful people usually *are* involved in many things. They're in demand. **What makes them in demand is the fact that they care about people and they show it. People want to do business with those people**. They do things that get them someone's attention. They do the things that get them noticed by people who want to make things happen. So when you meet someone, you should do something that keeps you in front of them. At some point in these relationships, you're going to discover that those people are going to want to know more about you and what you're doing. They're *not* going to know as much as you, in many cases, so they're going to come to you for assistance or help. And that, as far as I'm concerned, is the seed of any relationship.

Mike Lamb sometimes does this thing that I find a little funny. Sometimes he'll get a call, and it'll be a wrong number — but instead of blowing them off, he'll just say something cordial like, "Well, I have a couple of minutes here. Let me see if I can help you find the person you're looking for." Most people don't do that. So right away, at dinner that night, the person who called you accidentally is probably going to say, "Well, I dialed this wrong number today, but it's really funny. I started talking to this guy and he picked up the phonebook and looked up the number for me," or, "We had this very nice conversation. It turns out we know some of the same people," or, "We're doing some of the same things." Believe it or not, **Mike has actually had people who called wrong numbers give him their credit card number because they wanted to buy something about which he was talking or was selling. Sometimes he sends them to a website and they sign up on his list and, eventually, he ends up selling something to them,** or starts some kind of a relationship with them. In other words, sometimes he turns those wrong numbers into clients, simply because he spends some completely unexpected time with them. Sometimes he just so impresses somebody with his knowledge or enthusiasm that they want to involve him in something they're doing in some fashion.

This concept of 365 new relationships a day is the most important thing in Mike Lamb's life. He tries to treat every relationship that he has as gold, and that's a great idea. Not every single one works out the way he wants, and not every relationship makes him money. But it's the law of large numbers: the more people you meet, the more people who find out about you, some of those people will eventually want to work with you. **Mike documents everything about a new relationship on a page in a three-ring notebook on the day he meets a person: whether it was a phone call, whether it was a meeting, a chance encounter, a referral, whatever. He tries to document where he met them or how he met them, so he can reference that later. No, no one is going to remember all that stuff with every person; but if you write it down at that moment, and make a list of the notes and the things that you talked about, the next time you talk to that person — on purpose or by accident, or just because the timing was right — they're going to be very, very impressed that you've remembered these little nuances about your conversation.**

Mike admits that he didn't learn that on his own; he used to

FREE GIFT! Go to www.RuthlessMarketing.com/freegift

work for a long distance company, and he talked to business people all over the country. He had a computer screen that allowed him to type in all the information about who they were, and the last time they talked. One day a woman said to him, "I'm sorry, I've got to go now. My daughter was in a car accident." The next time he talked to her, three weeks later, the first thing out of his mouth was, "How is your daughter?" She was so impressed she gave Mike all of the phone business for eighteen flower shops she happened to own. It wasn't because of their rate; it wasn't because of the company. It was because of the relationship he'd started with her. You never know, as I said earlier, how many people are going to come to you and be so impressed — because you do something little like that that shows you really care about them — that they end up giving you all their business or becoming your best friend for life, and end up doing all kinds of things for you that you never ever would have seen coming.

Mike's approach is a good one. He's a "people person," so he's out there meeting people all the time, everywhere. He shows interest in them. He makes notes about certain characteristics or something about them that he can bring up at a later date. This is a very clever way to do things. As I said before, Bill Clinton is a master at this. I don't know about Clinton's sincerity, but with Mike, it's genuine. **It's a great way to let people know that you acknowledge and value them.** Here's how Mike sees it, and I happen to agree: he wants to make a huge amount of money so he can go out and do a lot of things with his money. We're only on the Earth for a certain period of time, so we need to have a lot of money to do anything we want — and very likely, we want to create a legacy, too. The idea of creating a system of relationship checks and balances in business helps. We keep track of our credits and our debits on the financial end — or at least, we should — so we know how much we make, how much money we spend, how much money we have, how much money we profited by doing what we do. Mike's idea is that the same thing holds true with relationships.

Here's how the best business relationships work: "Here's

what I can do for you, if you'll do this for me." In other words, it's a mutually advantageous, mutually profitable relationship, the good old mutual back-scratching approach that's common to human relationships. I don't think you have to be best friends with everyone with whom you have this kind of relationship; but I think if you say, "Look, I'm here to help you and I'd like some help from you as well," and it's mutually profitable, then that makes for the perfect business relationship. If you can create that relationship with people you like, then it's even easier; but you can even build that sort of relationship with people you're not that close with, because there's a greed factor involved. I think that's what makes it mutual, and that's what makes it powerful.

I believe in my heart that every time I do something for somebody, I shouldn't automatically expect anything in return. Some people never give you anything in return. But what you're doing is, essentially, building a universal bank account. I'm a big believer in karma. I'm a big believer in asking the universe for something and having the universe give it back to you. If you constantly put things into a positive category, if you're positively creating credits, then sooner or later all those things are going to come back to you. It may not be from the person with whom you're building a great relationship, but it may be from somebody connected to them, or it just may be because your intent is sincere and genuine. You *do* want to help them make more money, and sooner or later, Joint Ventures and other relationships are going to come around to help put that money right back in your pocket.

Whatever you might think of most career politicians, from this relationships perspective **there's no better role model out there than a major politician who really knows how to work a crowd** — or heck, just successful people in any field. It does require some big thinking, especially when you're talking about establishing long-term relationships with other ambitious people. You have to think win-win, and it takes some skills to develop these skills. You have to learn how to give people a break every once in a while, and hope they do the same for you every once in a while. The bottom line is, **everything we value in life must come from other people. I don't care whether it's money or power or sex or love. Humans are emotional creatures, and I know it's a cliché, but you really do have to win people's hearts before you can win their business.**

Give Them Some Attention

With relationships, in Joint Venturing or otherwise, the personal touch is absolutely critical. You have to make yourself accessible not just to your client, but to your partners as well — at all levels, at all times. You have to stay connected. That's what the word "relationship" means when you look it up in the dictionary. It's a connection — whether it's an emotional connection between two people, or some type of an association or involvement. When I did a study of this word "relationship," I looked under all of the synonyms — alliance, connection, a bond with customers, an affinity, an interdependence or a friendship or a closeness. **All of us want to do business with people we feel are our friends, people who care about us, who are looking out for our best interests. We all want to do business with people we feel respect us and appreciate us and care about us. You've got to develop this kind of a bond with your customers and your partners both.**

Of course, the results of any business venture really rests upon the strength of the relationship between the person who has the list — that's the host — and the people who are on that list — the clients. It stands to reason that cultivating a strong relationship with your clients is just like putting money in the bank. I want to tell you **six ways to cultivate and to nurture those relationships with your clients.**

- **Respond**. The first thing you should do is to send a letter to every person who makes a purchase of your product or your service. Send it out immediately; don't wait. It's a "thank you" letter; it reassures them that they've made a good decision, and that you're going to deliver what you promise.

- **Thank them again.** The next thing to do is to send a "thank you" letter with the package when you ship it, or when the service is fulfilled or delivered. Send along a physical letter to the client. It reassures them of the value of what they've just purchased, and also reinforces the value of your company in their mind.

- **Always over-deliver.** Everyone likes to get more than they bargained for, so give them a bonus. That's especially important when doing Joint Venture deals. **When you give more than the person bargained for, that really endears you to them in their heart, and sets you apart** in their mind as someone who not only provides what they promised, but who goes beyond that and gives more.

- **Survey your clients**. Ask your clients and customers, "What do you want? What do you need? What are your problems? What can I do to help you solve those? What are your desires? How can I help you fulfill those?" Don't be afraid to ask your clients what they want. Let them know you care about them; let them know you're interested in them.

- **Tele-marketing.** Here's something most people *don't* want to do, but it can really help your business. Actually pick up the phone (it won't bite you!), call them, follow up, and say thanks. **Nobody does that. It makes you special. It puts you at a different level above and beyond what most people in business are doing today,** especially if it's just a simple product or a service that you sold. Today, the most personal way you can communicate with people — other than eyeball-to-eyeball — is by telephone.

- **Segment your client list.** You can do that either by the product they've purchased, or by how much they've spent with you. Then do special things for special groups of clients. Make them feel special. Make them feel important. **You've got to know from where most of your profits are coming, and you've got to do things to give your best people some special care.** Develop things for them that you're not going to have for anyone else.

When you cultivate and nurture that relationship with your clients, your list obviously becomes more valuable, and you become more attractive as a host when other people want to do Joint Ventures, because you've got a responsive list. That is, you've got a list that responds well to endorsements from you for other people's products. If you really appreciate and understand the value of Joint Venture marketing as it applies to maintaining a good relationship with your clients (or with someone else's), then it is really like going to the gold mine — or like having a license to legally print your own money.

It's Good to Be Honest

When it comes to working with other people, not everybody out there (and I'll be on this list) is as nice as Mike Lamb. I believe that **business should be honestly selfish.** I'm looking out for my best interests, and I try to make it a point to let all the people with whom I do business know that. Hey, I know they're trying to do the same themselves! To me, the relationships can be developed out of this foundation of honesty... where we can enjoy each other's company because we share a lot of the same interests. But you know that I'm looking out for me, and I know that you're looking out for you. I'm trying to watch your back; you're trying to watch mine. **We're both trying to make money we never would have made had we not gotten together,** pooled our resources, and found a way to combine to create something much more important. What could be simpler than this?

At a client-relationship level, I believe **you have to give special preference and special treatment to your best customers, because most of the money you make will probably come from 10 to 20% of them. They're your superstars, to use the coach analogy** again. So, be accessible to everybody, but especially accessible to the really, really good customers. The more you give, the more you get. It's a universal principle. All that said, there's another side to the relationship road. If your business is large, you just might find yourself spending too much time talking on the phone, and not enough time developing products or Joint Venture situations with other companies, which is where you're really going to derive the most money out of the situation. If you had to talk to ten or a hundred different people in addition to what you're already doing today, that may be a lot more of a headache than you can afford.

FREE GIFT! Go to www.RuthlessMarketing.com/freegift

I'm not saying to lock yourself in a closet and never talk to your customers. But if you're going to be optimal in your business and you're going to make the most possible profit with your business, you've got to keep both sides in check. I'm advocating caring for your business and your own well being, as well as for your customers. Obviously, don't throw karma to the wind and just let it take care of itself. But you've got to be focused on the goal of building your business and building your profitability at the same time.

There are optimal ways to deal with this problem; for example, you can outsource your Customer Support, put up FAQs — Frequently Asked Questions lists — on your website, and manage your customers' expectations without physically managing every single customer. If you can't talk to every single person, you can still create an environment where you care and are still addressing your clients' concerns, on the whole. **You can also use approaches like tele-seminars and groups to communicate with your group of clients more effectively, and still keep it personal.**

A little trick that still lets you show you really care about your clients and want to cater to their needs is to use opinion polls. Don't feel bad about sending out a little audience poll that says something like, "Thank you for being a client. I appreciate your business. In order to serve you better in the upcoming year, I would like to know what you think about X, Y, and Z." You just poll them, get their information, and tally it up. Even if you've got 80,000 or 100,000 clients, you can play to those individuals and listen to their needs and adapt your business.

Working within Existing Relationships

Developing effective relationships requires a long-term view to be effective, whoever it is with whom you do business — whether they're complete strangers at first, or people you've known and loved for years. I have the benefit of working closely with a couple of my family members, whom I love and care for. They're people who mean a lot to me on a personal level, and I've found ways to work with them. **Elsewhere in this book I've talked about the fact that friendship and business don't usually mix if they're pre-existing friendships, but I don't think it *always* has to be that way. I've got a good working relationship with a couple of my family members, and I know some other people who have done it quite successfully.**

Earlier, I mentioned our printer, Steve. He works in a family operation, and he's found a way to make it very, very successful for him and his in-laws. I have another friend named Jeff McManis, who's got a nice sideline business. He's getting ready to hire his son-in-law, who's going to come to work for him and help build the business, and do it together as a team. I think this is part of relationship building that's often overlooked. You'll always do more for the people that you love and care for the most.

But let me caution you here: working with people you care for doesn't always work. When my mentor Russ von Hoelscher went into business over 30 years ago, he opened up a bookstore; eventually he had four bookstores, but he started with one, and he hired all his friends to work there. That was a terrible mistake. About half of them he hired just because he liked them; they had no skills that were valuable to him. They were terrible employees, and he kept some of them on for a long time before he had to fire one of them and another one decided to quit... and he lost their friendship. So, yes, you can hire relatives and you can hire friends, and some of these small mom-and-pop businesses do this. But don't do it unless the person has shown you they have some skills that will be advantageous to your business, because if you're hiring someone just because you like them, and you have doubts about what they can do that will be beneficial, you'll soon find out they won't do anything that really helps your business. So while it works sometimes, you have to be careful. Make sure that person understands that there's friendship, and there's business. Point out that you're making them a part of the business so that they can contribute to it — and that, of course, benefits both of you.

FREE GIFT! Go to www.RuthlessMarketing.com/freegift

Here's the key: if you can, you establish the friendship around a business model where there's something in it for both parties. **If a business relationship ever becomes lopsided, where one person feels like they're putting in more effort and the other person is benefiting more, and there's not a mutually beneficial relationship there, there will be problems. That's why a lot of people lose their clients,** for example. If a client doesn't feel like they're getting a benefit from the relationship in working with you, pretty soon that client is going to go hang their hat somewhere else. It's the same thing with the inner workings of your business as well. This is more of a partnership, I guess, than an employer-employee situation. But that's the reason why a lot of big companies give their people really great benefits: they want to make sure that the employee, in that situation, feels they're benefiting from working there.

Bringing Complementary Skills to the Table

Relationships permeate every aspect of your business. Besides your clients, I'm talking about employees, suppliers, consultants, partners — anyone with whom you work. I think you should always find people who are very talented, very smart — people who have things you lack. There has to be something they bring to the table that's of great value to the business, that contributes at a higher level of success. I had two partners before I met my wife, Eileen, and she became my ultimate partner. I'm grateful for both of my partners for their help in the beginning, because they played a role in helping me get started, and we worked together and it was nice. But ultimately, both of those two guys were exactly like I was: they were sales types. They could go out there, knock on doors and talk to customers all day long and sell stuff, just like I could, **but they were weak in all the same areas that I was; and therefore, both businesses dissolved rather quickly.** Then I met my wife, Eileen, and she's my exact opposite in so many ways. She has all those complementary skills and abilities I don't have. Together we hooked up and we got a relationship going in more than one way. Complementary skills

MARKETING SECRET #80

Spend most of your time working on your business — not in it. And make sure that part of that time is spent on doing nothing but thinking, planning, dreaming, and scheming about newer and better ways to make more money!

and abilities are part of this whole relationship building.

Besides looking for people with complementary skills, I also think you need to look at the person and what their passion is, and what their skill set is, and what it is that they might not contribute *today*, but might contribute tomorrow. **How can you make it a win-win situation for both of you?** My friend Eric Bechtold hired a gentleman last year for his business; he didn't have the money to hire him, and so he said, "Look, I'll hire you for this amount of money. But I can't pay you yet." Eric put it right upfront; he said, "I think you can help me make some money, and I think I can help you make some money, and I think that we can work together — not as partners, but if you come aboard and put in an effort in what we want to do here, you can make some good money." The new hire was very excited about working with Eric, and he wanted to get out of the situation he was in; and so he was willing to take the chance, knowing he wasn't going to make a paycheck immediately.

Of course, later on he made a lot more money than they thought they were going to make in the first place! Part of that was due to his commitment to the project and his ability to do the things Eric needed him to do. I'm not saying you should hire people for free, but there are other situations where you can both profit, such as bringing an intern into your business, or gradually giving a part-time hire more responsibility in order to see if they can run with it. If somebody steps up and gives you what they have to give, then you can reward them in various ways. You can split the profits with them, or give them some restaurant coupons or whatever in addition to paying them what you're going to pay them. **You can do things that let people know you care about them.** In fact, a lot of people say they'd rather have a pat on the back than a raise in salary. When people respond to what you need them to do, then you know they're going to be part of your organization, hopefully, for a long time, and it's going to be a beneficial relationship.

Relationships in a Nutshell

I hope you've benefited from the foregoing chapter. I've talked about relationships as they apply to customers, suppliers, and Joint Venture partners, and I wrapped it up with employees. In the relationship game, it's all about dealing with people. **You have to remember that you're dealing with emotional creatures, not creatures of logic. With every single person with whom you want to do business, you have to win their hearts first — and then you win their business.**

MARKETING SECRET #81

Inspiration comes in the midnight hour. When the deadlines are creeping in — and your back is against the wall. When the gun is pointed at your head and you're forced to solve the problem.

- The key: You must consciously put yourself in these do or die situations!

SECRET ELEVEN:
What Ruthless Really Means

In this chapter, I'm going to tell you what you have to do to become a truly ruthless marketer. I'll teach you how to stock up on your ruthless ammunition, how to treat your customers and competitors both, and how to become the center of attention in your marketplace. Along the way I'm also going to tell you more about what ruthless means — which may not necessarily be what you *think* it means. For example, **when I talk about "ruthless" marketing, what I really mean is** *aggressive* **marketing — it's just that "ruthless" sounds better!** But there's more to it than that, so sit tight, read on, and I'll reveal how you can become the most ruthless marketer you can be.

Positively Ruthless, In Every Way

First of all, "ruthless" isn't necessarily a negative term; a lot of people don't understand that. If you look at the dictionary meaning of the word "ruthless," you'll see that it *can* mean a lot of bad things; for example, somebody who is ruthless can kill a person without a second thought, because they have no conscience. But that's not exactly what I'm talking about here. **Ruthlessness can, in fact, be a positive thing for both you and your customers, though your competitors will never thank you for it.**

In a way, one of the easiest ways for me to describe ruthless marketing to people is by telling them that truly ruthless marketing occurs when we cater to the self-centered emotions of our customers. What I mean by that is this: people buy for emotional reasons. We've covered this before: you've got greed, guilt, fear, pride, and love. Basically, if you think about it, everybody is a self-centered individual living in a mostly self-centered world. From the client-side perspective, ruthless marketing focuses on the emotional reasons people have for purchasing. Yes, you can create a negative situation if you really play to somebody's fear and make them scared to the point where they think they must have your product to safeguard themselves: "Oh my gosh! I've got to run out and buy that because I'm fearful that my house may get broken into next week!" You can almost slap the consumer around and make them pay attention to what you're saying — that's one way to define ruthless marketing.

Ruthless marketing also means doing things differently than your competition. A lot of people are timid marketers, or they're "me too" marketers: they're only willing to do what everybody else is doing in terms of their marketing. You can't blame those people, because **whenever you get into a new business, the only thing you know to do is to copy the people who are in that exact same business.** So all the Yellow Page ads look the same, and all the mailers look the same, and so do the door hangers and the business cards; it all looks the same. That's timid "me too" marketing. It's not very exciting, and it really doesn't set you apart from your competition.

That's the root of the issue for me. Ruthless marketing means doing things that set you apart from the competition, that get you a bigger market share, more customers, and more profits. **It's the activities that make your competitors fear you, because you're stealing their customers and the money they want.** And you shouldn't think that's a bad thing, because in doing that, you're building a strong business of your own, thereby serving a lot more customers with the best quality products and services possible. Better yet, you're also building up your income for your own dreams for your family.

Again, in this sense, ruthless marketing is a great thing, not a negative thing. When a lot of people hear the word "ruthless," it

FREE GIFT! Go to www.RuthlessMarketing.com/freegift

conjures images of some kind of ruthless pillager — a Viking who just goes out there and takes whatever he wants. In some ways, that's true: as competitive an environment as the marketing world is, sometimes you've just got to do it that way. You have to tell yourself, "Okay, I'm going to do these things in order to capture my market share, in order to make the profits that I want and need to keep my business afloat." Oftentimes we've got employees to whom we have an obligation; we've also got families who depend on us. The ruthless mindset is just a means to an end, in that we're developing the skills that focus on those human factors that get people to give us their money.

The bottom line is, a ruthless marketer is not paid for his *methods*, but for his *results*. **If you're going to concentrate on manipulating and coercing people's emotional factors and psychological frames of reference in order to get them to spend their money with you, well, yes, that does sound very ruthless. But the reality is that it's just part of capitalism. It's part of being competitive, and part of doing what needs to be done to create a thriving marketing business.** When it comes to marketing in general, you don't want to be timid; you don't want to be shy. Sometimes you don't even want to be nice! So when I hear the term "ruthless marketer," I think it's a good thing that's attached to the end of my name. It's not something of which to be afraid or ashamed. It's actually a point of pride for me that I've invested in the skills necessary to become a ruthless marketer.

That said, **let me tell you a little about what ruthless marketing is** *not*.

1. **It's not taking advantage of people.**

2. **It's not lying, cheating, or stealing.**

3. **It's not ripping people off.**

Ruthless marketing isn't all the things you think of when you think of "ruthless" as it applies to a personal attribute. When you're talking about relationships among friends, the term "ruthless" might conjure up images you find unpleasant. But when it comes to business, especially when it comes to your competition, it's a necessary mindset. **The ruthless marketing mindset is that there's a whole lot of money out that's being spent, and you deserve to make as much of it as you can get. Your goal is to serve customers and make a profit. One of the ways you do that is by charging in there with the overall mindset of "take no prisoners" — this mindset that you want as big a market share as you can possibly get, and you want to make as many profits as possible while playing the game *right*.** It's not about taking advantage of people or ripping them off. It's about having this mindset that, of all the discretionary income out there, you want the largest market share, the biggest piece of the pie. That's what ruthless marketing is all about.

It's more about being aggressive than anything else. When I was a kid there was a rock-and-roll song called, "No More Mr. Nice Guy." I used to love that song! Plus, I like what Carl Icahn used to say: "If you want a friend, get a dog." You've got to be ruthless! You've got to be aggressive! **You've got to develop the heart of the lion and the mind of the fox. You've got to be bold and audacious, and even a little bit cunning, in order to seize the greatest opportunities for sales and profits.** Like I said, it's not about lying to people or cheating them: it's about mastering the art of getting the largest number of people in *your* market to give *you* the largest amount of *their* disposable income.

When you study the secrets of all great marketers, you'll see that they've all got this ruthless marketing mindset: the mind of the fox and the heart of the lion. Your job is to get as much money out of your marketplace as you possibly can. Your job isn't to be friends with your competitors, and it's not to be worried about what other people are going to think about you. I mentioned earlier that most businesspeople are far too timid. At an early age, we learn that it's not a nice thing to blow your own horn and toot your own whistle. We learn at an early age that we shouldn't be cocky or arrogant or egotistical. Even worse, I think there are too many people in this world who have what I call an "employee mentality." **Even people who've been in business for a number of years... in their hearts, they still think like an employee. I don't mean that as disrespectful to employees, because not all employees are alike; but most employees are waiting for other people to appoint them, to tell them what to do.**

When you look at the people who are the most aggressive and are achieving the largest amount of success in the marketplace, you'll see that they're not waiting around for anybody to appoint them to anything. They're out there tooting their own horns or ringing their own bells. Some of them, in fact, set out to be a little controversial. They're not really concerned about what other people are going to think about them. Their primary focus is doing all kinds of bold and audacious, outside-of-the-box, wild and crazy kinds of things that get the best customers attracted to them, because they know their competitors are all after the best customers too. So you've got to do something to completely separate yourself from everyone else, and get all of the money that could and should be yours, and not your competitor's.

On another note, the ruthless mindset is to **treat business as a something like a sport or game,** as I've mentioned in other chapters. We're in this game to win. It's almost like playing Monopoly. We're not just going to continue to move around the board just for the fun of it. We need to put up our houses, and then put up hotels. That's how we win that game. Ruthless marketing is taking that concept of winning a game like Monopoly into your business. How can you get the houses in the right places? How can you get your marketing in front of the people who need to see it, ahead of all of your other competitors? *We're here to win.* **Never forget that.**

There's an old fable about a gazelle that gets up in the morning. The gazelle has to run faster than the lion behind it — or, at least, it has to run faster than the slowest gazelle, because if it doesn't, the lion will catch it and eat it, and then it's out of the game. The lion, on the other hand, must run faster than the slowest gazelle, or it'll starve to death. It's the same thing in business. When the lion eats up those weaker competitors, you're next in line. If you're the gazelle, you need to get in front of the herd, and the only way you do that is through ruthless marketing. "Ruthless" is really "aggressive." But I also think that **to be really good at ruthless marketing, you need to have courage. Courage is going to put you at the front of the pack in everything you do.** You can't be timid, because then you're that last gazelle, just waiting to be eaten by the next lion that comes along.

Ruthless Ammunition and the Psychological Edge

My friend and colleague Eric Bechtold talks about something he calls "getting your ruthless ammunition for your business." The definition of "ruthless ammunition" is going to be different for every business, so you really need to internalize this and focus on how it applies to your business in order to understand what it means. Basically, Eric's goal in marketing any program or product or service is to put it into his advertising formula. This is where the ruthless marketing part comes in, because first, in order to perform a good marketing push out there, in order to connect with your customers, you always need to try to figure out what the biggest problem is, or the biggest solution you're providing to your customer. **Think about your product or service from your customer's standpoint, and try to figure out how you make their lives easier.**

Let's say, for example, that you're selling car seats for parents to put their little kids in when they're driving to work or school or wherever. You can broadcast a TV commercial that shows the plain statistics: about how 85% of children who are injured in car accidents are injured because their parents didn't put them into the proper seating. To be most effective, you need to focus in on all these scary statistics, and play to their fear for their kids' safety. This is just one example of how you could get yourself into this ruthless mindset, simply by **figuring out what problems — or worries — drive your consumers. Focus on that, and identify those issues. Obviously, the above example is a very specialized situation, but it illustrates the general method. You want to agitate those issues, bring them to the surface, and really get your consumer feeling the pain.** Make them scared. Make them want to say, "Oh man, I really wish I could do that or have this. My life would be so much better." If you make them feel their pain, you can sell them the solution.

That's one example of ruthless marketing, and that's Eric's advertising formula for handling that situation. But there are also other psychological influences that you can play to, factors that influence how people buy. These include:

- Scarcity
- Authority
- Social proof
- Consistency
- Liking

- Reciprocity

These are all things on which you can focus when you're searching for those problems that you're going to agitate in order to get people to buy. I've talked about this before in several previous chapters, but it bears repeating as I wrap this book up: you've absolutely got to know your customers better than they know themselves.

There's a book out there called *Non-Manipulative Selling*. I know that sounds like a joke — like it would be a completely blank book, on the order of *Everything Men Know About Women* — but it's not, which I find a little mind-boggling. I can just imagine all these people buying that book who want to be nice people, who don't want to take advantage of others and don't want to manipulate others. But guess what? ***All selling and all marketing is manipulation. You're trying to get people to spend money with you instead of your competitors. You've got to know all the tricks in the book. You've got to line up your ruthless ammunition and have it ready at all times. Having the best product and service is not enough; the marketplace is unfair in every way. Many times, the people who do a better job of marketing are the ones who are going to make all the money, not the company that delivers the best product and service. That's the reality of the marketplace.*** But if you're committed to quality products and services, then you've also got to know all these other little tricks and secrets that other marketers are using to try to get the best prospects in your market to give the money to *them* rather than you.

Take scarcity, for example. I don't think that you must have one of your products for every one of your customers. That may be nice and fair, but life's not fair. Scarcity is something that moves people to make a decision to buy your product. Maybe there's a limited number of free items you're giving away; maybe it's limited access to consultants. **There's got to be some sort of scarcity that moves people off the couch to come and give you a call.** But it really has to be honest scarcity! You often see those commercials nowadays where they say, "You have to order in the next 30 minutes to get this bonus." You'll see this on an infomercial, and you'll see that infomercial every single night and it says the same thing, every single night. Eventually, no one believes it anymore.

But there *are* some really smart companies that train their customers that the scarcity is real, and if you plan to use this tactic, you have to be like them. Say, for example, you only have seventeen of a particular item and a customer is the eighteenth person, or the twentieth or the fiftieth to contact you. What do you say? Tell them, "I'm sorry, but all those bonuses are gone. We do have these great gifts for you, but all the big bonuses are gone." What you teach them is to respond to scarcity when you put it out there. If you train people to do that, they'll be more responsive whenever you make new scarcity-based marketing offers.

Car dealerships have a big problem with using scarcity tactics; they use them completely the wrong way. A lot of the major manufacturers have special sales, and they're always ending. Then the next week, you see an ad on TV — and the same sale is still going on, or it's been extended, and you find out it's been extended indefinitely — or at least until people stop responding to it. Then they come up with a new deadline or something.

To go ahead and pick on the car industry some more — talk about your ruthless marketers! Car dealers routinely use reciprocity in their message. Have you ever sat there while you're buying a car and the salesman you're dealing with says, "Okay, hold on. Let me go check with my sales manager and we'll see if we can do this for you." He comes back and says something to the effect of, "Well, we were able to do this for *you*." Now, what's that doing in the mind of the consumer who's sitting there thinking about buying a car? It's saying, "Wow, they did this for me; now I should do something for *them*." It's using human nature against that person. "We were able to take $2,000 off this price and give you a better warranty. We were able to do this for you." They're going to be asking for you, the consumer, to do something for them. That's a good example of reciprocity as used in a car dealership. You can use that psychological influence in many different settings with your business, regardless of what it is. All you have to do is identify that it's something you'd want to do in your marketing, and then dream up ways to utilize that psychological influence on people.

Use your ruthless ammunition to declare war against all your direct competitors. There are only two types of competitors: indirect competitors who are selling to the same types of people that you do, but aren't selling the same exact products and services; and direct competitors that are selling the exact same things you are, to the exact same people. **Those people are your enemy!** Start thinking about them that way right now. **Learn how to hate them, if you have to — but just as a psychological tool. You've got to see them as trying to take money away that should and could be yours.** I see a lot of people who don't consider their direct competitors their enemies, and I think in some marketplaces, you can afford to have a better attitude about it. But in other marketplaces there are only so many good prospects and customers to go around, and the pond is not being replenished much. If you're not trying to go after those people, you know your competitors are.

You *cannot* be timid about any of this! You've got to be very aggressive. If you're timid about it, it's only a matter of

time until you hang out your "Going Out Of Business Sale" sign, because at some point a competitor will come along and take all your customers. I've seen it happen in the small business world over and over again. A business owner sits and says, "Oh, I've got all this business coming in. I don't have to do any marketing. I'm making so much this year." They never figure out that they need to continue to market. What happens is, either a competitor comes in nearby, or maybe they have to move and can't take their customers with them. They no longer have the right storefront, and they just go down the tubes — and they go down fast.

If you're not a ruthless marketer, you need to change your attitude, even if you're doing well — because success is a temporary state that'll last no longer than it takes for an aggressive competitor to come in and take your market share. **You can't just sit back and enjoy life, because business is too competitive these days.** It's no longer a situation where you can start a business, hang out a shingle, and people will come. That's a common fallacy. You need to aggressively, ruthlessly go out and grab customers off the street and drag them into your business. It's the only way you're going to stay in business long-term.

Make Audacious Promises

Eric Bechtold told me once that what "really slapped me around and made me change the way I was thinking ruthlessly," as he put it, was something he heard at a Direct-Marketing conference. Someone pointed out that **in every offer you make, you've got to make a bold, audacious promise to your customer — something that you're going to have to struggle like hell to actually produce.** Sure, you're going to have to work really hard in order to fulfill that commitment, but that makes you that much more likely to go out there and over-deliver.

That person also pointed out that, when you make these bold claims, some of your customers aren't going to be 100% happy with what you're offering if it doesn't completely meet their expectations. **You have to make it clear to them that you're going to back your promise with a guarantee:** so you say something like, "If you do such and such, you're going to increase your business by 200%, or I'll guarantee I'll give you every dollar you gave me back." Some people who are going to come back to you and say, "Well, I wasn't happy with what it was you sold me. I want my money back," and you're going to have to give their money back. The philosophy here — and this is what I thought was really ruthless — was that if you're not making enough refunds, you're not selling hard enough. I've always been taught that when you sell anything to your customer, you need to make sure you've got it right there ready to deliver, and that you're managing every expectation, and you want to make sure that *there are no refunds at all*.

But in a ruthless mindset, if you're not making a certain amount of refunds, you're not selling hard enough, and you need to be happy to make those refunds consistently, so you're *still* managing the expectations of your customer and making them happy. That's extremely ruthless, because you actually go into it knowing, "I'm not going to make a lot of my customers happy. I'm going to make a whole lot more money because of it, because a lot of people are going to want my product and will buy it... but I might have as much as 20% refunds

FREE GIFT! Go to www.RuthlessMarketing.com/freegift

on this individual item."

The whole concept of being bold and audacious (and, yes, ruthless) reminds me of the Solo-Flex story. For the first twenty years of his career, the guy who started Solo-Flex was a charter jet pilot who flew people from Los Angeles to Las Vegas and back. He worked for a company that had a rich clientele and he was probably making a good six-figure income, just taking the same small client-base from L.A. to Vegas so they could gamble. They didn't want to spend five or six hours to drive to Las Vegas, and didn't want to take a commercial flight. In any case, he got to know these people, and after a while they were all on a first name basis — but he was still making a six-figure pilot's income. **Many of these people were worth many tens of millions of dollars, and there were probably a couple of billionaires in the mix, too. One morning the pilot asked himself a simple question: "I wonder what it is, really, that separates me from these guys?"**

The answer was that these guys all had a certain level of audacity. They were just a little bit bolder than most people. It was in the way they carried themselves, the way they thought, the way they acted, the way that they took on everything in life and went after their dreams and whatever they wanted. **Once he realized that, his whole life changed. Within a matter of just a few years, he started the Solo-Flex Company and became a multimillionaire himself.** He was bold; he was audacious. You need to be that way, too. There's a famous book out called *Timid Salespeople Raise Skinny Kids*; it was written by Zig Ziglar's brother. I like that title, because it emphasizes part of what we're talking about with this ruthless mindset. **You have to have courage to take that next, audacious step: to advertise in a new, untested way, to reach out to a new segment of the market, to be willing to lose customers by making audacious claims. It's not an absence of fear. It's moving forward in spite of your fear, and that's really a lot of the secret right there.**

Here's something that helps me get in the ruthless mindset,

and it may be a good little drill for you, too. **Sit down with a pen and paper and think about your business, and some audacious, bold promises you could make to your consumer. Write those down, and be really outlandish; just write down whatever comes to mind. If you were the consumer, what could I say to you that would make you sit up and take notice?** Regardless of who else is in the field, regardless of the competition, they're going to want to figure out about what it is you're talking and want to pay attention to you. **Write those all down and then go back and weed out the ones that are literally impossible. It will be a good exercise to open up your mind. Focus on picking a couple of those, and then work them into your marketing strategies in some way.** Make sure, if it's audacious and bold, that you offer a guarantee so that any customer who's not happy with the results can definitely get their money back. Or offer some sort of a guarantee to ease the strain, in case it's too much for you to possibly deliver. Try to go out there and do everything morally and ethically, but try to make bold promises that make you stand out.

Pay Your Dues and Open Your Mind

One thing that'll boost your confidence and get you going courageously and boldly is working hard to develop your abilities. When you look at life, you can always tell those people or teams who've put in the time to be confident at what they're doing. Go out there and check the difference in the confidence level. **The people who've paid their dues, who've worked hard at being good at what they're doing, are out there taking on the world and accomplishing everything they want to accomplish, whether they're a courageous entrepreneur or part of a championship team.**

A ruthless marketer has to develop a mindset that continually motivates and encourages them to go out there and take those confident steps, to do those things they need to do to capture that market share. It all starts with study and learning and education: learning from the best, building a library that's filled with all kinds of books, tapes, and programs so you're learning from proven, successful people. There aren't actually a lot of people who go out and buy the books and programs they need to succeed. They'd rather sit down and watch a TV program every night and veg out. A ruthless marketer, on the other hand, goes out and grabs a book, reads it and gets some of these skills, or listens to a tape or studies a program to help him or her develop skills they need to succeed in their business. **It only takes one good idea, sometimes, to impel you into a marketing campaign that's going to return thousands, hundreds of thousands, or millions of dollars — but starting out, you usually can't tell what that idea is, or from where it will come. It all starts with education and study: paying your dues by doing some brain-work, then going out there and trying out some of the ideas you find, and maybe failing a lot more often than you succeed.**

On top of all that, you definitely need to keep an open mind. Nothing will close you down faster than thinking you already know it all, whether it's dealing with colleagues or clients or competitors. The main point I want to make about keeping an open mind is that you have to realize that your peripheral vision isn't as wide as you think it is. Many people go through life with such arrogance that they think they know it all; they know everything, and they don't need to go back to school to learn anything, or get a book or tape or a program, because they think their peripheral vision is so great — when in reality, they're looking through binoculars, and have tunnel vision about a lot of things. I've seen that over and over again — people who use arrogance to cover up their ignorance.

Even though a truly ruthless marketer may appear arrogant, that arrogance is usually backed up by study, research, and a firm understanding of marketing. **So focus on those things that help you become a better marketer, and develop the commitment, the dedication, the discipline, and the desire to learn. That's part of the ruthless mindset: making up your mind that you *don't* know it all, that you need to keep an open mind, that you need to expand your horizons so that next ruthless marketer**

MARKETING SECRET #85

The stronger your "marriage" between the front-end and the back-end — the more money you'll make.

- The secret: Develop your back-end first! Then build your front-end promotion.

doesn't catch up to you. If you're not putting in the time to learn and to study, someone else is.

Bad things happen to a businessperson who's been in business for a while and thinks they know it all. Here's something that many people like that do: they forget how to listen, to really listen, to teach themselves the value and to understand the ideas and the opinions of others before criticizing those ideas and opinions. Because even when you know, deep in your heart, that someone doesn't know about what the hell he or she is talking, you can still learn what *not* to do. It's a good idea to keep your ears open — that's why God gave you two of them — and to teach yourself to value and understand the ideas and opinions of others before you criticize: to learn from them.

If you set things up in your daily life so you're expanding the things you need to expand and you're learning the things you need to learn, you're going to have an overall mindset that allows you to consistently think outside the box and do those things you need to do to succeed. **You'll have the courage to be bold in the marketplace, because your knowledge is grounded in solid, proven marketing strategies, and a mindset that keeps you on the cutting edge.** Now, it's not easy to stay there on the cutting edge. If you're going to be super-successful — year in and year out — you have to keep learning

FREE GIFT! Go to www.RuthlessMarketing.com/freegift

and growing.

That, right there, is your basic ammunition for becoming a ruthless marketer. That, and the fact that **you have to be disciplined: you have to know what you want and how to define your goals, and can't just expect great things to happen by chance. You have to put in the effort it takes to develop this kind of mindset, and simply believe you're going to be the best.** Last year, my buddy Chris Lakey's daughter, Ashleigh, was in a spelling bee. Every night she'd come home and talk about how she did in school that day. They practiced every day: they'd do these mock spelling bees, and she would constantly tell her Mom and Dad how she did, and about how she wanted to win. If she won, she got to go to the next level and participate in a spelling bee against a bunch of kids from other schools. Chris would tell her that if she wanted to win the spelling bee, she had to study better and harder than everybody else, and she had to continuously put in the effort to practice, to study the list of words on which they were going to be quizzed. So she knew the parameters of the spelling bee — but she just wouldn't practice. She wanted it, but not bad enough to put the time in to practice, and so she finished second. Chris told her, after she finished second, that he was proud of her for finishing second — but that she couldn't be too upset when she didn't finish first, because she knew she hadn't put in the time it took to be Number One and to overtake that other person.

Now, that may seem a little harsh when applied to a little kid, but it's the same whether you want to win in kickball or in a spelling bee or in business. **If you don't put in the time and effort it takes to be Number One, then don't get mad when your competitors keep taking your business away from you. You have to put in the time, and you have to do more than say, "I want to be Number One in my marketplace." You have to do what it takes to be there. It's not just a matter of thinking it and writing down your goals; it's about doing what it takes to get to that top position in your marketplace.** You have to have that ruthless mindset that you're going to take as much business

---

out of this marketplace as you can, and that you're going to be Number One. If you'll have that mindset to do that, then you can get there.

Let's use a sports analogy again. My colleague and friend Chris Hollinger used to be a basketball coach. I know for a fact, having spoken to him about it, that he saw players who weren't nearly as talented as others who ultimately performed better and more consistently than the rest. He told me how **he once coached a team that was made up of some extremely talented players; on paper, it looked like no one should have been able to touch them out on the court. But they really had to struggle in some games, simply because there were other teams that worked harder and had more discipline.** They had more dedication to the craft of basketball, and were more serious about coming together as a team than Chris' team was. Because the team Chris coached was so talented, the team members thought they could just walk out on the court and beat everybody with no problem. That's not always the case. As a matter of fact, they got second at State that year with a super-talented team to which no one should have even been close.

This only goes to show that having the right mix of skills and ability can actually be a downfall in some ways, because it makes you complacent sometimes. That's why you have to go back and be true to your craft and put in the time and the effort that it really takes to develop your talent even further. You see that in a lot of sports — and in a lot of businesses as well. You may not realize this, but the great Michael Jordan was *not* the best basketball player in his high school; he was good, but he didn't have all of the talent. By the end of his career, though, he'd trained so much and had worked so hard that he did. Tiger Woods is another example of someone who continued to work at his skills, to hone his craft into something extra special. **It works the same way with businesses, small or large. The people that continue to practice their skills, to work at their craft —whether it's marketing, or running a business as a whole — continue to make their businesses better, bit by little bit. It's an ongoing process increasing their sales** and making their profits grow by leaps and bounds.

One of the things I find interesting about most business owners is that they seem to want to be *out* of their business desperately. Whenever five o'clock rolls around, they all want to leave. Whatever they're doing — whether it's plumbing or maintenance or carpet cleaning — they've started this business because they want a certain type of lifestyle, a certain type of income. They want to be self-employed, but they get buried in the day-to-day minutia of running that business, and so they all want to be out of it desperately. Now, one of the great things about being a ruthless marketer is that there's a lot of creativity involved; you've got a competitive spirit, and so you're always trying to do a little bit better and a little bit better. Instead of getting involved in the minutia of what cleaning products you're going to order this month, all of a sudden you've got your own little game going. **Being a ruthless marketer is like creating your own game, where you're always trying to do better than the competition, or you're always trying to put out better marketing materials, or you're always trying to be a little bit better than everybody else. In doing that, you get to become more passionate about your business. You get to rekindle the passion about what you're doing.**

I think it's very important for you to step outside of that mindset of being the business owner. A lot of people, when they start a business up, fall into that business-owner mindset. You know: "I run a carpet cleaning business." Or, "I run a pet store." Or, "I'm a lawyer... an attorney." Don't fall into the trap. Instead, step into the ruthless marketing mindset where, "I'm a marketer." *That's* where the money is, along with the joy of the chase. **You're a marketer of whatever products or services you're currently promoting; you're not just a carpet cleaner. As I've said before, that seems like a tiny little difference on the surface, but there's really a big gap between being, say, a carpet cleaner and a marketer of carpet cleaning services.** Keep that in mind, and you'll be able to build a much larger, more successful business.

The Case of the Fan Company

I have a little story I wanted to tell about a case study I've been following now for a little while, one about which I've heard marketing coaches and other people talk. **It regards a company that's within one of the most mundane industries you could ever imagine — but they've turned their business around by using ruthless marketing tactics, and by not being scared to try something different. This is a company that sells, of all things, great big fans.** I think it's a good example of a company that wasn't scared to do something different, to go out there and shake up the industry a little bit. The name of the company is actually "Big Ass Fans."

I'm not kidding. That's the reason I wanted to bring this case study to your attention, because... well, think about that name: "Big Ass Fans." This is a company that focuses their attention on developing large fans for cooling down warehouses and other big buildings. The reason I find this to be a great example of ruthless marketing is that somebody really had to be daring, really had to have some *cojones*, to go out there in this quiet little industry and change the company's name to what it is now. It was something really mundane before. But they listened to their customers — and **whenever their customers they saw their product, they tended to say,**

"Man, that's a big ass fan!" You see, these fans are six feet or more across, and they have to be, since they sit up in the ceilings of really big buildings and keep the air circulating.

At some point, they took the plunge and changed the name of the company to Big Ass Fans from whatever it was before (I think it was something like Industrial Air Coil Flow Systems). Now, whenever you call the company, they'll answer the phone, "Hello, this is Big Ass Fans. How can we help you?" They're on the Internet; check them out. **At the time they changed their name, it was an action that was completely foreign to this industry. To do something like that that completely shakes up the industry and almost alienates you, because it's so odd. People think, "Man, those guys are weird. The name of their company is Big Ass Fans." But once they embraced the name, they got so much press and so much exposure that their company has since seen phenomenal growth.** They were in an industry where they were just plugging away with a plain name, and then they did something a little bit different and a little bit edgy and fun — and **they captured a huge percentage of the market share, just because they weren't scared to go out there and shake things up a little bit.**

Why Be Timid?

The Big Ass Fans example goes to show that **no matter how mundane your business is, if you're thinking ruthlessly, you can find an edge that'll let you get ahead.** Sometimes this ruthless marketing stuff is actually the *fun* stuff, because you're doing something different and exciting and new, and not necessarily worrying about what your competition is doing. It's all about being controversial. The key can be as simple as just shaking it up and making people question what you're doing. You might get some negative press — but sometimes negative press turns out to be good press anyhow. Be the innovator: I think that's another way to look at being a ruthless marketer as well.

Some people think that timid marketing is also safe marketing. Well, yes, that's true; but sometimes you have to be not so safe. You need to say to yourself, "Okay, I'm doing the same safe stuff everybody else is doing. What could I do, in terms of marketing, that would really push the envelope? **What could I do that would wake people up, slap them in the face and get their attention?" You might have to get a piece of paper and ask yourself that question, and jot down dozens and dozens of ideas. Go crazy. Just brainstorm. In doing that, you're really training your brain to have that ruthless mindset.** Because, really, that's what you're going to have to do: you're going to have to push the envelope, go beyond everybody else, and come up with that one idea that really makes you stand apart from everybody else. No, it's not safe. People are going to say, "I can't believe he's doing that!" But you really don't care what people say. What you care about are those numbers in your bankbook. Believe me, **it's the ruthless marketers, the people who are pushing the envelope, that are making a lot more money than all of the safe, timid marketers in those same industries.**

And here's something else about taking chances: it can be fun. As I've said again and again, most businesspeople are working *in* their business and not *on* their business. They're not having fun. I've got all kinds of friends who get up and go to work and they never have fun at all. But **ruthless marketing is one of the most enjoyable things I've ever done professionally, and I know many of my friends and colleagues feel the same. Done right, marketing is fun stuff! The energy and the ideas that flow out of my office, and the colleagues I talk to all the time, keep me busy enjoying life — and the next thing I know, twelve hours has gone by while I've been working on this marketing campaign, and now I can't wait to get it out there and get it going. Ruthless marketing is such a fun thing to do for a living, and it pays well if you're doing it right.**

That means you've got to get out of the employee mindset, as I've emphasized before. A lot of businesspeople just see their business as a job. You get to talking to them about their business, and you listen to the way they describe what they do, and it doesn't sound much different than most employees. There are plenty of exceptions out there, but with most employees, it's just a job; it's just something they do. It's the same with most business owners. They're involved in the day-to-day aspects of their jobs and they've got no ability to pull back away from it and see the whole thing as if it were more of a war or a sport or a game. I love the example of the Big Ass Fan Company, because you've got to do things that are aggressive and create wild and crazy guarantees and promises. You've got to do things that just blow people away! **Nobody is going to blow your horn for you. You've got to be the one that does it.** Truly ruthless marketers are so dedicated and focused on trying to do things that extract the largest amount of sales and profits out of their marketplace as possible, that they really don't give a damn about what other people think about them, or what other people say about them.

The older I get, the less aggressive I become, and it's really sad. I'm getting close to 50 years old now. I've been in business for twenty years, and I have to fight myself now to be more aggressive. What came natural to me ten or fifteen years ago I now have to do consciously. So I just want to say this: recently, I was scared about something that had to do with the marketing of a certain promotion. What I wanted to do was kind of aggressive and bold, but I was afraid of upsetting the people I was targeting, of turning them off. But then I realized just how unaggressive that was. **The phrase I want to give to all of our listeners now is something that has helped me so much, and here it is: "It doesn't matter who you piss off. It only matters who you *sell*."**

You can't do what I did. I was getting ready to make a bad mistake by playing it too safe, by holding back and being too conservative, by worrying too much about what other people were going to think about me, and how I was going to upset a few customers. **What I should have been focused on, and what I'm focused on now, is extracting the largest number of sales from**

Don't bog the prospect down in a bunch of details... Sell the sizzle — not the steak!

- Sell that new car smell!

- Sell the excitement of some future dream!

This works with ordinary plain-Jane products and services too.

that certain lead group of people who responded to an initial invitation — and forget about all the people who are going to be upset. No offense to my good customers who may be reading this, but come on! The tendency is always to hold back more than you should. People are always worried, thinking, "Gosh, am I going to go too far? Am I going to push it too far?" Hey, the truth is, no matter how hard you push it, you probably aren't pushing it far enough. Too often, people go for bland vanilla marketing. They think they're trying to sell to everybody, so they try to be everything to everybody.

In doing that, you really don't create a strong basis for your business. In setting yourself apart and in making a stand, and in ticking people off, you're able to create a connection with those people who *do* like what you've got to say — or like whatever controversial thing you've put out there. They like the bold attempts you're making in your marketing. In doing that, you create better customers who are going to do more business with you. You're going to have a stronger business. Those are people who aren't going to run off to your competitors if they offer sales or discounts or things like that. You have to change your mindset and say, "I'm not going to be everything to everybody. I'm going to be the best I can for this particular section of the market and if other people don't like it, I'm not the best one for them. They need to find somebody else." If the Big Ass Fan

Company hadn't thought that way, they'd still be some boring fan company of which no-one outside the industry had ever heard.

No Doesn't Necessarily Mean No in Marketing

I compare just about everything that has to do with marketing with social situations. **Let's take dating, from a male perspective at least. There are plenty of guys, from the younger teens on up, who are very successful in the dating game. They sure don't let a "no" stop them. Fifteen "no's" just means they keep going at it from a different angle, until finally they get the answer for which they're looking.** You have to be nice but aggressive to get the dates you want, and the same thing is true in marketing. I see so many people out there who are just aren't aggressive enough when it comes to marketing. They're weak. They wait around for business to come to them. They constantly take "no" for an answer way too soon. Whether it's in the dating game or in business, the people who do the best are a little aggressive. They may even keep asking the same person the same thing more than once. If you're a guy and you ask a beautiful woman to marry you, she's probably going to say no right away, especially if you don't know her well. In fact, maybe the first time she's going to slap you in the face, if you ask her too soon. But if you're really in love with her, you don't necessarily take that "no" as a final answer. I'm not talking about stalking her — just not giving up right away.

Here's a great example of something similar from the marketing field. My friend Kris Solie-Johnston once made a pitch to a large billion-dollar bank, and when they came back and said no, you know what? She didn't even hear "no." She heard, in her mind, "Not now." Think of it not as an N-O but as a K-N-O-W. It's not a "no;" it's an "I don't know enough to say yes." Make like you have selective hearing: that one word, "no," you just don't understand. You understand all other English words, except for that word one. "No" is not an option.

There are plenty of people who are very aggressive marketers who really won't accept a "no" as an answer. Because they're so passionately convinced that their product or service is right for their marketplace, nothing in the world is going to stop them. I think that's probably a better way of describing this. It's not about just trying to suck money out of people's bank accounts and trying to get people to hand over their money; it's about being so sure that what you have is so perfect for the people you're trying to reach, that they're just blown away by your total conviction, enthusiasm, and passion.

When you take that type of stance with your prospect or your customer, you're setting yourself up as an authority; you're basically saying, "Here's what you should do and here's why. I'm the expert." I've mentioned this before in other chapters. A lot of people will say "yes" if you just tell them, "Here's what you need. This is what you need to do." You get a lot more yeses that way than if you go out there and say, "I really think it would be good for you if you did this, because this will help your business." You don't want to do that: instead just state bluntly, "I think you should do this because if you don't, here's what going to happen, and you're going to regret it later. Do it now. I'll guarantee your results." That type of authoritative approach works well, as opposed to just going out there and stumbling around. **People respond to authority. It doesn't even have to be hardnosed, highhanded authority, either.**

Consider Oprah Winfrey, for example. Everybody knows Oprah's story and understands a little bit about her past, and how she rose to stardom, and how she comes across as a genuinely nice person who's happy to help people out. But that doesn't mean she's not in charge! She's got this Book Club, and I think it's interesting that **every time she says to read a book, millions of people run out and buy it. She's not some literary expert: she's a woman who has a talk show. But anytime she tells people they need to buy this or that book, they go out and do it, because she has authority and command over her audience base.** It doesn't matter what she tells them to do, either, because she's got so many

FREE GIFT! Go to www.RuthlessMarketing.com/freegift

loyal followers. She can say, "Everybody needs to go down to the store and buy this brand of orange juice," and a large percentage of her audience will go down and buy that brand of orange juice.

That's what you need to strive for with authority, too. If you take that stance and increase your credibility and build yourself into your consumer's mind as the ultimate authority, they'll pretty much do whatever you tell them to do. If you set out to grow that authority and build that rapport in order to use it in that capacity, well, that really is pretty ruthless — but it's very effective. **You want to build emotional bonds with your customers that are so strong that people are not only compelled to buy more of whatever you sell, but they'll feel guilty if they do business with one of your direct competitors.** I have such a relationship with a couple of the people with whom I do business — where it would almost be like cheating on a spouse if I was to do business with any of their competitors. How can you develop those bonds with your customers? That's the question that should keep you up at night.

Ruthless is as Ruthless Does

As I was doing research for this book, I went to my trusty Google to check out the definition of "ruthless." According to Google — which, by the way, I use for everything — "ruthless" means: pitiless, without mercy or pity. I started thinking about that; you know, if it's piti*less*, that means it would be the opposite of having pity. So, the opposite of ruthless to be full of pity for someone. So I went and looked up the definition of "pity" and Google told me lots of things about pity. But the best definition I could find was, "An emotion, usually resulting from an encounter with an unfortunate, injured, or pathetic person or creature." I thought that was a pretty good definition of the word. But this is usually a term that's reserved for person-to-person encounters, or you and me on the street, or someone about whom you see or hear or read a story.

I drew the conclusion from this that a lot of people get

MARKETING SECRET #88

Developing Marketing Systems:

1. You find out what works best through testing.

2. Then you expand those activities as far as possible. You do more testing to discover "how high is high?"

3. Then you focus on the areas that bring you the best results. You create procedures that make those things work automatically.

confused about "ruthless," and what we mean by ruthless marketing. Business is different from everyday life. Of course, in business your goal should be to serve your customers and make a profit. If you have pity on your competitors, you'll do all kinds of things to help them out. When someone steps foot in your door, you stop them and show them where your competitors are located, tell them why they should *not* do business with you, and why they should go down the street and do business with your competitors. Right? Well, of course not. That's preposterous — you'd never do that! No business would. Yet, without that ruthless mindset, that's exactly what you're doing. Every time you approach your customers with this lethargic attitude and think, "I'm just going to sit back and let the customers browse. I'm not going to do anything proactively," then you're pitying your competitors. **If you really are in business to make a profit, you've got to maintain the ruthless mindset that says, "Whatever it takes — legally, morally, and ethically — I'm going to get the most profits possible."**

It's the same thing with sports. In sports, your goal is to win. It doesn't mean you don't care about your competition as people; they're fellow humans. If you're watching a football game or playing in a football game, you don't try to kill the other guy. You just try to knock him down and do what you can to win the game within the framework of the rules. Your goal is to win,

FREE GIFT! Go to www.RuthlessMarketing.com/freegift

whether it's an individual competition like tennis or golf or whether it's football or baseball, where you're working within a team. In sports, the second place winner really is just the first loser. You can say, "Well, they still came in second place," if they didn't win — but that just means they were the first losers.

In business, **there really is a lot of money floating around out there being spent by your prospects and your customers. They're either going to be spending it with you, or they're going to spend it with your competition.** It's just a fact. Having a ruthless marketing mindset means that you play the game of business to win. You won't get all the money; no business ever does. But you want the largest share of your market's expendable income — the biggest share of the money they're spending — and you've got to have that ruthless mindset to get it.

I once heard someone say, "I don't want all my clients' and prospects' income. I just want all of their *disposable* income." That's the kind of ruthless mindset about which we're talking. It's not about making your customers suffer or sending them to the poorhouse. **It's not about taking the money they should have spent to pay the car bill or the gas bill. It's just about getting the largest share of the money they're already spending on all that extra stuff on which they're going to continue spending money.** You need to think about the term "ruthless" not as it applies to people, but as it applies to other businesses. If you can develop that ruthless mindset about your business competition, then you can succeed, you can be Number One in your market, and you can do the things that produce a winning edge in your business.

This morning I looked up the word "aggressive," and one of the definitions was: "making an all-out effort to win and to boldly and assertively move forward." I like that! It's about being on the offense — not on the defense — by staking your claim, by claiming your greatness. One of the guys **I admire a lot is the General Manager of my best friend's business. They've got over a hundred competitors in their local area, and it's not that big** an area. He always says, "I have lots of competition, but I have zero competitors." I like that attitude. That's how I see it, too — and I see a lot of other people who have that aggressive kind of mentality. I think business is not for the weak-hearted. You've got to be strong, you've got to be aggressive, and you've got to think of it as if it were a war or a sport or a game.

Nice Guys Really Do Finish Last

Although I perform information marketing now, I often talk to people who run actual physical businesses — for example, veterinarians, or folks who have dry cleaning businesses. One of the things I get from them is they all want to be nice and have a community and not be aggressive or ruthless. Now, everyone advertises, but they all have this mindset of not going after anybody, of not being aggressive, of not competing against everybody else. All the ads in the Yellow Pages are exactly the same size. Everybody's trying to be nice. We're all trying to be friendly. We're all members of the Chamber of Commerce. Yeah, flowers and peace and all sorts of good stuff.

But that's not a way to run a business, and so I think **there has to be a shift in your mindset if you want to succeed.** What you'll find is that's how it is in most marketplaces. **Everybody believes they have competition, but no one is being competitive.** If you think that way, then you really have to develop a different way of thinking. When you understand not only that you have competition, but that you need to be actively competitive yourself, you really change your mindset. In most industries people aren't doing that. Your focus in business (as it's been said before) is to deliver great products and services you honestly believe in, to the most people possible, and to make as much money as possible. It's not to be friendly with your competitors. It's not to send Christmas cards to them and be able to say "Hi" to them in the grocery store. It's to be able to build a large, growing business. In many cases, that means being aggressive, being ruthless, and having that competitive mindset. It doesn't mean you're a mean person; it doesn't mean you're a bastard. Your relatives can still love you; your kids can still love you. But it does mean changing your mindset. And believe me, I've talked to enough business owners who have this friendly-friendly mindset that I do understand it takes some effort to go from not wanting to rock the boat to becoming a truly aggressive marketer.

Let's go back to the sports analogy. One of the things I want to point out is that **you can never defeat an opponent you don't define.** You shouldn't think about your competition as, "I want to go out there and kill my enemy!" It's not like that at all, and that's what really makes it fun for me and for a lot of the marketers I know. We sit around every day thinking, "Okay, if I do this, I wonder what my biggest competitor is going to do? Or, if I do this, I wonder how they're going to react?" Because I'm thinking about their business and what they're doing and I'm thinking, "Man, I can really shake things up if I do this or that." That's what makes it fun! It's ruthless because you're thinking, "This is going to make these people sweat when I do this." You're not out there to say, "Here's the ball. Go run it into your end zone and make a touchdown." You don't want to watch people run by you! If you're in the game, you've identified your competitor. Then you're going head-to-head, and you're formulating plans and strategies that are going to help you get ahead and get into the end zone and make you all the money you want to make. That's how you gain market share.

For example, **here's a strategy. I was recently talking to somebody about this;** they're involved in an industry that's very chummy. They all put their arms around each other and say, "Let's go eat donuts together and get involved in these different community networks." **Even though they're competitors and they're all going after the same dollar, they get involved in these little organizations and network meetings where they all sit around and drink coffee. What's funny is, the smart, ruthless marketers are joining those little committees and looking around, and learning what they can, and taking it back to their little laboratories (if you will), and putting it to work against**

their competitors — who have been lulled into this attitude of, "Oh, everything's happy and I'm sitting here drinking my coffee and eating my donuts and talking about marketing." The ruthless marketers are using those environments as learning environments to figure out what they can do next. My advice is, if you're going to join one of these things, don't do it just to become part of this little community and give away your best ideas. **Join it so that you can get in tighter with your competition and learn their insider secrets, so you can apply them to your business and help you gain market share on those same people.**

My colleague Chris Hollinger recently told me about an interesting experience he had. He went to a convenience store just right around the block, and when he pulled up in the parking lot, there were two plumber vans sitting there out front. One van just had the guy's name on it — something like "Joe's Plumbing." The other van looked a little nicer; it was a little cleaner, and maybe it was newer. The name on the side of this van was, "The Clog Father." The Clog Father van caught Chris' eye; it was a neat name. So he walked into the store, and there was a guy sitting over there sipping coffee out of a Styrofoam cup, in an untucked flannel shirt, playing Keno. The guy in the Clog Father shirt was buying something at the register and talking on his cell phone, conducting business. This guy had a nice shirt on that said "Clog Father" on it. Now, I don't know how successful both plumbers are; but who would you rather have come to your house and open your drains? **The Clog Father guy has done some thinking about how he wants to go about capturing his market share.** There's his competitor over there drinking coffee, playing Keno. That's all that Chris saw, and we don't know any of the details, but obviously the Clog Father has something going on. He's really considered what he's doing in the marketplace, how he's positioned himself, and how he presents himself. So you see, ruthless marketing can be done in every single business there is! You'd be surprised how many people are sitting out there, not really thinking creatively with their marketing. You may be one of them. Ultimately, to me, that's what ruthless marketing boils down to: thinking creatively about how you can go out there and capture that market share.

I think anybody reading this can take comfort in the fact that *most of your competitors are weak marketers.* Most of them are doing what I suggested in the beginning of this chapter: they're following the follower. They're doing exactly the same thing as all their other competitors are doing. Most people are like me. As I've mentioned before, I was a carpet cleaner for another company, and that's how I got into the carpet cleaning business. I started my own business because I was cleaning carpets for another guy, and then I decided I was tired of making him money and I wanted to be self-employed. But, basically, I was still just a carpet cleaner at heart.

Most business people are still employees, even if they're their own boss. I don't mean any disrespect to employees, but as I've shared in other chapters of this book, **the business you're in and the things that your business does — the products and services that you provide to your marketplace — are two entirely different things. Most businesspeople still show up for work every day to punch their clock. They put in as little time as they have to, and then they leave. They're not thinking about this thing strategically.**

Ruthless marketers, on the other hand, are constantly focused on getting as much business as they can. No company — except for an isolated few that got tangled up in personal or legal issues — ever went out of business because their sales and profits were too high. People go out of business because they get tired of working so hard for so little money. So you've got to be aggressive. **You've got to realize that there are a lot of forces working against you. There's the competition, and then there's the overhead. The markets are changing constantly. The solution to all these problems is to increase your sales and profits.** If you think aggressively and practice some of the ideas I've shared with you in this chapter, your business will continue to thrive and grow; your profits will continue to increase year after year.

Now, if you're struggling with the concept of competition and the "ruthless" way of going after someone else — maybe you're having a moral issue with it — then it might be better for you to try competing against yourself. When you're tracking the leads or customers you're bringing in on a weekly basis, ask yourself: how can you get more of them into your business? **Work to continually compete with yourself, instead of everybody else.** Compile your metrics and try to do better every week, and eventually it's going to get to a point where you're bringing in so many clients that the competition will be irrelevant. As you improve your business, one step at a time, the competition will no longer exist for you.

This is the End

Your job as a marketer and businessperson is to do as much business as you can with your customers, to penetrate as much of the marketplace as you can. **Every new customer must be won over, and sometimes you have to do something bold to attract them to you.** Either you get their business or your competitor gets their business; it's your choice. When you study effective marketers, you'll see that they've got this ruthless marketing mindset. They're very aggressive. You need to do the same: **you've got to strike fast, strike hard, and strike often!** Stay in touch with your best customers. Keep trying to do things to do more and more business with them, and they'll be happy to give you more and more of their money.

That Brings Us to the End
of This Book

Please keep this book close by and refer to it often. Take notes. Think. Find all the ways you can to use these powerful tips, tricks, and strategies, and in no time at all you will DOUBLE or even TRIPLE your profits!

PLUS, as I also told you at the beginning of this book...

Your FREE business-building gift
is waiting for you!

As I told you in the Introduction, I have just finished writing a new eBook, called: *"265 of the Greatest Marketing Secrets You Can Use to Dominate Your Market."* This Electronic Book normally sells for $27.95 — and is worth every penny. But for a limited time it can be yours — absolutely FREE — by simply going to my Web-Site and giving me your contact information. Remember, I am giving you this $27.95 eBook for free because I have other business-building products and services about which I would love to tell you. So I'm more than happy to give you this brand new Electronic Book that gives you 265 of my greatest marketing secrets if you'll give me your contact information (which I will not give out to anyone). Just go to **www.RuthlessMarketing.com/freegift** and immediately download this very special Electronic Marketing book. And don't worry, although I <u>will</u> add your name to my mailing list and send you additional information, there is NEVER any cost or obligation for you to purchase anything else from me, now or in the future. This FREE gift will be my way of thanking you for taking the time to read and study this book.

MARKETING SECRET #90

The best marketing ideas for your business are evolutionary... It takes time.

- A marketing promotion must breathe... It must grow and develop... It goes through many stages before it is complete... You can't rush it too fast.

- In many ways, building a business is an artistic development that takes time, work, faith, creativity — and lots of thinking and intuition.

FREE GIFT! Go to www.RuthlessMarketing.com/freegift

www.ingramcontent.com/pod-product-compliance
Lightning Source LLC
Chambersburg PA
CBHW022052210326
41519CB00054B/313